HISTORY'S GREATEST DECISIONS

HISTORY'S GREATEST DECISIONS

AND THE PEOPLE WHO MADE THEM

Bill Price

METRO BOOKS

NEW YORK

METRO BOOKS
New York

An Imprint of Sterling Publishing
387 Park Avenue South
New York, NY 10016

METRO BOOKS and the distinctive Metro Books logo
are trademarks of Sterling Publishing Co., Inc.

© 2013 by Quid Publishing

This 2013 edition published by Metro Books, by arrangement with Quid Publishing.

Conceived, designed, and produced by
Quid Publishing
Level 4 Sheridan House
114 Western Road
Hove BN3 1DD
England

www.quidpublishing.com

ISBN: 978-1-4351-4582-5

For information about custom editions, special sales, and premium and corporate purchases,
please contact Sterling Special Sales at 800-805-5489 or specialsales@sterlingpublishing.com.

Manufactured in Singapore

3 5 7 9 10 8 6 4 2

www.sterlingpublishing.com

To Sean and Sarah, with love.

CONTENTS

INTRODUCTION

In a previous book in this series, *History's Worst Decisions*, Stephen Weir took us on a journey through his selection of the worst decisions made in history, a catalog of errors of judgment and acts of sheer stupidity of the sort that most of us are probably capable of making given the chance. This book, *History's Greatest Decisions*, could be regarded as a companion piece to Stephen's work in that it looks at the opposite side of the coin in an effort to establish that, at least on a few occasions, there have been people who, when faced with difficult circumstances or apparently impossible choices, were capable of making a big decision and getting it right. So here we have 50 of these decisions, set out in chronological order and spanning the entire length of our experience, beginning in the far distant past with one of our earliest ancestors, who, in making a stone tool about 2.6 million years ago, demonstrated the cognitive capability not only to make a decision, but also to act on that decision, in the process exhibiting one of the defining characteristics of human beings: rational thought.

From that starting point, we then move on through some other examples from prehistory, such as the beginning of farming, when the decisions made by our unnamable ancestors had enormous consequences for humanity, until we arrive at the invention of writing by Sumerian scribes in the ancient Mesopotamian city of Uruk. From this moment, prehistory gradually becomes history and we can start to put names to those people who made the decisions, beginning in the Egypt of Ramesses II and then moving on to Classical Antiquity to look at decisions made by the likes of Julius Caesar and Constantine the Great. From there, we continue to the Medieval period to look at the birth of the Magna Carta and then on to the Renaissance—that remarkable period in history when, it could be argued, the modern world was invented.

The opening up of the New World to European colonization by Christopher Columbus provides us with another strand of historical decisions, those involved in the creation and expansion of the United States of America, described in chapters on the Declaration of Independence and the Monroe Doctrine. We then arrive at the nineteenth century to look at Charles Darwin's decision to sail round the world and Lincoln issuing the Emancipation Proclamation during the American Civil War. Then we move on to the twentieth century of technological advances, world wars, and the civil rights and independence movements. This brings us up to the modern world and the invention of the World Wide Web by Tim Berners-Lee as well as, in the last chapter, the end of the Troubles in Northern Ireland marked by the signing of the Good Friday Agreement, part of a peace process that continues today.

As well as arranging the decisions covered here by date, each has been placed in one of seven categories depending on the nature of the decision discussed. So we have those political decisions that have occurred in individual countries, like President Franklin D. Roosevelt's introduction of the New Deal in America in an attempt to drag the country out of the Great Depression, and diplomatic ones that have impacted on large parts of the world, such as the reorganization of European states after the end of the Napoleonic wars at the Congress of Vienna. Then there are those important military decisions that have changed the world, none more so than the one taken by Eisenhower to give the order to go on D-Day, despite the weather. On a more peaceful note, we have decisions that have led to great changes in religion, like that of Siddhartha Gotama to leave his family to go in search of enlightenment, becoming known as the Buddha in the process. In the category of social change, we look at those people who were prepared to take a stand against injustice, like Rosa Parks and Nelson Mandela, while in science and innovation we examine the work of Copernicus and Isaac Newton as well as the rather more recent achievements of Steve Jobs at Apple. Finally, we take in those decisions that have led to great moments in culture: the French writer Michel de Montaigne giving up his job to devote himself to writing or George Martin signing the Beatles to EMI after they had been turned down by every other record company.

When I first began to consider writing about great decisions, I must admit that I was initially at something of a loss to think of any examples at all. After doing some research, I began to get my eye in, so to speak, and discovered a great many more examples than I had been expecting to find, making the process of settling on the final 50 an exercise in the decision-making process in itself. In compiling my list, I have made a few assumptions about the type of decisions included; that peace is better than war, democracy is better than tyranny, equality is better than the oppression of minorities, innovations in science and culture are better than everything remaining the same. I hope the decisions chosen through this method are a reasonable interpretation of the book's title, but in the end, it can only be a subjective process. We all make decisions every day of our lives and, while most of those may not have too many long-term consequences, a few people have made decisions that have affected many millions of others and may still affect us all today. Here is my selection of those big decisions, which are, in my opinion at least, the greatest made in the history of humanity.

DECISION

Social Change

Science and Innovation

Culture

Politics

Diplomacy

Military

Religion

THE FIRST STONE TOOLS

ca. 2.6 million years BP (Before Present)

Circumstances: The changing environment of East Africa during the Pliocene/Pleistocene transition

Protagonists: *Homo habilis* or another species of early humans

Consequences: The evolution of our ability to make decisions

Every animal leaves traces of what it was; man alone leaves traces of what he created.

Jacob Bronowski, *The Ascent of Man*

The oldest artifact on display in the British Museum is a piece of dark gray volcanic rock small enough to fit comfortably into the palm of the hand. It is, at first sight, a little less than impressive and for anybody too lazy to read the accompanying label it could easily be taken for a lump of coal that has somehow found its way into its own display case in a prominent position in the museum. Needless to say, there is rather more to it than that; it is a stone tool, found in 1931 in the Olduvai Gorge of northern Tanzania by the archaeologist Louis Leakey and it was made about 1.8 million years ago by one of our very distant ancestors. Once this provenance has been appreciated, it quickly becomes apparent that the sharp edges on the rock have not been formed by natural processes, but have been intentionally fashioned to produce a cutting or chopping blade. Somebody held this stone in their hand all that time ago and made the decision to alter its shape, most likely by hitting it with a harder stone to make it into a more useful tool and, in doing so, demonstrated the sort of mental abilities and thought processes—the cognition, as it is known by scientists—that marked them out as being different from other animals. The person who made that stone tool was a human being and inadvertently demonstrated that to us not just by exhibiting a capacity to make the stone tool, but by having the intelligence to decide to make the tool in the first place.

CHOPPING TOOL
The sharp edge around the top of this stone tool in the British Museum can only have been made by a human being.

© Babel Stone | Creative Commons

The Olduvai Gorge cuts across the Serengeti Plain, forming part of the Great Rift Valley in East Africa. It holds a central place in the study of human evolution because so many archaeological discoveries relating to our ancient ancestors have been made there, leading to it becoming known as the "Cradle of Mankind." Excavations in the stratified layers of sediment at the bottom of the gorge have uncovered numerous indications of early human inhabitation, including fossilized remains of a number of different species as well as a variety of stone tools. The tool in the British Museum was found in the bottom layers of sediment, indicating that it is of the earliest type to be found at the site. These tools are named Olduwan by archaeologists, after the gorge where they were

OLDUWAN TOOLS

first described, and are also sometimes known as pebble tools because of the simplicity of their manufacture. They represent the earliest known style of stone tools from prehistory and, since those first ones were excavated at Olduvai, even older examples have been found in other parts of East Africa. Currently, the earliest known finds are those from Gona in Ethiopia, which have been dated to 2.6 million years ago.

THE DATE OF THESE EARLIEST TOOLS IS SIGNIFICANT BECAUSE IT COINCIDES WITH A MAJOR CHANGE IN THE ENVIRONMENTAL CONDITIONS IN EAST AFRICA

The date of these earliest tools is significant because it coincides with a major change in the environmental conditions in East Africa, known in scientific terms as the transition from the geological epoch of the Pliocene to that of the Pleistocene. The climate became much drier, causing the tropical forests formerly occupying the region to retreat toward the south to be replaced by the more open grassland of the savannah. This change is thought to be one of the main driving forces behind the evolution of early humans, who adapted to these different conditions by becoming more upright in stance. As well as allowing early humans to walk and run on two legs, this also meant that their hands were free to be used for other purposes, such as making tools.

The fossil record from this period is fragmentary and no skeletal remains have yet been found in close proximity to tools, so it has not been possible to establish for certain which of the various species of early human were the first to make use of them. A likely candidate is *Homo habilis*, one of the earliest members of the genus *Homo*, given a name that literally means "man the maker." The problem with this designation is that the oldest known fossils of *H. habilis* date to about 2.3 million years ago, leading some evolutionary biologists to propose that one of the more archaic australopithecine species, such as *Australopithecus gahri* or *Paranthropus boisei*, could have initiated the technology, which was then taken up by later *Homo* species. This has become a controversial subject in human evolution, not least because of the difficulty of assigning any new fossil discoveries to a particular species. It is further complicated by the possibility that an entirely different species, one that has either not survived in the fossil record or has yet to be discovered, was the first tool maker, but, whatever the truth of the matter, the debate looks set to continue until more definitive evidence has been discovered.

One argument in favor of *Homo habilis* as the first tool maker is that these early humans had brains that were 50% larger than those of the australopithecines, giving them the sort of enhanced cognition required for the task. The reason why early humans had larger brains is also a controversial subject and, at least according to one theory, may be a consequence of early humans living in larger groups on the savannah than their forebears had done in forests. The most successful members of these larger groups, so the theory goes, were the ones who exhibited the greatest social intelligence, the ability to understand and deal with others in complex and ever-changing situations, and, as those with more advanced social intelligence would be those likely to have the most offspring, this would give them an evolutionary advantage.

As well as leading to a greater degree of social intelligence, a larger brain size confers further evolutionary advantages because of an increase in general intelligence. Evidence of these great changes in our ancestors comes in the form of the first emergence of stone tools simply because these are the artifacts that have survived from this period. If people were capable of making tools out of stone, then they must surely have used other materials as well, such as wood, bone, and leather, but these have rotted away over time. The importance of the tools that have survived, like the one in the British Museum, thereby becomes more apparent because here we have a demonstration, literally carved in stone, of the cognitive abilities that differentiate us from other animals. Looked at in this way, this seemingly insignificant object is not only the oldest in the British Museum, but one of the most remarkable as well.

Most of the events discussed in this book concern either an individual or a small group of people who, when faced with a particular problem, have come to a decision about how best to deal with it. Here, we are concerned with a much more general aspect of the decision-making process: of when it first evolved in our distant ancestors and why it was a vital part of our development. The combination of intelligence and dexterity, which enabled early humans to make tools, represents one of the qualities that defined them as human and that continues to define us today. That lump of rock in the British Museum, then, not only tells us about where we came from, but also offers us a fleeting glimpse into the mind of one of our earliest ancestors, allowing us to get a better appreciation of ourselves and of what it is that makes us human.

DECISION

Social Change

Science and Innovation

Culture

Politics

Diplomacy

Military

Religion

THE MIGRATION OUT OF AFRICA

ca. 70,000 BP

Circumstances: People looking across a stretch of water wondering what the land on the other side is like

Protagonists: A small band of early modern humans in East Africa

Consequences: The spread of human beings around the world

Although fossil remains show that anatomically modern humans dispersed out of Africa into the Near East ~ 100 to 130 ka [thousand years ago], genetic evidence from extant populations has suggested that non-Africans descend primarily from a single successful later migration. Within the human mitochondrial DNA (mtDNA) tree, haplogroup L3 encompasses not only many sub-Saharan Africans, but also all ancient non-African lineages, and its age therefore provides an upper bound for the dispersal out of Africa.

Soares, P. et al, "The Expansion of mtDNA Haplogroup L3 within and out of Africa," *Molecular Biology and Evolution* **vol. 29 (3)**

In *The Descent of Man*, published in 1871, Charles Darwin proposed that human beings first evolved in Africa. He based this theory on the presence of gorillas and chimpanzees on the continent, observing that, in numerous places around the world, living species of mammals were closely related to similar extinct species from the same region and going on to say that he expected examples of extinct species of apes to be found in Africa. It was a controversial theory at the time and remains so today, at least to those who refute the whole idea of evolution in the first place. Over the years, evidence has accumulated to support Darwin, including the discovery of fossils of our early ancestors and, as we saw in the previous chapter, evidence of their cognitive abilities in the form of stone tools. So, if we accept that human beings originally evolved in Africa, then people must have migrated out of the continent at some point because we now live in almost every available inhabitable place on Earth and, in order for this migration to take place, difficult decisions must have been taken for people to leave behind their homeland and head out into the unknown.

OUT OF AFRICA

The most widely accepted theory of human migration is known as the Out of Africa theory, which suggests that modern humans evolved in East Africa about 200,000 years ago before spreading out across the continent and then migrating farther afield. Fossil evidence of bones of anatomically modern humans found in Israel dating to 125,000 BP indicate an early migration took place from what is now Egypt and across the Sinai, the peninsula of land separating the Mediterranean Sea from the Red Sea, but signs of habitation only continue here for about 10,000 years, so this is usually taken as a false start. The earliest date supported by good evidence for a sustained migration out of Africa is at about 70,000 BP, when people crossed the relatively narrow Bab el Mandeb strait at the southern end of the Red Sea, which separates the African state of Djibouti from Yemen on the Arabian Peninsula. At present, the strait is about 12 miles (20 km) wide, but 70,000 years ago the sea level was 250 ft (80 m) lower as a consequence of the Ice Age, which locked up huge quantities of water at the poles as ice, making the crossing at the time almost half the distance. Today the coast of the Arabian Peninsula is mostly barren desert, but at the time of the migration it consisted of a low-lying plain, now underwater, where numerous freshwater springs created a band of green vegetation.

Presumably this lush plain would have been visible across the narrow strait and must have looked very inviting to those people on the much drier African coast.

IN THE GENES

The interior of the Arabian Peninsula was an arid and inhospitable desert throughout the Pleistocene, as it still is today, so the people who first made the decision to cross over the strait probably stayed in the coastal region. As the climate began to warm at the end of the Ice Age, about 12,000 years ago, sea levels rose and covered any signs they may have left behind, preventing the discovery of any material evidence to support the Out of Africa theory. Since the late 1980s, however, advances in the field of genetics have meant that the theory has been corroborated by research into the distribution of specific genetic markers known to have first arisen in Africa in various populations of people from other parts of the world. Much of this research has concentrated on investigating mitochondrial DNA — strands of genetic material in the mitochondria of cells (organelles involved in respiration and energy production) that are passed down exclusively through the female line of inheritance. Mitochondrial DNA is relatively stable compared to the DNA in the chromosomes of the cell nucleus, which can be subject to a greater degree of mutation during the process of cell division so can vary much more over time. This relative lack of change makes it possible to track sections of mitochondrial DNA, known as haplogroups, back over long periods of time, allowing geneticists to unravel the route specific haplogroups have taken as people have moved around the world.

One of these haplogroups, known as L3, arose in East Africa, making it possible to differentiate between people from this region and those from the south and west of the continent, who most commonly have the L1 and L2 haplogroups rather than L3. Everybody else in the world outside of Africa has a haplogroup derived from L3, indicating that they are all descended from people of East African origin rather than from anywhere else on the continent. The relatively high level of genetic conformity between people who are not African in origin compared to the much greater differences between those from different parts of Africa also suggests that a small number of people left the continent in the first migration, perhaps as low as 200 but more likely a few

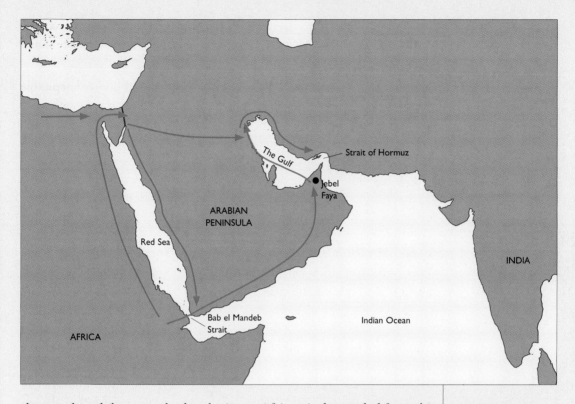

thousand, and that everybody who is not African is descended from this small genetic pool. As mitochondrial DNA does vary over time, if only slightly, it has been possible to date this first migration to approximately 70,000 years ago based on the amount of variation that has occurred. Going further back still, this slight variation in mitochondrial DNA has also been used to propose the theoretical existence of a single woman, known as Mitochondrial Eve, who was the common ancestor to all of us and lived about 200,000 years ago somewhere in East Africa.

The Out of Africa theory may be the most widely accepted theory, particularly since it has been backed up with genetic evidence, but it is not supported by everybody working in the field of human evolution. A competing idea, known as the Multiregional theory, suggests that modern humans evolved in separate parts of the world as a result of a much earlier migration out of Africa, occurring at around 1.5 million years ago, by an older species of human known as *Homo erectus*. According to the theory, *H. erectus* was effectively the same species

OUT OF AFRICA
Modern humans most likely first migrated out of Africa across the narrow Bab el Mandeb strait, but could also have crossed the Sinai Desert.

© Aki | Dreamstime

LAKE TOBA
The volcanic winter resulting from an eruption here in about 74,000 BP resulted in a drastic reduction in human populations.

as modern humans and, after migrating out of Africa, it adapted to the different conditions it encountered in various parts of the world, thereby giving rise to the diverse populations of people we have today. The relative conformity of DNA found in people who are not of African origin does not support this theory because it indicates that they are descended from a small group who migrated much more recently. Supporters of the theory have attempted to account for this by suggesting that migrations occurring after that of *H. erectus* have had the effect of mixing genes from different populations so that, while they show local adaptations, their genetic make-up has remained very similar.

Recent research, published in the journal *Science* in 2011, also challenges the Out of Africa theory as it stands at the moment. Stone tools found in the United Arab Emirates have been dated to 120,000 BP and are consistent with those being used in Africa at this time by modern humans, suggesting a much earlier date for the first migration into the Arabian Peninsula than previously thought. No fossil remains have been found, which would convincingly prove the case, and this might be another instance, like the finds from Israel, of people existing outside Africa for a limited period rather than going on to migrate around the rest of the world. One possible explanation is that the Toba event, one of the largest ever volcanic eruptions, which occurred in Sumatra in about 74,000 BP, caused a major reduction in the human population as a consequence of a prolonged volcanic winter, in which dust and ash in the atmosphere caused a significant drop in temperature and a corresponding fall in the available food resources. Any people who had migrated out of Africa before this, it has been speculated, either did not survive or, if they did, remained in such small numbers that they have left few traces behind them.

THE BEACHCOMBER MODEL

Whatever the truth of the matter, genetic research has shown that people certainly began to spread out across the world 70,000 years ago, most likely by moving along the coasts in what is sometimes known as the beachcomber model of human migration. This coastal route was followed because this is where most resources were available, but has again made archaeological research difficult because of the rising sea levels at the end of the Ice Age. What we can say is that people appear to have moved along this coastal route quickly, getting to India a few thousand years after leaving Africa and continuing to spread through South East Asia before arriving in Australia by about 50,000 BP. This rapid expansion eastward is in sharp contrast to a much slower migration to the north. Modern humans only began to enter Europe about 40,000 years ago, perhaps as a consequence of the colder climate in this region during the Pleistocene glacial periods or perhaps because the territory was already occupied by Neanderthals (*Homo neanderthalis*). The first peopling of the Americas took longer still, occurring, according to current estimates, at some point between 20,000 BP and 15,000 BP, after people first began to cross a land bridge between Russia and Alaska, across what is now the Bering Straits.

We still have a long way to go to fully understand the nature of human migration around the world, but over the past few decades advances in technology, particularly in DNA analysis, have begun to fill in many of the gaps. As the body of knowledge increases, the more it tends to confirm Darwin's theory of an African origin of modern humans, who then migrated out from there, first across the Red Sea into the Arabian Peninsula and then on into Asia and the rest of the world. It is, of course, impossible to know now exactly what motivated those first migrants to embark on such a dangerous adventure, exchanging the comfort of the familiar for the uncertainties of the unknown, but it is not hard to imagine people looking across the Bab el Mandeb and wondering what the land on the other side was like. That sort of insatiable curiosity, together with a desire for a better future and, perhaps, our general dissatisfaction with our given lot, has been the driving force behind many decisions made throughout the course of human history. Alternatively, the final decision to leave may have been made out of necessity, if, for instance, people were forced from their land by a prolonged drought and the ensuing famine, causing them to make a desperate bid for survival by taking to boats or rafts and heading for the land they could see across the water. With no chance of knowing for certain, all we can really say is that those people who first set out on humanity's long journey around the world were demonstrating our innate capacity to consider the options available to us and make a decision about what to do.

AS THE BODY OF KNOWLEDGE INCREASES, THE MORE IT TENDS TO CONFIRM DARWIN'S THEORY OF AN AFRICAN ORIGIN OF MODERN HUMANS

THE FIRST FARMERS

ca. 12,000 BP

Circumstances: The right conditions for the first adoption of farming

Protagonists: Hunter-gatherers and farmers in the Fertile Crescent

Consequences: The greatest social change in the history of humanity

The development of agriculture around the globe entailed innumerable historically contingent decisions by individuals and communities confronted by what they perceived as risks and opportunities. But they took those decisions, of course, without knowing the likely outcome. It is important that we do not fall into the trap of evaluating those decisions with the benefit of hindsight—a tendency that has characterized so much thinking about the reasons for the agricultural revolution—from, as it were, the perspective of the supermarket checkout counter.

Graeme Barker, *The Agricultural Revolution in Prehistory*

It may be hard to envisage for most of us, but almost everybody living in the world today is part of a society fundamentally based on agriculture. In the more developed countries, less than 1% of the population is directly involved in farming, so it is hardly surprising if the vast majority of people give little thought to the role it continues to play in the modern world. In terms of the overall history of humanity, agriculture is actually a recent development, going back for only about 12,000 years of the 200,000 years since human beings first evolved as a separate species on the East African savannah. For most of that time, we have existed as hunters and gatherers, as a very small number of people still do, finding sustenance from the natural world. The change from this foraging way of life to one based on farming has been described as the greatest social upheaval human beings have ever been through. It is known to archaeologists as the Neolithic transition, after the period in which it occurred, when the adoption of farming was accompanied by a whole array of related changes: people began to live in more settled communities, use more advanced stone tools, and develop methods of making pottery. As the transition began thousands of years before the invention of writing, we can only get an idea now of how these momentous changes occurred from an interpretation of the archaeology left behind, making it impossible to know for certain what was going through the minds of people during this critical turning point in human history. But the decisions made during this process had a huge impact at the time and continue to be relevant today, making them among the most important in all of human history.

Agriculture has arisen independently on a number of occasions around the world, but was first practiced in the region known as the Fertile Crescent, an arc of land straddling an arid interior, beginning in the foothills of the Zagros Mountains of modern-day Iran and extending across Iraq and Syria and on into southern Turkey along the valleys of the Tigris and Euphrates, before continuing southward through the Levantine Corridor of Lebanon, Israel, and Jordan. Many of the cereal crops that still form the basis of agricultural systems around the world, including wheat, barley, and rye, were first domesticated from their wild ancestors here, as were a number of other important food crops, such as various varieties of peas, beans, and lentils. A similar story can be told for livestock; cattle were first domesticated from aurochs, their wild

THE FERTILE CRESCENT

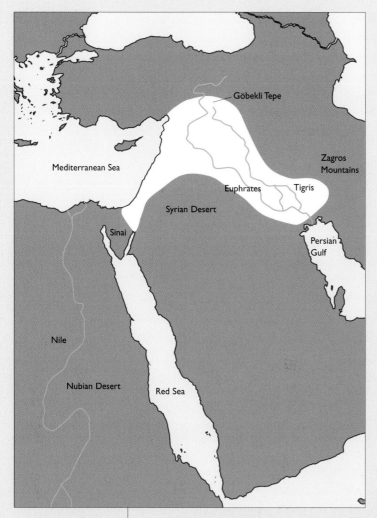

Göbekli Tepe

Zagros
Mountains

Mediterranean Sea

Euphrates   Tigris

Syrian Desert

Sinai

Persian
Gulf

Nile

Nubian Desert   Red Sea

FERTILE CRESCENT
Farming first began in the
crescent-shaped region
between the deserts and
mountains of what is now
the Middle East.

and now extinct ancestors, in this region, while both sheep and goats have their origins in wild species from the Taurus Mountains.

The reason why farming first began in the Fertile crescent, as opposed to anywhere else, has been a hotly debated subject in archaeology throughout the history of the discipline and numerous theories have been put forward to explain it. One of the most widely supported theories suggests that climate change at the end of the last Ice Age, beginning about 15,000 years ago, was instrumental in bringing about the adoption of farming. The warming climate created favorable conditions in the Fertile Crescent for those species of animals and plants used by hunter-gatherers, leading to a rise in their population, before a sudden cold snap, beginning in about 12,800 BP and known as the Younger Dryas, returned the region to the climatic conditions of the Ice Age. This change appears to have happened very rapidly, perhaps in the space of only a few years, and it lasted for more than a thousand, during which time the amount of food available to hunter-gatherers would have been much reduced. In this situation, the adoption of farming can be regarded as a response to these changing conditions because it provided a more reliable source of food than could be obtained solely from hunting and gathering, so the decisions involved in the transition were ones made out of necessity.

Archaeological research has found that hunter-gatherers from this period were healthier than farmers, living to an older age and suffering from fewer diseases, while farmers were exposed to a wide range of diseases passed on to them by their livestock and were also more likely to develop health problems associated with repetitive labor, like arthritis and lower back pain. Comparative studies of modern hunter-gatherer societies, most

© Louriv | Dreamstime

FARMING TODAY
A valley in the Fertile Crescent of eastern Turkey, where agriculture has been practiced for many thousands of years.

famously by Marshall Sahlins in his paper *The Original Affluent Society*, first published in 1966, have shown that hunter-gatherers spend less time and effort providing food for themselves than farmers do, which, taken together with the archaeological research, lends support to the theory that people only adopted agriculture in the first place because they were forced into it by climate change. Why, the argument goes, would anybody voluntarily choose to live in a way that involves long hours of back-breaking work when an easier alternative was available, unless a desperate situation, like the prospect of starvation, left them with no other choice?

SEDENTISM

In his influential book *The Birth of the Gods and the Origin of Agriculture*, the French archaeologist Jacques Cauvin formulated an alternative theory for the adoption of agriculture. He observed that human beings are rarely passive participants in the way they live their lives who are forced into a course of action entirely by circumstances outside of their control. In his view, people have the ability to make calculated decisions about fundamental issues, leading him to propose that the domestication of livestock and crops was not a necessity dictated by adverse conditions, but a conscious choice made as a consequence of sedentism, the phenomenon of people settling down to live permanently in one place. Sedentism, according to Cauvin, was accompanied by a corresponding shift in religious belief from the veneration of animals and places characteristic of nomadic hunter-gatherers to the worship of the ancestors and sky gods commonly found in more settled communities. Rather than seeing farming as the first stage of sedentism, Cauvin thought that people first settled down to live in one place as hunter-gatherers, leading to a shift in their belief system that facilitated the adoption of agriculture.

The Natufian culture of the Levantine Corridor, which existed from about 14,000 BP to 10,000 BP, spanned the transition from hunter-gathering to farming, or, as archaeologists would say, from the Epipaleolithic to the Neolithic, and provides some support for Cauvin's theory. At the beginning of the Natufian, some hunter-gatherers were living in permanent villages of about 200–300 people, while others in the more marginal areas on the edge of the desert continued to be semi-nomadic. Archaeologists have found stone sickles and grinding stones, used in the harvest and processing of wild cereals, in Natufian villages, together with granaries for storing grain, showing that the technology needed for farming was already present before cultivation began. This implies that the transition to agriculture could well have been quite smooth, taking place over a relatively long period of time rather than occurring in one revolutionary moment. So, instead of people making a momentous decision that would have completely changed their lives and from which there was no going back, the transition to agriculture could well have involved a series of small incremental changes that resulted eventually in farming without those people making the decisions at each stage in the process being aware of the final outcome.

GÖBEKLI TEPE

The chronology of sedentism as envisaged by Cauvin is further supported by the excavation currently underway at Göbekli Tepe, a site in southeastern Turkey considered to be one of the most important archaeological discoveries made in recent times. Only 5% of the site has been excavated so far, but what has been found indicates that it contains the oldest religious buildings discovered anywhere in the world. The lowest layers have been dated to 12,000 BP and are made up of 20 circular enclosures, which, as no residential buildings have been found, are thought to have been used entirely for ritual purposes. Each enclosure is composed of an outer ring of 12 T-shaped standing stones, connected to each other by stone benches, with two taller stones of a similar shape in the middle of the circle, some of which reach 16 ft (5 m) in height. Most of the standing stones have been decorated with carvings of animals and, in a few cases, with human arms and clothing, suggesting that they are symbolic representations of ancestors or gods.

Large numbers of animal bones and cereal grains have been found within the site, all from wild species of animals and plants rather than domesticated ones, suggesting that it was constructed and used by hunter-gatherers rather than farmers. The sophisticated nature of the symbolic art found here and the degree of social organization required to build such monumental structures are both remarkable and unparallelled from a site of such early date. The amount of work required to construct the complex, and the number of people needed to do it, is an indication of the importance that must have been attached to it and, while the exact nature of their belief systems remains a mystery, the huge quantities of animal bones and cereal grains found makes it likely that the rituals performed here involved feasting on a very large scale. One speculative theory even suggests that this sort of ritual feasting, which included the consumption of a large amount of beer, could have been what led to the invention of agriculture in the first place, because herding livestock and cultivating cereals may have been the only way of ensuring the supply of sufficient resources of food and beer at the moment when they were required for a feast.

Klaus Schmidt, the German archaeologist leading the excavation at Göbekli Tepe, has estimated that it will take another 50 years to excavate the whole site, and there are numerous other potential sites in the region that have yet to be investigated at all. The picture emerging from this ongoing research is of a highly organized and complex society experiencing a fundamental transition; while climate change and population growth must surely have played a role, the main driving force appears to have been the people themselves and the decisions they were making. It is impossible to point to a single key decision that led directly to the adoption of farming; more likely, it was a long process involving many choices and with an eventual outcome not envisaged by those who were making the choices. But it is no coincidence that the region where farming originated was also the one where people first began to live together in towns and cities, where what we might now describe as civilization first developed, because such societies relied on farming to provide a sufficient supply of food. And, as far removed from farming as most of us have now become, much the same remains the case today.

DECISION

Social Change

Science and Innovation

Culture

Politics

Diplomacy

Military

Religion

THE SUMERIANS BEGIN TO WRITE

ca. 3400 BC

Circumstances: The need for a method of keeping track of an increasing amount of information in an expanding city

Protagonists: The scribes of the Sumerian city of Uruk

Consequences: The first use of true writing

His speech was substantial, and its contents extensive. The messenger, whose mouth was heavy, was not able to repeat it. Because the messenger, whose mouth was tired, was not able to repeat it, the lord of Kulaba patted some clay and wrote the message as if on a tablet. Formerly, the writing of messages on clay was not established. Now, under that sun and on that day, it was indeed so. The lord of Kulaba inscribed the message like a tablet. It was just like that.

From "Enmerkar and the Lord of Aratta," a Sumerian myth dating to the third century BC containing one of the first known references to the beginning of writing

Writing has developed independently in a number of different parts of the world, but it is generally agreed to have first been used in Uruk, the largest of the city-states, known to us today collectively as Sumer, that developed in southern Mesopotamia during the fourth century BC. Despite technically being the moment at which prehistory becomes history, we still have to rely on the interpretation of archaeological evidence to get an idea of how this major advance in human culture occurred, because writing was initially used solely as a means of record-keeping in the administration of the city. The first written documents were made by those professional scribes in Uruk who were employed to keep track of the quantities and movements of agricultural produce and manufactured goods. They appear to have hit upon a way of simplifying their method of record-keeping by using what is known in linguistics as phonetic symbols. The decision to adopt these symbols, which may have been taken collectively by a small number of scribes or could possibly even have been the invention of a single individual, would lead to what might be described as true writing. But before going on to consider the decisions taken by these Sumerian scribes and the wider consequences, perhaps it would be as well to pause briefly to discuss what constitutes true writing.

A LINGUISTIC INTERLUDE

In linguistics, true writing involves the use of phonetic symbols, such as the letters of the alphabet, to stand for spoken sounds that, when put together, make up the words of a particular language. Before the advent of this form of writing, people were using simpler methods of recording information, beginning with pictograms, which were straightforward drawings of an object. As more complicated writing systems began to develop, pictograms evolved into logograms—more abstract symbols representing entire words—so that, as long as people knew what each symbol meant, more complicated pieces of information could be written down. The disadvantage of this method is that spoken languages are made up of thousands of words, so thousands of symbols are required to represent them, making the process of learning to read and write a long and complicated one, and even with all these symbols it is difficult to write with the same grammar used in speech. Splitting words up into their constituent sounds greatly reduces the number of symbols required, making the learning process and the use of grammar much easier. The innovation achieved by the Sumerian scribes of Uruk in the fourth century BC was to introduce phonetic symbols, indicating particular sounds rather than complete words, into the logographic writing system they were already using. While this cannot be classed as true writing, which technically must consist of a complete phonetic system of both vowels and consonants, it is nevertheless reasonable to say that it was the beginning of the process that would eventually lead to true writing.

THE URUK PERIOD

At its height in the fourth century BC, Uruk had a population in excess of 50,000 people, making it by far the largest city in the world at that time and allowing it to dominate the whole of the Mesopotamian region. The administration of such a large city was the driving force behind the innovations in record-keeping, which were initially made by using a pointed wooden stylus to make marks on a wet clay tablet. Once these tablets had dried in the sun, or had been baked in an oven, they proved to be much more durable than later writing on prepared animal hides (parchment and vellum) or paper so that, today, huge archives, some containing thousands of tablets, have been found in archaeological excavations of numerous ancient cities in Mesopotamia and beyond.

© Jakub Cejpek | Dreamstime

CLAY TABLET
An example of cuneiform writing in the Sumerian language made by pressing a reed into clay to make a wedge-shaped mark.

The earliest clay tablets date to about 3400 BC and have been found in what is known to archaeologists as the Uruk IV level of excavations in the city. Unfortunately, a clear progression of writing systems has not been established because the archaeological evidence indicates that a number of different systems were in use at the same time, but the most likely scenario is that the use of clay tablets developed out of an accounting system that employed clay cylinders. Small discs of clay, each impressed with logographic symbols to represent a certain quantity of goods, say a number of sheep or a certain quantity of cloth, were placed in a cylinder, which was then sealed with wet clay. A city official would then use an inscribed cylinder seal to impress their own identifying symbols in the clay, guaranteeing both the contents of the cylinder and the transaction that was being enacted. What appears to have happened is that, as the tokens were sealed inside the cylinder, a separate record was made on a flat piece of clay to keep track of the transaction and, at some point, it was realized that the cylinder and tokens were actually not necessary at all as long as everybody concerned recognized what had been written on the clay tablet. The symbols used for sheep and cloth, and for whatever else was being transacted, were gradually simplified so that, rather than drawing a sheep every time a deal was struck, a scribe could make a mark indicating a sheep with a few marks of the stylus.

Over time, the symbols became more abstract, and easier to write, establishing a logographic system of writing in which only these stylized symbols were in use. The leap from this to using abstract symbols to represent sounds rather than complete words might have been first accomplished by using the same symbols for homophones—words that are pronounced in a similar way but mean different things (such as "deer" and "dear" in English)—and then putting a number of these together to make a completely different word. This establishes the principle that a symbol stands for a sound rather than being directly related to an object and, from this point, it is not such a great step to invent symbols for any further sounds needed to make up a particular word. In this way, a phonetic writing system begins to emerge, even if in Uruk words constructed in this way were used alongside logographic symbols rather than replacing them completely.

By about 3000 BC, the influence of Uruk was beginning to diminish in Mesopotamia, but by that time the writing system first developed there had spread to other city-states in the region. By about 2500 BC, documents were being written on clay tablets in a number of different languages in what is known as the cuneiform script, including in Akkadian, the region immediately to the north of Sumer. The Akkadian language had the advantage over Sumerian of being more closely related to a number of other Mesopotamian languages and so became much more widely used because it could more readily be understood by a larger number of people. The method of writing also changed as the cuneiform script became more widely adopted; documents were written by impressing the end of a piece of reed into the clay to make a characteristically wedge-shaped mark (cuneiform literally means "wedge-shaped"), which was much easier and quicker than scratching out a mark on clay with a pointed stylus.

Cuneiform was in use for the next 1,500 years and, despite retaining some logographic symbols as well as phonetic ones throughout this period, it is widely regarded as being the earliest example of a true writing system.

CUNEIFORM

It was gradually superseded by the much simpler Phoenician alphabet from about 1000 BC, which consisted of only about 20 symbols and was fully phonetic, even if it did not originally contain any vowels. The seafaring Phoenicians, who were from what is now the coast of Lebanon, developed extensive trading links around the Mediterranean and their writing system was widely adopted throughout much of this region. The Ancient Greeks used the Phoenician alphabet and added vowels to it, which greatly increased the capacity of the written language to reproduce the same sounds as existed in the spoken language. From Greece, the alphabet would eventually spread to Rome, where it was adapted into the form that many of us use today.

THE DECISIONS MADE BY THOSE SUMERIAN SCRIBES IN URUK MORE THAN 4,000 YEARS AGO CAN BE SEEN AS THE FIRST OCCASION WHEN WRITING BEGAN TO DEVELOP

The development of writing, then, was by no means a straightforward process that can be traced by a direct line from Sumer through to the Phoenicians and then on to the Greeks and Romans. But the decisions made by those Sumerian scribes in Uruk more than 4,000 years ago to simplify their accounting method so they could deal with an increasing amount of information can be seen as the first occasion when writing began to develop in the direction that would eventually lead to true writing. Some academics consider that Egyptian hieroglyphics are at least as old as Sumerian writing, and a debate continues among them as to whether hieroglyphics arose independently or were the result of contact and cultural diffusion between Egypt and Mesopotamia. Some have also argued that the Phoenician alphabet arose out of hieroglyphics via an intermediary script known as proto-Sinaitic and had nothing to do with the cuneiform script at all. If this were the case, then the path toward fully phonetic writing had nothing to do with the Sumerians. Nevertheless, even if cuneiform was an evolutionary dead end in the history of writing, it takes little away from the decisions made by those Sumerian scribes more than 4,000 years ago, which demonstrated that necessity is a great motivating force for innovation and change.

THE EGYPTIAN AND HITTITE PEACE TREATY

ca. 1259 BC

DECISION

Social Change

Science and Innovation

Culture

Politics

Diplomacy

Military

Religion

Circumstances: An attempt by warring empires to find a peaceful way of settling their differences

Protagonists: The Egyptian pharaoh Ramesses II and the Hittite king Hattusili III

Consequences: A mutually beneficial peace treaty

Now Ramesses, the great king of the country of Egypt, has established this bond by treaty on a silver tablet with Hattusili, the great king of the country of Hatti, his brother, starting from this day, to settle forever among them a good peace and a good fraternity. He is a brother to me and he is at peace with me and I am a brother to him and I am forever at peace with him. We are united and a bond of peace and fraternity exists between us and it is better than the bond of peace and fraternity that used to exist between the country of Egypt and the country of Hatti.

From the Hittite version of the Peace Treaty

PEACE TREATY
The original Hittite version of the Egyptian–Hittite peace treaty, found in Turkey in 1906 and now in Istanbul's Archaeological Museum.

The United Nations Security Council meets in permanent session in an attempt to fulfill its role of maintaining peace and security in its member states through diplomacy and, where that approach has failed, has the power to authorize further measures of intervention in conflicts through the use of sanctions, peacekeeping forces, or direct military action. Immediately outside the chamber where it meets in the UN Headquarters in New York, there is a scaled-up copy of a clay tablet hanging on the wall that contains the text, written in the cuneiform script, of a peace treaty negotiated in about 1259 BC between the representatives of the Ancient Egyptian pharaoh Ramesses II and those of the Hittite king Hattusili III. The original was found in 1906 during archaeological excavations of Hattusha, the capital city of the Hittites in central Turkey, and, taken together with the corresponding inscription on the wall of an Egyptian temple, it is the earliest known example of a peace treaty that has survived into the modern age. The copy was given to the UN by the Turkish Government in 1970 and, by hanging it in such a prominent position, the intention was presumably to inspire modern diplomats as they entered the Security Council chamber and show them that negotiating peace between warring states has had a very long history. It might also suggest that, if the Egyptians and Hittites could decide to sort out their differences in such a sensible manner more than 3,000 years ago, then surely it is not beyond us to do the same today.

COMPETING EMPIRES

Little was known about the Hittites before the discovery of Hattusha, where monumental building work and huge city walls were uncovered by archaeological excavation, together with an extensive archive of over 10,000 clay tablets that contained details of many aspects of Hittite society and included a library of diplomatic documents and letters concerning relations with their neighboring states. By about 1500 BC, the Hittites had expanded beyond their original homeland in central Anatolia to occupy territories in northern Mesopotamia and the Levantine region of what is now Syria, Lebanon, and northern Israel. Some of this territory in the Levant had formally been under Egyptian control, leading to a long-running conflict between the Hittites and the Egyptians that came to a head in about 1274 BC at the Battle of Kadesh. Ramesses II had come to the throne in Egypt five years previously and, in an effort to regain the territory lost to the Hittites by his ancestors, personally led his army against the forces controlled by the Hittite king Muwatalli II, the elder brother of Hattusili III. The ensuing encounter is thought to be the largest chariot battle ever fought, with as many as 6,000 chariots taking part, and was proclaimed afterward by Ramesses as being a great victory for the Egyptians.

Up until the discovery of the Hittite archives, the account given by Ramesses, inscribed on the walls of a number of Egyptian temples, was taken as being accurate. As more details have come to light, it appears that Ramesses may well have been exaggerating the success of his forces and, in reality, the battle had been fought to a stalemate in which the Egyptians had been unable to capture the strategically important city of Kadesh, but had nevertheless prevented any further incursions by the Hittites into Egyptian territory. Over the following 15 years, numerous other smaller military encounters between Egyptian and Hittite forces occurred in this disputed region, without either being able to gain a decisive advantage, and it is against this background of constant low-level warfare that the two sides would eventually negotiate a settlement that would put an end to hostilities between them.

A PRAGMATIC DECISION

Hattusili III came to power in Hattusha in about 1267 BC after deposing his nephew Mursili III, the son and heir of Muwatalli II, and appears to have wanted to legitimize his position as king of the Hittites among both his own people and the surrounding states. One of the ways he tried to achieve this was through establishing diplomatic relations, apparently in the belief that, if neighboring states were prepared to deal with him, then it created the impression at home and abroad that he was really in charge. The Hittite archive contained numerous examples of correspondence between Hattusili and other rulers from all over the region, but, as much as he proclaimed his right to be king, by no means all of his own subjects accepted him. As well as this uncertainty over his legitimacy as king at home, he was also facing the rising power of the Assyrian Empire on the eastern borders of his empire, so the last thing he needed was more trouble with the Egyptians on his southern border.

The mood in Egypt was not so obviously in favor of reaching an accommodation with the Hittites. Ramesses II was certainly not facing any challenge to his authority at home; he was widely regarded at the time as being one of the greatest of all the pharaohs. In line with the traditional practice of Egyptian pharaohs, he had embarked on a huge and expensive program of monumental building projects to further enhance his reputation and ensure that he would be remembered in the future. But the constant state of war with the Hittites had placed a great strain on his resources and he was well aware of the potential threat posed by the rising power of the Assyrians in the Levant, so he may well have been more open to the idea of a peace treaty than first impressions might indicate. The stumbling block that he faced was that, as he had boasted about winning a great victory over them at Kadesh, he could hardly approach them 15 years later to propose a peace settlement without having to admit that the battle had not gone quite as well as he had claimed.

We don't know exactly how the peace treaty came about, but in the circumstances it appears likely that Hattusili made the first move, perhaps sending an envoy to Ramesses to suggest the start of negotiations. The resulting treaty was written in the usual diplomatic language of the period, stressing the sort of ideals of brotherhood and eternal peace that are a feature of international agreements today, but there can be little doubt that what led to the settlement were pragmatic decisions that had mutual benefits for both sides. As well as all the flowery language, the treaty contained provisions ensuring that neither side would invade the territory of the other and would come to each other's aid if either was attacked by a third party, which, without actually saying it, meant the Assyrians. The wording of the treaty allowed both sides to present it as a significant victory at home; Ramesses could claim that the Hittites had come to him asking for peace, while Hattusili could say he had dealt on equal terms with the great pharaoh, the most powerful man in the world at the time, and had come away with the settlement he had set out to achieve.

Relations between the Egyptians and Hittites remained cordial, if not particularly friendly, for a long period after the treaty came into force, enabling both states to pursue their own agendas without interference from the other. Contact was maintained by a regular correspondence, and, 13 years later, Hattusili sent one of his daughters to Egypt where she was married to Ramesses, becoming one of his many wives and given the title of Great Royal Wife. After Hattusili died, in about 1237

BC, peace was maintained, but the power of the Hittite Empire began to decline as it faced challenges from the Assyrians and from raiders from the west collectively known as the Sea Peoples. It would not be long before the terms of the treaty carried little meaning because the Hittites had ceased to present a threat to the Egyptians. In about 1200 BC, Hattusha was abandoned and the Hittites disappeared from history completely until their capital city was rediscovered in the early twentieth century. The Egyptians were faced with similar threats from the Assyrians and Sea Peoples and, even though their empire persisted for much longer, they also entered a period of decline and would never regain the power and prestige that Ramesses II had enjoyed during his reign.

The decisions of the Egyptians and Hittites to negotiate a peace treaty was, then, more about the self-interest of the parties involved than it was about any great desire for peace for its own sake. So, if the diplomats of today take the time to contemplate the clay tablet hanging on the wall outside the chamber of the UN Security Council, perhaps the lesson to be learned from it is that it is possible to negotiate a peace settlement between opposing states no matter how long or acrimonious the dispute, but to be effective it has to be mutually beneficial. It is a terrible irony that the most intractable conflict of the modern age, between Israelis and Palestinians, has developed over much of the same territory as was being fought over more than 3,000 years ago. As there are few indications that either side today is willing to compromise to find a peaceful solution, perhaps it is possible to point toward those decisions made by the Egyptians and Hittites as an example of a way forward. The Egyptians and Hittites may not have liked each other very much, but, in the end, at least they found a way of living together in peace.

THE DECISIONS OF THE EGYPTIANS AND HITTITES TO NEGOTIATE A PEACE TREATY WAS, THEN, MORE ABOUT THE SELF-INTEREST OF THE PARTIES INVOLVED

DECISION

Social Change

Science and Innovation

Culture

Politics

Diplomacy

Military

Religion

THE ATHENIANS CHOOSE DEMOCRACY

508 BC

Circumstances: The city-state of Athens emerges from a period of tyranny

Protagonists: The citizens of Athens

Consequences: The first attempt at a democratic system of government

Many forms of government have been tried, and will be tried in this world of sin and woe. No one pretends that democracy is perfect or all-wise. Indeed, it has been said that democracy is the worst form of government except all those other forms that have been tried from time to time; but there is a broad feeling in our country that the people should rule, continuously rule, and that public opinion, expressed by all constitutional means, should shape, guide, and control the actions of ministers who are their servants and not their masters.

From a speech given by Sir Winston Churchill in the British House of Commons on November 11, 1947

In the Gettysburg Address, Abraham Lincoln set out with clarity and concision his vision of a democratic government, which, he said, should be "of the people, by the people, for the people." He overtly eluded to the Founding Fathers of America who signed the Declaration of Independence in 1776 and may have also made a more subtle reference to ancient Athens, widely considered to have been the first democratic state. The historian Garry Wills has pointed out the parallels between Lincoln's speech at Gettysburg and a funeral oration given by the Athenian statesman Pericles (495–429 BC) during the Peloponnesian War, fought between Athens and Sparta. There is no way of knowing if Lincoln really drew inspiration from this source — and some reports of the occasion suggest he composed the speech while traveling on the train from Washington to Gettysburg, writing it out on the back of an envelope — but, if he had, then it would have been entirely fitting to have evoked

CLEISTHENES
A modern bust of the father of democracy by Anna Christoforidis. No ancient likeness is known to exist.

the beginnings of democracy at a moment when he was looking forward to the period after the end of the Civil War, to a renewal of America and what he called a "new birth of freedom." Whatever the truth of the matter, Lincoln's words stand as a powerful and eloquent reminder of the importance of a system of government in which citizens are free to make their own decisions, either directly on particular issues, as they did in Athens, or by holding elections to appoint specific individuals as representatives, as most democracies do today.

THE ATHENIAN WAY

The roots of the word "democracy" are in the Greek words *demos* and *kratos*, which taken together literally mean "people power." It is generally agreed that the first truly democratic system of governance was established in Athens by Cleisthenes in 508 BC, making this the date usually given for the beginning of democracy. The reforms introduced by Cleisthenes appear to have been based on a previous attempt at introducing democracy in about 594 BC by the Athenian statesman Solon, who rarely gets the credit for his actions because the system he introduced only lasted for a few years before being overthrown by Peisistratus, a member of one of the noble families of Athens who, after taking power by force, went on to rule as a tyrant. The democracy established by Cleisthenes, on the other hand, lasted for almost 200 years, up until the period of Alexander the Great, and encompassed the golden age of classical Athens, considered by many to be the birthplace of Western civilization.

The democracy instituted by Cleisthenes after the tyranny established by Peisistratus had been overthrown involved a fundamental reform of Athenian society, from the city being divided into four tribes led by members of noble families to a more egalitarian system based on the division of the city and the surrounding countryside into ten areas known as demes, which are comparable to modern electoral constituencies. The idea was to reduce the influence of the nobility, who had been responsible for instituting tyranny, by encouraging Athenian citizens to be loyal to their deme rather than to a particular individual within a tribe. Democracy was exercised through three bodies: the assembly, at which every Athenian citizen was entitled to attend and vote; the council of 500 citizens, selected by lot and consisting of 50 citizens from each deme; and the courts, which presided over legal cases and were made up of jurors numbering in the hundreds who were also selected by lot from among the demes.

The important issues, such as those involving war and peace, were dealt with through the assembly, which met once a month in a large flat area on the Pynx, a hill overlooking Athens, which, it has been estimated,

could accommodate 6,000 people. Any citizen had the right to speak at the assembly and decisions were reached by a show of hands, making it very democratic, even if not all of the 30,000 citizens of Athens could have attended an assembly meeting at the same time. Setting the agenda for the assembly was one of the responsibilities of the council, which otherwise dealt with the more routine decisions required for the day-to-day administration of the city. Selection by lot for both the council and the courts was adopted because it was thought that elections would favor the wealthy and powerful families of Athens, who could exert influence over others by appealing to their loyalty or by bribery. Drawing lots was obviously random and would ensure people from all sections of society were represented, although the positions were unpaid up until the system was reformed by Pericles in about 457 BC, so it favored those who could afford the time to take part.

ATHENS
A view across the city from the Pynx, the hill where Athenian citizens met to exercise their democratic rights.

© Klaas Lingbeek | iStockphoto

At first sight, this system of direct democracy in which all eligible citizens could take part in the decision-making process may appear to be as close to being perfect as possible, and it certainly led to a long period of stability in Athens that allowed the city to flourish. But the truth is that only 20% of the population of Athens were considered to be citizens, leaving all the rest, including women and people who were not born in the city, without any rights at all. The prosperity of the city was also based on slavery and, of course, slaves had no rights either. Rather, they were the ones who did all the work, allowing citizens, at least those wealthy enough to own slaves in the first place, free to spend their time attending meetings and exercising their democratic rights. The idea of equality, then, may have been central to the Athenian system, but it only applied to those who were, in George Orwell's words, "more equal than others."

It is, perhaps, too harsh to judge the Athenian experiment in democracy by comparing it with the liberal democracies of today, in which the right to vote and universal suffrage normally form a core part of the constitution. Before dismissing what the Athenians achieved, it is also worth remembering that universal suffrage only became law in Britain in 1928, when women were given the vote, and had to wait until 1965 in America, at which point civil rights legislation guaranteeing the right to vote for everybody became enshrined in the constitution. And there are, of course, plenty of countries around the world today where democracy either doesn't exist at all or has been hijacked in an attempt to legitimize despotic rule. So, if we can assume that democracy is a good thing, then it is not unreasonable to regard the Athenian version as the first step in a very long and ongoing process that continues today. It might not have been perfect, and the democracy that some of us enjoy today might not be perfect either, but at least the citizens of Athens could make their own decisions, so that, if it all went wrong, they had nobody else to blame but themselves.

A LIMITED DEMOCRACY

DECISION

Social Change

Science and Innovation

Culture

Politics

Diplomacy

Military

Religion

SIDDHARTHA GOTAMA GOES IN SEARCH OF ENLIGHTENMENT

ca. sixth century BC

Circumstances: A young man leaves his family to search for enlightenment

Protagonists: Siddhartha Gotama, aka the Buddha

Consequences: The beginnings of the Buddhist faith

Firm in his resolve and leaving behind without hesitation his father who turned ever toward him, and his young son, his affectionate people, and his unparallelled magnificence, he then went forth out of his father's city.

From the epic poem *Buddhacharita*, one of the earliest known accounts of the life of Siddhartha Gotama, composed in the first century AD by the Sanskrit poet Aśvaghoṣa

The earliest accounts of the life of Siddhartha Gotama were written down in the first century AD, more than 400 years after he is thought to have lived, so even though these accounts may well be based on much earlier stories preserved in the oral tradition of the region of northern India where he lived, it is difficult to know if they were really intended to be an accurate portrayal of the man who became known as the Buddha, an honorific title meaning "the awakened one." It is equally likely that these accounts were presenting a mythologized version of the Buddha's life, a story adapted over generations of its telling to place an emphasis on those important spiritual events that would give shape to the emerging Buddhist faith. One of these key events, recounted in all the stories, is how, as a young man of 29, Siddhartha made the decision to leave his comfortable home and become a mendicant, a wandering monk who relied on the charity of others to sustain him. It was a decision that would determine the entire course of his future life, setting him out on the path toward enlightenment and, through his subsequent teaching, would lead to the establishment of the central tenets of Buddhism.

SIDDHARTHA LEAVES HOME

Siddhartha was, we are told, born in the town of Lumbini in the foothills of the Himalayas of what is now southern Nepal. In some accounts of his life, his father is described as being the king of the Sakya people, making him a prince, but there is little evidence to support the assertion that Sayka society actually included a royal family and it has become more usual to suggest that Siddhartha's family were in fact aristocratic and wealthy rather than royal. He grew up in the family home in Kapilavatthu, near where he was born, and lived a very comfortable early life, sheltered from the outside world by his father and protected from any signs of human suffering. This easy life continued until he was 29, when he began to take trips away from his home on his own and, as he encountered for the first time people who were sick and dying, was suddenly confronted by the reality of human suffering.

The realization that the world is filled with pain and suffering appears to have had a profound effect on Siddhartha. He became intensely dissatisfied with his life of comfortable domesticity and could find no pleasure in the birth of his first son, seeing only the inevitability of all the people he loved living in sorrow before eventually growing old and dying. On his next trip away from home, Siddhartha met one of the many mendicants traveling the roads and pathways of northern India at that time and decided there and then to become one of them and to search for a solution to the suffering he had seen at the heart of humanity. That same night, at least according to some accounts of his life, he is said to have taken one last look at his sleeping wife and their newborn son, knowing that if he lingered he would not be able to go, before leaving his family and everything else that was tying him to the life he could no longer bear to live.

ENLIGHTENMENT

Over the course of the next six years, Siddhartha lived the life of an ascetic, denying himself worldly pleasures and traveling extensively around northern India to study under a number of different religious teachers. He became adept in the techniques of meditation, but this still did not lead him toward the awakening he was seeking, so, in apparent desperation, he tried to live an even more austere life by hardly eating anything at all. After almost dying of starvation, he realized that this was not the right path either, but he was not prepared to give up his search. He recalled a moment from his childhood when his father had taken him to see the ceremonial first ploughing of the fields before a crop was planted in the spring, and realized that, when he had been left alone and was sitting under a tree, he had unconsciously entered into a meditative state in which he had been completely calm and happy but, at the same time, had retained complete awareness and was capable of deep reflection. He resolved to find a suitable tree where he could meditate in solitude using this new "middle way" he had discovered within himself, which took a path between lavish self-indulgence and extreme austerity, and, once he had found the right place, remain there until he had achieved enlightenment.

© Traveler | iStockphoto

BODHI TREE
The shrine in Bodh Gaya around a descendant of the sacred fig tree where the Buddha is said to have achieved enlightenment.

Siddhartha found the secluded spot he had been seeking under a bodhi tree—a variety of sacred fig—near what is now the town of Bodh Gaya in the Indian state of Bihar. During the first night of meditating, he achieved enlightenment by gaining a full insight into the causes of human suffering and the way in which it could be overcome. It has become the most important pilgrimage site in Buddhism, and the bodhi tree that grows there today is believed to be a direct descendant of the original one. The Buddha, as he can now be called, spent the following seven weeks at the bodhi tree thinking over what he would do next. He decided to teach what he called the Four Noble Truths, which he described to his first pupils in a discourse known in English as *The Setting in Motion of the Wheels of Dharma*. These truths form the fundamental teachings at the center of the Buddhist faith, and the Buddha would spend the remaining 45 years of his life discussing, explaining, and elaborating on them as he continued to travel around northern India.

In her book simply entitled *Buddha*, the religious scholar and writer Karen Armstrong explains the Four Noble Truths in a straightforward way:

> The first of these verities was the noble truth of suffering (*dukkha*) that informs the whole of human life. The second truth was that the cause of this suffering was desire (*tanha*). In the third noble truth, Gotama asserted that Nibbana (Nirvana) existed as a way out of this predicament, and finally, he claimed that he had discovered the path that leads from suffering and pain to its cessation in the state of Nibbana.

STANDING BUDDHA
A first century AD statue of the Buddha from Gandhara in northern Pakistan, now in the Tokyo National Museum.

It is a little beyond the scope of this book (and a long way beyond the understanding of its author) to attempt a full explanation of the Buddhist faith, but, for anybody wanting to find out more, Armstrong's book would be a good place to start. As far as Siddhartha's original decision to leave his former life behind is concerned, then, to our modern sensibilities, it might appear to have been a rather self-indulgent one, to abandon his wife and newborn child to go in search of an entirely personal enlightenment. Needless to say, none of the accounts of his life mention what his wife thought about his decision, but perhaps to look at it from this perspective is to take the biographical details too literally. When faced with having to decide between continuing to live comfortably with his family or leaving that life behind in order to search for a way of ending the pain and suffering of the human condition, Siddhartha chose the more difficult and uncertain path. This tells us that such an undertaking will not be an easy journey for anybody else seeking to emulate the Buddha and that personal sacrifices will have to be made in order to achieve enlightenment. But, in making his great decision, the Buddha not only transformed his own life, but initiated a system of belief that would transform the lives of many millions of other people as well.

DECISION

Social Change

Science and Innovation

Culture

Politics

Diplomacy

Military

Religion

ASHOKA THE GREAT RENOUNCES WAR

ca. 262 BC

Circumstances: The man who started a war of conquest becomes disgusted by its terrible consequences

Protagonists: Ashoka the Great and the people of the Mauryan Empire

Consequences: Empire ruled on the principles of nonviolence and tolerance, the spread of the Buddhist faith

Ashoka was at first disposed to follow the example of his father and grandfather and complete the conquest of the Indian peninsula. He invaded Kalinga (255 BC), a country on the east coast of Madras, he was successful in his military operations and—alone among conquerors—he was so disgusted by the cruelty and horror of war that he renounced it. He would have no more of it. He adopted the peaceful doctrines of Buddhism and declared that henceforth his conquests should be the conquests of religion.

H. G. Wells, *A Short History of the World*

At its height during the reign of the emperor Ashoka the Great (ca. 304–232 BC), the Mauryan Empire extended over almost all of the Indian subcontinent and beyond into modern-day Afghanistan and eastern Iran. It was the largest empire ever to exist in the region, and nothing approaching its size would be seen again until the establishment of the British Raj more than 2,000 years later. On ascending to the throne in about 274 BC, Ashoka at first continued the military campaigns and empire-building of his predecessors, either occupying new territories by force or by the threat of force. After eight years, he appears to have made the momentous decision not to continue with his campaigns of conquest and colonization and, instead, renounced the use of any further acts of war. From that time onward, he began to espouse the Buddhist way of nonviolence and tolerance, becoming what we might now call a missionary by promoting the Buddhist faith within his empire and sending emissaries to those states he may formerly have considered invading to spread the knowledge of Buddhism by entirely peaceful means.

Much of what we know about Ashoka and his transformation from a warrior into a man of peace derives from Buddhist texts written centuries after his death, but there are also some primary sources still in existence today, scattered across the territories of his former empire. These are known as the Edicts of Ashoka and mostly take the form of inscriptions carved into stone pillars and rock faces. Many deal with the concept of *dharma*, the Buddhist teachings of natural and moral law, covering such concerns as how to live a good life and, in Ashoka's case, how to run an empire in accordance with the principles of Buddhism. But some of the texts also provide us with insights into the reasons why Ashoka took what was, at the time, a radical and unprecedented decision to adopt the principle of nonviolence, one that, at least among kings and emperors, has few parallels in history.

A ROCK EDICT
An impression of the first rock edict of Ashoka from Girnar in Gujarat, written in the Brahmi script.

THE MAURYA DYNASTY

The dynasty was founded by Ashoka's grandfather, Chandragupta Maurya, who rose from obscurity to become a military leader and, in about 322 BC, led a successful plot to depose the king of the Nanda Empire in Magadha, formerly a kingdom in the east of India. As soon as he had taken control of the empire, Chandragupta began to mount campaigns of conquest against the states to the west of Magadha, taking advantage of a power vacuum that had developed after Alexander the Great withdrew his Greek and Persian armies from the region and left them under the control of his subordinates. Alexander's death in 323 BC led to a period of turmoil in these regions, giving Chandragupta the opportunity to take possession of them and extend his own empire westward, right up to the Persian border. Chandragupta's son and heir Bindusara succeeded to the throne in about 298 BC and continued the expansionist policies of his father, capturing territory to the south and adding much of peninsular India to the empire.

According to the Buddhist sources, Bindusara had many wives, who together bore him 100 sons. Ashoka—born in Pataliputra, the capital of the empire (now the city of Patna in the state of Bihar)—was one of them, and as one of the younger sons, born to a junior wife, he was by no means the most obvious candidate to succeed his father. But from a young age he began to gain a reputation as an intelligent and talented military commander, being sent by his father to put down rebellions in parts of the empire while still in his teens. Bindusara died in 272 BC, when Ashoka was 22 years old, and, with Shushima, the oldest son and heir apparent, absent from Pataliputra, he seized the opportunity to claim the throne for himself. Shushima, we are told, was killed on his return to the capital and, after Ashoka became emperor, he had all of his other brothers killed as well, except for the youngest one, who was his full brother and had become a monk, so presumably did not pose any threat.

KALINGA At the start of his reign, Ashoka proved to be ruthless and brutal, repressing any opposition and further expanding his empire by conquest, leading to him becoming known as Ashoka the Cruel. After eight years, he decided the time had come to invade Kalinga, a coastal region in the east of India that had resisted both his father and grandfather. One of the best known edicts, known as the Rock Edict No. 13 and quoted here from the version given in Charles Allen's book, *Ashoka: The Search for India's Lost Emperor*, describes what happened:

> Beloved-of the-Gods, King Piyadasi [the titles and name adopted by Ashoka], conquered the Kalingas eight years after his coronation. One hundred and fifty thousand were deported, one hundred thousand were killed, and many more died from other causes. After the Kalingas had been conquered, Beloved-of-the-Gods

came to feel a strong inclination toward the Dharma, a love for the Dharma, and for the instruction of the Dharma. Now Beloved-of-the-Gods feels deep remorse for having conquered the Kalingas.

The remorse shown by Ashoka after the mass slaughter and deportation of so many people in Kalinga appears to have been genuine. For the remainder of his 40-year reign as emperor, he refrained from any further military campaigns, despite having by far the most powerful forces in the region. He could easily have overpowered the last remaining region of the subcontinent that he had not already conquered, the tip of the Indian peninsula in what is now Kerala and Tamil Nadu, but he appears to have shown no inclination to do so.

The exact moment when Ashoka converted to Buddhism is unclear, and it could possibly have come at an earlier time than the Kalinga war, but from that point onward he committed himself to following the teachings of the dharma. As well as ruling his people with tolerance and benevolence, he stopped hunting animals and became a vegetarian, extending the new-found compassion to all living things. It was the beginning of an attitude that still exists in many parts of the Indian subcontinent today and also one that would be recognized by anybody who follows the Buddhist faith. This new approach may have been nonviolent, but it was by no means passive and, while he did not use force or intimidation to spread Buddhism, he did everything else he could to promote it within the empire and in regions beyond its borders. He sent his eldest son, Mahinda, to Sri Lanka where, according to the Buddhist chronicles, he first converted the king and queen and then established the faith more widely among the people of the island. Missionaries were sent out elsewhere to perform similar tasks, spreading Buddhism far beyond the region of northern India where it originated and leading some people to describe Ashoka as being the second most important person in the history of the faith after the Buddha himself.

The tolerance displayed by Ashoka toward people of other religions is widely admired in India today. The wheel at the center of the Indian flag is the Ashoka Chakra, a symbol representing the eternal wheel of life that was inscribed alongside many of the Edicts of Ashoka. It can be seen on the base of the Lion Capital of Ashoka, a sculpture of four lions that originally stood on top of a pillar in Sarnath, the place

© Ekaratch | Dreamstime.com

LION CAPITAL
A thirteenth-century replica of one of the Pillars of Ashoka from Sarnath with the Ashoka Chakra on top of four lions.

near the city of Varanasi where the Buddha first began to teach the dharma, and it is now in a nearby museum. In 1950, a depiction of the Lion Capital was chosen as the emblem of the newly independent Republic of India and it has since appeared on currency, stamps, passports, insignia on government buildings, and for just about every other purpose imaginable for which an official symbol of India is required.

Ashoka died in 232 BC at the age of 72 and was succeeded by his grandson Dasaratha. The empire may already have been in decline by the time of Ashoka's death and it gradually unraveled over the next few decades until, 50 years later, its last emperor was assassinated and it fell apart completely. The achievements of Ashoka disappeared into obscurity, where they would largely remain for the next 2,000 years, until serious research into the early history of the subcontinent began in the nineteenth century. The major breakthrough was made by James Prinsep (1799–1840), a British scholar and employee of the East India Company, who deciphered the Brahmi script in which the edicts had been written. This allowed researchers to read the text written on pillars and rock faces during Ashoka's reign and compare the information uncovered with the Buddhist text that described the exploits of what had previously been thought to be a purely mythological king. But even after the man himself had been long forgotten, he left a tangible legacy in the widespread adoption of Buddhism and the teaching of the dharma, along with the observance of the principles of nonviolence and tolerance that continue to this day.

JULIUS CAESAR CROSSES THE RUBICON

49 BC

DECISION

Social Change

Science and Innovation

Culture

Politics

Diplomacy

Military

Religion

Circumstances: Julius Caesar, standing on the banks of a river, thinks about what to do next

Protagonists: Caesar, Pompey, and the citizens of the Roman Republic

Consequences: The Roman Empire replacing the Roman Republic

Coming to the banks of the Rubicon, the boundary of his province, Caesar halted for a while, and considering the importance of the step he was about take, turned to those with him and said, "We may still withdraw, but if we cross this little bridge, we will have no choice but to fight it out." While he was caught in two minds, a man of noble bearing and graceful aspect appeared close at hand, who sat down and played a shepherd's pipe. Soldiers gathered to listen to him, trumpeters among them. He took a trumpet from one of them, ran to the river with it, and sounding the advance with a piercing blast, crossed to the other side. On seeing this, Caesar was roused from his thoughts and shouted out, "Let us accept this as a sign from the gods and follow it to wherever the iniquity of our enemies will take us. The die is cast."

Suetonius, *The Lives of the Twelve Caesars*

To cross the Rubicon is, proverbially, to decide on a course of action from which there can be no going back; by doing so you may, to employ a few more expressions, pass the point of no return or burn your bridges. The Rubicon itself does not present much of an obstacle. It is a minor river in Italy, flowing eastward out of the Apennine Mountains to the coast between Rimini and Cesena, and it is no more difficult to cross today than it was on January 10, 49 BC, when Julius Caesar stood on its northern bank with the soldiers of one of his legions, apparently hesitating while he decided what to do next. The decision he faced had nothing to do with how to get to the other side — he was standing right next to a bridge; it was what the river represented that was giving him pause for thought. It marked the boundary between the Roman province of Cisalpine Gaul, then under his own governorship, and Italia, the region surrounding Rome itself and directly governed from the city. Military commanders were expressly forbidden by Roman law from entering Italia at the head of an army, as Caesar was about to do, and he was well aware of the consequences of his actions. To cross the river was a capital offence for both himself and for anybody who accompanied him, so, if he crossed with his legion, he would either have to seize control of the city by defeating the forces loyal to Rome commanded by his former ally and now bitter rival Gnaeus Pompeius Magnus, better known as Pompey, or face the death penalty. After taking a moment to reflect on the enormity of the decision he faced, Caesar crossed the Rubicon, igniting a civil war and, at least according to the historians Plutarch and Suetonius, both writing more than 100 years after the event, coining his own phrase as he did so; *alea iacta est*, the die is cast.

THE PATH TO THE RIVER

Gaius Julius Caesar, to give him his full name, was born in 100 BC into an old aristocratic family of the patrician class that had lost much of its former wealth and power. From an early age, Caesar appears to have set himself the target of regaining his family's past glory and set out to achieve his aims by distinguishing himself as a military commander. By 60 BC, he had made his reputation as an outstanding general in the Roman army and his achievements had propelled him into the political spotlight. To further his ambitions, he entered into an agreement of mutual understanding with two other successful military commanders who had also crossed over into politics, Pompey and Marcus Licinius

Crassus, an alliance that would become known as the First Triumvirate. As a direct result of this alliance with the two men who would otherwise have been his biggest rivals, Caesar was elected as Consul of Rome, the highest elected political office in the republic. The controversial nature of the election, in which bribery and corruption had been rife, together with suspicions about his conduct during the one-year term of the office, led to his opponents demanding that he be held to account after his term had expired. While in office, Caesar had been immune from prosecution and, again with the help of Pompey and Crassus, as his term was drawing to a close, he was awarded the governorship of three provinces: Cisalpine Gaul, Transalpine Gaul in the south of France, and Illyricum on the eastern coast of the Adriatic. Provincial governors were given immunity as well as the Consul, allowing Caesar to continue to avoid the prosecutions his political opponents were intending to bring against him.

JULIUS CAESAR
A bust of the Roman general, consul, and dictator, now in the National Archaeological Museum of Naples.

The governorships came with the command of four legions, which Caesar used over the course of the next ten years to complete the conquest of the remainder of Gaul—a victory that made him both very wealthy and very popular with the citizens of Rome. When Crassus died in 53 BC, Pompey seized his chance to outmaneuver Caesar, who was still in Gaul, by forming alliances with his former opponents in the Senate, a group known as the Optimates. He was also well aware of Caesar's popularity as the conquerer of Gaul so, together with the Optimates, he pushed for an order to be issued by the Senate to relieve Caesar of his command and recall him to Rome to face the prosecutions he had managed to avoid. Caesar had expected to return in triumph after his victory and to be appointed as Consul again to ensure he would still not face any charges, but in 50 BC the Senate did what Pompey wanted and summoned him back to Rome. If he were to comply without the protection of immunity he could have been charged with the capital crime of treason, thereby risking not only his political career but also his life.

The Senate had effectively backed Caesar into a corner; he could either submit to the law of Rome, give up his army and political ambitions, and be put on trial for his life, or he could fight it out with Pompey while he still retained the command and loyalty of his legions. This was the apparent dilemma he faced as he was standing on the banks of the Rubicon; however, as he had one of his legions with him, it would appear likely that he had already made the decision to fight. In his own account, *The Civil War*, Caesar doesn't even mention crossing the river. All he says is that, because of the injustices he had suffered at the hands of Pompey and the Senate, he marched the 13th Legion from Ravenna in Cisalpine Gaul to Rimini in Italia, a route that required him to cross the border between the two at the river. By omitting an account of the river crossing, he may have been attempting to avoid acknowledging that, by entering Italia at the head of a legion, he was breaking Roman law, even if this would have been obvious to his contemporaries. Caesar's account, in truth, is more an exercise in self-justification than an attempt to establish an accurate portrait of events, in which he presents himself not so much as leading a rebellion against Rome, but as freeing the city from the dictatorial rule of Pompey.

BY OMITTING AN ACCOUNT OF THE RIVER CROSSING, HE MAY HAVE BEEN ATTEMPTING TO AVOID ACKNOWLEDGING THAT HE WAS BREAKING ROMAN LAW

As Caesar's single legion, a force of 6,000 men, advanced toward Rome, Pompey decided to abandon the city and retreat to the south of Italy, despite having a much larger army at his disposal. Caesar pursued him and again he refused to fight, this time escaping to the Roman provinces in Greece. Before going after him, Caesar made a remarkable forced march to Spain, where Pompey had additional forces stationed, leaving Mark Antony, his closest ally, in command in Rome. After easily defeating Pompey's forces in Spain, Caesar took his legions to Greece and engaged Pompey in a number of battles before decisively defeating him in 48 BC at the Battle of Pharsalus. Pompey fled to Egypt, with Caesar not far behind, and was assassinated there on the orders of the young pharaoh Ptolemy XIII, who could not have been more than 14 years old. Ptolemy was involved in civil war himself, fighting with his sister Cleopatra for overall control of Egypt, and appears to have thought that, by murdering Pompey, he would ingratiate himself with Caesar, who would make a powerful ally against Cleopatra. When Caesar arrived in Egypt, he was presented with Pompey's severed head, a gesture that had exactly the opposite effect. Caesar was enraged that a Roman citizen could be assassinated and the body disrespected in such a manner, so, rather than allying himself with Ptolemy, he famously went on to forge an alliance with Cleopatra.

The death of Pompey all but ended the civil war. Caesar quickly dealt with the few supporters of Pompey who refused to submit to him and pardoned those who did. In 46 BC he returned to Rome and this time celebrated in proper style with a triumphal entry into the city. He became dictator of Rome for a period of ten years, an unprecedented term for a role previously only thought necessary in times of crisis, and used the power he had been granted to begin widespread reforms in the administration of the city and empire. At the beginning of 44 BC he was made dictator in perpetuity, becoming a king in everything but name. A group of 60 senators, including Caesar's friend Marcus Junius Brutus, opposed the idea of one man having so much power and began to plot a conspiracy to kill him. On the Ides of March (the 15th), he was stabbed to death in the Senate—the only place where his bodyguards were not with him—by numerous members of the conspiracy, including Brutus. If he spoke any last words, they were not recorded at the time and those most often attributed to him now, "Et tu Brute?", were actually put into his mouth by Shakespeare. In his will, Caesar left his estate to his 18-year-old great nephew and adopted son Octavian who, despite his youth, would prove to be ruthless and calculating in the power struggles and civil wars that erupted after Caesar's death. Octavian eventually came out on top, defeating Mark Antony, his main rival, at the battle of Actium in 31 BC and becoming the first emperor of Rome under the name of Augustus Caesar.

It is impossible to know now if Julius Caesar had intended to become the supreme leader of Rome when he initiated the civil war with Pompey by crossing the Rubicon. On defeating Pompey, he certainly became very powerful, but did not resolve the dilemma of how best to exercise that power, which would have ultimately required him either to dissolve the Senate and declare himself emperor or to relinquish some of his authority and abide by the laws of the Republic. The only thing we can be certain of is that, in making that decision to cross the Rubicon in 49 BC, Julius Caesar began a sequence of events that culminated in the establishment of the Roman Empire, whose preeminence would survive in one form or another for a further 1,500 years.

© Giovanni Antonio Pellegrini

CAESAR'S DISGUST
The Head of Pompey Presented to Caesar by the Venetian artist Giovanni Antonio Pellegrini (1675–1741).

DECISION

Social Change

Science and Innovation

Culture

Politics

Diplomacy

Military

Religion

PAUL ON THE ROAD TO DAMASCUS

ca. 32–36

Circumstances: A man sets out on a journey from Jerusalem to Damascus

Protagonists: St. Paul and the early Christians

Consequences: The development of Christianity into a major religion

Meanwhile Saul, still threatening murder against the disciples of the Lord, went to the high priest and asked him for letters to the synagogues at Damascus, so that if he found any who belonged to the Way, men or women, he might bring them bound to Jerusalem. Now as he journeyed he approached Damascus, and suddenly a light from heaven flashed about him. And he fell to the ground and heard a voice saying to him, "Saul, Saul, why do you persecute me?" And he said, "Who are you, Lord?" And he said, "I am Jesus, whom you are persecuting, but rise and enter the city and you will be told what you are to do."

Acts of the Apostles, 9: 3–6

What we know today of the life of St. Paul comes solely from the Acts of the Apostles and the Epistles in the New Testament of the Bible, which were letters written by Paul himself to the churches he had founded in various places around the Mediterranean. In the Epistles, Paul only writes about his life where biographical details have some relevance to the theological point he is making, so we have not been left with anything like a full biography from this source. The Acts are traditionally said to have been written by Luke, the author of the third Gospel, who apparently knew Paul personally and has provided us with more information about him, even if some of what Luke says does not exactly match the version given in the Epistles and we are still left with some large gaps. But his conversion to Christianity on the road to Damascus, in which he saw a vision of the risen Christ, is described on a total of five occasions, twice in the Epistles and three times in Acts, indicating that it was regarded by both Paul and Luke as being the pivotal moment in his life. The event itself is described in both sources as being a miraculous occurrence and, if we accept these versions of the story, then Paul did not make a decision to convert to Christianity; rather, he was being directed by Christ to do so. Regardless of how the conversion occurred, Paul's subsequent decision about what to do in its aftermath would have profound consequences because it would lay the foundation for the transformation of Christianity from being a minor sect into a major religion in its own right.

SAUL OF TARSUS

If we accept the nuggets of information we are given about Paul's life in the Epistles and Acts as being accurate, which not all religious scholars do, it is possible to get at least some idea of Paul's early life. He was born in the first or second year after the birth of Christ and came from a wealthy Jewish family in Tarsus, a Greek city within the Roman Empire in what is now southern Turkey, and was most probably known by the Jewish name of Saul. His father was a tent maker, a trade for which Tarsus was well known, and it is reasonable to assume that he followed his father into that business. The city was also known as a center of learning and Paul, who both spoke and wrote in Greek, appears to have received a good education there before going to Jerusalem as a young man, possibly to study Jewish law under the eminent scholar Gamaliel, a leading authority in the discipline at that time.

Paul tells us that before his conversion he had been a Pharisee, making him a member of a Jewish sect committed to maintaining a strict interpretation of the Law of Moses. At that time, the Jewish faith was coming under increasing pressure to change thanks to radical new ideas, not least those articulated by Jesus, who was regarded as the Messiah by his followers, thereby making him a heretic in the eyes of the Pharisees. Paul says that he did not actually meet Jesus, although he may have been in Jerusalem at the time of the Crucifixion, and afterward, as a Pharisee himself, became involved in the persecution of Christians, including being present at the stoning of St. Stephen, one of the earliest Christian martyrs. It was in this context, as a persecutor of Christians, that he decided to travel from Jerusalem to Damascus, intending, he tells us, to arrest any Christians he found there who had fled to the city to avoid persecution and bring them back to Jerusalem in chains.

ON THE ROAD | While traveling to Damascus, Paul was subjected to a sudden flash of light that blinded him and caused him to fall to the ground. At the same moment, a vision of the risen Christ was revealed to him, causing him to instantly convert to Christianity. In the vision, Jesus asked Paul why he had been persecuting Christians and said that, when he got to Damascus, he would be told what to do next. Once there, he was approached by a follower of Jesus called Ananias, who had also experienced a vision telling him that Paul had been chosen to spread the name of the Lord. Despite any misgivings Ananias may have had over Paul's reputation as a persecutor of Christians, he cured Paul of his blindness and, after instructing him in the faith, baptized him as a Christian.

CARAVAGGIO'S PAUL
The Conversion of Saint Paul by Caravaggio (1571–1610), depicting the moment of revelation on the road to Damascus.

Over the years, numerous attempts have been made to explain Paul's conversion experience in rational terms rather than miraculous ones. It has been suggested that he had some kind of seizure or an epileptic fit, while others have theorized that he had become disillusioned with his role as a persecutor and, perhaps as a consequence of feeling guilt over the death of Stephen, was either consciously or unconsciously seeking a way of atoning for his actions. However it came about, once he had made the initial step of converting, Paul threw all his considerable energy into his new faith. In truth, we don't know a great deal about what he did over the course of the ten years following the conversion because neither he nor Luke has much to say about it. He appears to have spent time traveling in Arabia and also went to Jerusalem, where he met Peter, the apostle who would also have a huge influence on the development of the early Church, and James, who he described as being the brother of Jesus and who would go on to become the leader of the Christian Church in Jerusalem. Other than these fleeting glimpses from his so-called "lost years," we can only assume that he was studying the faith and developing the means he would subsequently use to spread it.

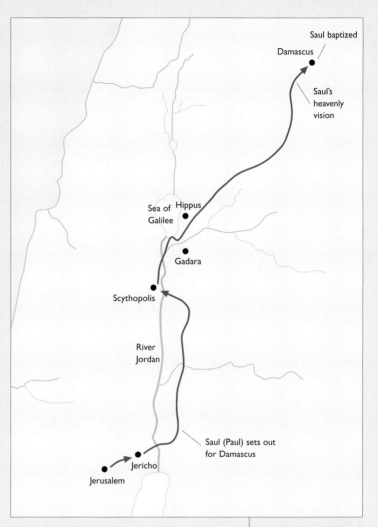

Paul reappears in about AD 45 at the beginning of his missionary work, which included traveling extensively around the Roman Empire to convert people to Christianity and to establish churches. He tells us about being involved in three shipwrecks on his missionary journeys and was also imprisoned on a number of occasions because of his beliefs, from which, Luke writes, he was released because he was a Roman citizen, making him subject to Roman law rather than the local law of those places where he had been arrested. Paul was preaching the New Covenant, a theology based on the belief that the route to salvation

ROAD TO DAMASCUS
The probable route taken by St. Paul on his journey from Jerusalem to Damascus showing the approximate location of the conversion.

was to be found in Jesus's death on the Cross and the Resurrection rather than through the Law of Moses. He had been involved in long debates with other figures in the early church, notably with Peter at what became known as the Incident at Antioch, in which he argued that Gentiles should be permitted to join the Church as well as Jews and that the Jewish law relating to circumcision and the proscribing of certain foods, which discouraged some Gentiles from converting, should be relaxed to make the faith more inclusive. In winning the argument, Paul ensured that Christianity welcomed everybody, no matter what their background or whatever sins they had previously committed.

Beginning in about AD 50, the Epistles were written in response to enquiries from some of the churches Paul had established. As well as being the earliest Christian documents in existence, predating the Gospels, the Epistles formed the foundation stones of Christian theology. In them, Paul developed the principle of universality, in which all churches held to the same core beliefs, thereby preventing early Christianity from splitting into obscure sects. So, as well as spreading the Word around the Roman Empire and opening up the faith to Gentiles, Paul greatly influenced the direction of early Christianity, separating it from Judaism and establishing it as a religion in its own right, one based on faith and inclusion rather than law and exclusivity.

© Tango 7174 | Creative Commons

PAPAL BASILICA
The interior of Saint Paul Outside the Walls in Rome, founded on the site where Paul is thought to have been executed.

The scriptures say nothing about Paul's death, which later traditions claim occurred in Rome in about AD 65. According to some stories, he was martyred during the persecutions of Christians initiated by the emperor Nero in an attempt to deflect blame away from himself for the great fire of AD 64, in which he is said to have fiddled while Rome burned. Paul is said to have been buried in a vineyard outside Rome in a site that was consecrated as a church by the Emperor Constantine in AD 324. The Papal Basilica of Saint Paul Outside the Walls now stands on the site and contains a sarcophagus where Paul's remains are thought to rest. But, even though Paul may have died in obscurity, the influence he had on the early Christian Church, both in its organization and its doctrine, was enormous. Many later Christian thinkers, including St. Augustine and Martin Luther, used Paul's writings as a starting point for their own theology, demonstrating his continuing importance, evidence of which was provided by the poet and clergyman John Donne in a famous sermon he gave in 1624 at St. Paul's Cathedral in London, in which he said:

> Wheresoever I open St. Paul's Epistles, I meet not words, but thunder, and universal thunder, thunder that passes through all the world... That that was done upon him, wrought upon all the world; he was struck blind and all the world saw better for that.

So, even if we were to concede that Paul's conversion was a miraculous occurrence rather than a conscious decision, his subsequent actions in devoting himself to Christianity would still rank among the greatest decisions ever made because of the impact he went on to have on early Christianity. It is, of course, impossible to know for sure, but without his energy and devotion, the Church may never have become established in the first place and, even if it had, would almost certainly not have developed into the major world religion it is today.

DECISION

Social Change

Science and Innovation

Culture

Politics

Diplomacy

Military

Religion

CONSTANTINE CONVERTS TO CHRISTIANITY

ca. 306–337

Circumstances: The early history of the Christian Church

Protagonists: Constantine, his mother, and the Christians of the Roman Empire

Consequences: Christianity became the official religion of the empire

When I, Constantine Augustus, and I, Licinius Augustus, met near Milan and were considering public welfare and security, we thought that, among those things which could be done for the good of the people, those regulations pertaining to the reverence of the Divinity ought certainly to be made first, so that we might grant to Christians and others full authority to observe whichever religion they preferred.

From the Edict of Milan, signed by Constantine and Licinius in AD 313

© Katie Chao | Creative Commons

For much of its early history, Christianity was very much a minority religion in the Roman Empire and Christians were the subject of state-sponsored persecution. The fortunes of the Church changed completely under the rule of the emperor Constantine the Great (ca. AD 272–337), when the religion not only became officially tolerated under the authority of the Edict of Milan, issued in 313, but would become the predominant religion throughout the empire over the course of the following few decades. The driving force behind this change is thought to have been the conversion of Constantine; if this is the case, then it was one of the greatest individual decisions in the history of the religion because it created the conditions under which Christianity could grow into the major world religion it is today.

The circumstances of the conversion are far from clear; Constantine himself later claimed that he converted during the Battle of the Milvian Bridge in 312 when, at least according to one version of the story, soldiers under his command reported seeing the sign of the Cross in the sky and, after painting crosses on their shields, went on to win the battle. No specifically Christian iconography was included on the Arch of Constantine—the monument erected to celebrate the victory, which still stands near the Colosseum in Rome—leading some to doubt the validity of this version of events. Constantine was not actually baptized until 337, 25 years after the battle, suggesting that, whenever he converted, it was either not politically expedient to publicize the fact at the time, as it surely would have been after winning a great victory, or that he was not as committed to the Christian faith during his life as was made out after he died. An alternative theory proposes that he was introduced to the Church at an early age by his mother, Helena, who is thought to have been a Christian at the time of his birth, so there was no great conversion event in his life at all because he was already a Christian, but had kept his beliefs to himself until he became emperor because of the discrimination he would have otherwise experienced.

Constantine was born in Naissus in the Roman province of Dardania, now Niš in Serbia. His father, Constantius, was a military commander

© Zsolt Farkas | Dreamstime

VICTORY ARCH
The Arch of Constantine, erected in Rome to celebrate victory in the Battle of Milvian Bridge, with the Colosseum in the background.

in the Roman army who rose to prominence under the emperor Diocletian. In AD 293, Constantius became part of the Tetrarchy, a system of governance developed by Diocletian that split the empire into eastern and western parts, each ruled by two men: a senior emperor to whom the title of Augustus was given; and a junior emperor who became known as Caesar. Constantius, who was appointed as Caesar by Diocletian, governed the western empire, which included Gaul, Britain and Spain; when he died in 306, Constantine was proclaimed as the new Caesar by his father's army. By this time, Diocletian had retired and a power struggle was developing between senior army officers in an attempt not only to gain a position in the Tetrarchy, but with the ultimate ambition of becoming the emperor of the whole Roman Empire.

Constantine's main opponent in the west was Maxentius and their dispute reached a head at Milvian Bridge, a crossing over the Tiber just to the north of Rome. In the ensuing battle, Maxentius drowned in the river, leaving Constantine as Augustus of the whole of the Western Roman Empire, with Licinius—the Augustus in the east—his only remaining rival for the position of sole emperor. Relations between the two initially appear to have been cordial and it was in this atmosphere that they met in Milan in 313, where Licinius married Constantine's sister and they both signed the Edict of Milan. Under the rule of Diocletian, the persecution of Christians had been particularly severe, so the edict represented a huge reversal of fortune and is now regarded as the biggest religious revolution in the history of the Roman Empire. The terms of the edict gave people of all religions the freedom to worship in whatever manner they chose, but also singled out Christianity for special treatment, both legalizing it and making provision for the return of property seized under Diocletian's persecutions.

MILVIAN BRIDGE
A fresco by Giulio Romano in the Apostolic Palace of the Vatican, painted in the early 1520s from a design by Raphael.

NEW ROME

In the east, Licinius continued to worship the pagan gods of Rome and, although Christians were no longer persecuted, they were not granted any special privileges either. Constantine, in contrast, actively began to promote Christianity in the west, beginning a program of church building in cities under his control, including the construction of the first church on the site of what is now St. Peter's Basilica in the Vatican City. By 320, Licinius had begun to renege on the terms of the edict by reinstituting persecutions, which was, in effect, a challenge to the authority of Constantine. A civil war ensued, ending in 324 with victory for Constantine at the Battle of Chrysopolis, making him the ruler of the whole of the Roman Empire. In the following year he decided to move the capital of the empire away from Rome to the Greek town of Byzantium in the eastern Mediterranean, renaming it as New Rome and beginning a huge program of construction that included massive new city walls, public buildings, and churches. By 330, much of the initial phase of building work had been completed and the new city was inaugurated in a ceremony that involved changing the city's name from Byzantium to Constantinople to honor the city's founder.

The manner of his baptism in 337, which only happened after it had become apparent that he was dying, has been the main cause of skepticism over Constantine's Christian convictions. To those who contend that Constantine was a cynical manipulator rather than a genuine convert, in which he only promoted Christianity because it suited his wider purpose of gaining control over the whole of the Roman Empire, his choice of the Christian religion was primarily due to it being monotheistic. This, the argument goes, fitted in with his intention of replacing the rule of the Tetrarchy with the rule of a single person, thereby leaving the empire with only one emperor and one God. A counterargument might suggest that, if Constantine was a Christian in name only, why did he bother to get baptized at all and why did he spend huge amounts of both his time and money on building so many churches when he could easily have professed his faith in a much simpler and less expensive way?

The Edict of Milan came into force when only about 10% of people in the Roman Empire were Christians, and most of them were from the lower classes, so it would appear that Constantine would have had little to gain politically by favoring the religion of a minority of poor people over the religions followed by the remaining 90% of the population. In 325 he was also responsible for convening the Council of Nicea, the first ecumenical council of representatives from all Christian denominations held to discuss matters of doctrine, which, among other things, established how the date of Easter would be calculated so that it would be the same for all churches. Taken together with construction of churches across the Roman Empire, this certainly looks like the actions of a true believer rather than somebody going through the motions for the sake of appearances.

LEGALIZING CHRISTIANITY UNDER THE TERMS OF THE EDICT OF MILAN WOULD BE THE FIRST STEP TO PLACING THE RELIGION AT THE HEART OF THE AFFAIRS OF THE ROMAN STATE

We may not be able to pinpoint the exact moment when Constantine converted to Christianity in the same way as we can for St. Paul, but if we can assume that his conversion really was an expression of his convictions, as the evidence suggests, then its significance for Christianity was almost as great. Legalizing Christianity under the terms of the Edict of Milan would be the first step to placing the religion at the heart of the affairs of the Roman state, as would happen in 380, when a later emperor, Theodosius I (347–395), recognized it as the official religion of the empire. The Western Roman Empire is conventionally said to have come to an end in 476, by which time Christianity was firmly established in Europe, while the Eastern Roman Empire, usually known as the Byzantine Empire today, continued for a further 1,000 years as a Christian state, right up until the fall of Constantinople to the Islamic Ottomans.

Constantine's actions certainly point toward a deeply held conviction and his apparently close relationship with his Christian mother suggest that he could well have been a follower of the faith from an early age. After he became emperor, she was given a prominent position in his imperial court, overseeing the church-building program he had begun. But, even if Constantine had always been a Christian and did not actually have to convert, his decision to instigate and sign the Edict of Milan would still rank as one of the greatest ever made in the history of the Church because of the consequences it would have for the development of the religion as a whole, which may otherwise have withered away under the constant threat of persecution. So, if we can say that St. Paul transformed Christianity from a minor Jewish sect into a separate religion in its own right, then Constantine brought the religion out into the open and set it on the path toward becoming the most widely observed faith today, now followed by an estimated 2.2 billion people around the world.

THE MAGNA CARTA

1215

DECISION

Social Change

Science and Innovation

Culture

Politics

Diplomacy

Military

Religion

Circumstances: The increasingly despotic rule of a monarch

Protagonists: King John, the barons, and the freemen of England

Consequences: The first expression of the constitutional rights and liberty of the individual

No free man will be taken or imprisoned or disseised [have their estate seized] or outlawed or exiled or in any way ruined, nor shall we go or send against him, save by the lawful judgment of his peers and by the law of the land.

To no man shall we sell, to no man shall we deny or delay, right or justice.

From the Magna Carta of 1215

Magna Carta literally means Great Charter in Latin and, in its earliest form, it is the text of a negotiated settlement reached between King John and a group of English barons who had rebelled at what they perceived to be his despotic rule and the heavy burden of taxation he had imposed on them. As every British schoolchild who was paying attention in their history classes should know, it dates to July 15, 1215, and was sealed by the king at Runnymede, an otherwise unremarkable field on the banks of the River Thames about 20 miles (30 km) to the west of London. It is comprized of a single large sheet of parchment on which 63 clauses setting out the agreement have been written in Latin. About 40 copies were originally thought to have been made, of which only four are known to survive today; one each in Salisbury and Lincoln cathedrals and two in the British Library. Although the true value of these national treasures cannot be gauged in purely monetary terms, their importance as historical documents was clear when a later version of the Magna Carta, dating from 1297, was sold in New York in 2007 for $21 million.

Over the years, Magna Carta has variously been described as the most important document in the world, the greatest constitutional document of all time, and the foundation stone of parliamentary government. The significance later attached to it was by no means apparent in 1215, not least because the terms of the settlement were broken within three months of it coming into force. It was not even the first charter sealed by an English king to define their responsibilities as monarch. The Charter of Liberties issued by Henry I at his coronation in 1100 was a direct forerunner of Magna Carta and set a precedent for monarchs to set out their duties in written form, even if they habitually went on to ignore them. What set Magna Carta apart was that it represented the first successful attempt by subjects of an English monarch to force their king to accept limitations on his power, compelling him to respect the liberties of so-called "freemen," who could not be punished solely on the orders of the king and, if accused of a crime, could only be prosecuted through the due process of the law of the land. It said nothing at all about the rights of women and children and, in restricting itself to freemen, specifically excluded serfs, those people who were held in a form of bonded labor that was little better than slavery and who made up something like 70% of the adult male population of England at that time.

But, despite its shortcomings, Magna Carta can be regarded as the beginning of the process of constitutional reform in English, and then British, history, that would eventually lead to the representative democracy of today. King John had little choice in the matter at the time, as he was compelled to accept the conditions in the document, so the historical decision we are dealing with here is the one made collectively by the barons who, rather than trying to depose the king, rebelled against his rule by presenting him with their terms to limit his power over them. The decision of the barons to rebel in this way may have been primarily motivated by their own self-interest, and their idea of liberty did not extend very much further than to themselves alone, but, whatever their motivation, the relationship between monarch and subjects changed and, once the door to reform had been opened, there would be no going back.

John was the youngest son of King Henry II, the first Plantagenet king of England, and Eleanor of Aquitaine, who, when they married, combined their lands to form an empire stretching from the south-west of France to southern Scotland, which included all of England and much of Wales and Ireland. As the youngest of five brothers, John was not expected to ascend to the throne, but three of them died before Henry II and in 1199, on the death of his only surviving older brother, Richard the Lionheart, John became king. After his coronation, he began a long and costly war in France against the supporters of Arthur of Brittany, the son of one of his older brothers and his only serious rival as a claimant to the throne. After Arthur was captured by John's army in 1203, he disappeared from history and, while we don't know exactly what happened to him, it is reasonable to assume that he was murdered on John's orders. But the removal of his rival did not put an end to the war and, over the next few years, John lost almost all of the territory he ruled in France. He would make a number of attempts to regain it. These culminated in 1214 with a decisive defeat at the Battle of Bouvines, in which King Philip II of France won control over the majority of the country for the first time.

The enormous cost of the war in France was one of the main sources of dissatisfaction among the barons of England, not least because John

KING JOHN

© Popperfoto | Getty Images

PLANTAGENET KING
An eighteenth-century illustration of King John showing him in about 1200, shortly after he ascended to the throne.

had extracted as much money as he could from them to pay for it. A particular irritant to a group of barons from the north of England, who would become known as "the Northerners," was scutage, a form of taxation the nobility had to pay in order to buy themselves out of military service. It was only one of numerous taxes and when these were combined with the king's other means of raising money, such as selling patronage and outright extortion, it led to a high level of opposition to his rule. The Northerners in particular gained little advantage from John's apparently endless war in France, yet it was costing them a fortune. Even before the war was lost, they had begun to organize themselves together to oppose his rule and when he returned from France in defeat, this opposition erupted into outright rebellion.

THE CHARTER

The barons assembled in January 1215 and, as there was no obvious candidate to replace John as king, they decided to force him to accept a list of their demands based on Henry I's Charter of Liberties. As more people joined them, momentum began to gather behind their cause, leading to a decisive moment in May when they approached London at the head of an army and, rather than having to fight, were welcomed into the city by its freemen. It was a disastrous turn of events for John, who now faced the very real possibility of losing his crown. Rather than risk any further defeats, and in order to buy time to gather his forces, he entered into peace negotiations with the barons at Runnymede. The barons were well aware that they had John over a barrel, so the terms contained in the peace settlement, which would become known later as Magna Carta, went far further than those of the original Charter of Liberties. Much of the detail contained in its 63 clauses is obscure today and relates to specific grievances, such as the scutage tax, but the two clauses quoted at the beginning of this chapter dealing with the freedom of the individual still resonate and also anticipate later laws relating to habeas corpus, the requirement for anybody who has been arrested to be charged and the evidence against them brought before a court. These two clauses, together with two others relating to the freedom of the Church and the freemen of London, are the only ones still to remain on the statute books of English law today, the rest having been repealed

© Antony McCallum | Creative Commons

RUNNYMEDE
A view across the River Thames of the meadow where the English barons met King John and where Magna Carta was sealed.

over the centuries either because they had become obsolete or because they had been replaced by more up-to-date legislation.

One of the most important clauses in the charter authorized the creation of a committee of 25 barons to oversee John's conduct and ensure that he stuck to the commitments he had made. It represented a direct threat to his authority and, almost as soon as he had placed his seal on the document, John appealed to Pope Innocent III to annul the whole charter on the grounds that it undermined his God-given rights as king and that he had only sealed it under duress. The Pope granted John's request, sparking a civil war, known as the First Baron's War, which continued into the following year. On October 18, 1216, John died, having contracted dysentery while campaigning, and was succeeded by his nine-year-old son Henry III, with Sir William Marshall acting as regent. Marshall was a widely respected man and he immediately reinstated the charter, although with the omission of the clause about setting up a committee of barons, bringing the war to an end.

ONE OF THE MOST IMPORTANT CLAUSES IN THE CHARTER AUTHORIZED THE CREATION OF A COMMITTEE OF 25 BARONS TO OVERSEE JOHN'S CONDUCT

The original Magna Carta, then, only came into effect for a matter of weeks before being annulled, but the principle of limiting the power of the king had been established and would lead to a gradual shift of power from the monarchy to the people in the form of an elected parliament. The influence of the charter eventually extended far beyond England. This was because English common law formed the basis of many constitutions in countries that had been part of the British Empire. The Fifth Amendment to the United States Constitution, for instance, states that people cannot be "deprived of life, liberty, or property, without due process of law," a phrase that can be traced directly back to the original clauses in the first document sealed at Runnymede. It could also be argued that Magna Carta provided, at least in some part, an inspiration for American rebels to break away from Britain during the American Revolution because they considered its terms protected them from what they saw as the unlawful interventions of the British Crown in their affairs. This explains why Magna Carta remains a revered document in America today, a fact recognized by Britain in 1965 by the gift of a patch of ground at Runnymede to the American people, where a memorial to President John F. Kennedy now stands.

As we approach the 800th anniversary of Magna Carta, it remains an important document, even if these days the significance has more to do with what it represents rather than what it actually said. In setting limits to the power of the king, the barons of England established a principle of liberty that retains its power today. Much of the detail contained in the original document may have faded into obscurity, but those few clauses that have not are as powerful today as they were in 1215. Nobody cites Clause 33 these days, which states that fish weirs must be removed from the River Thames, but when British politicians recently attempted to extend the legal period of detention without charge from 28 to 42 days for suspected terrorists, they were faced with counterarguments based on the liberty of the individual going back to Magna Carta. In 2010, the prominent civil liberties campaigner John Wadham wrote in reference to these proposals:

> Starting with the Magna Carta to the present laws, the individual has been granted and enjoys fundamental rights including liberty, protection against unlawful imprisonment, presumption of innocence, the right to be told promptly of the reasons for arrest and charge.

The principles contained in this statement are hard to argue against, demonstrating the continuing relevance of Magna Carta. As we understand them today, these fundamental rights apply to everybody, even those suspected of committing terrible crimes, but this is accompanied by recognition that nobody, whoever they are, should be above the rule of law. These ideals may be unintended consequences of the decision of a group of barons to fight for their own liberties in 1215, but they are consequences nevertheless and must surely be equally as worth fighting for now as they ever were.

THE MEDICI OPEN A BANK

1397

DECISION

Social Change

Science and Innovation

Culture

Politics

Diplomacy

Military

Religion

Circumstances: A commercial and artistic boom in fifteenth-century Florence

Protagonists: The Medici family and the artists of the Florentine Renaissance

Consequences: The conditions in which some of the greatest art in history was created

The causes of the Renaissance were as deep as they were broad. They can be related to the growth of cities and of late medieval trade, to the rise of rich and powerful capitalist patrons, to technical progress which affected both economic and artistic life.

Norman Davies, *Europe: A History*

During the great cultural flowering of the Renaissance, the learning of Classical Greece was rediscovered and the radical new ideas of humanism, which emphasized freedom of thought and expression, began to challenge the rigid and unchanging doctrine of the Christian Church. Most historians of the period agree that this movement began in the Italian city-state of Florence and reached its height there in the middle of the fifteenth century with the works of such great artists as Leonardo da Vinci and Michelangelo. But there is far less consensus over the question of exactly when the Renaissance began and why it first occurred in Florence rather than in any of the other Italian city-states, such as Milan or Venice. One theory suggests that the presence of so many talented people gathered together in one place was purely coincidental, while another sees it as being a gradual cultural development beginning in the early fourteenth century with, among others, the writer Dante Alighieri and the artist Giotto.

An alternative school of thought dates the beginning of the Renaissance to a specific moment in 1401 when a competition was held in Florence by the Cloth Importers Guild to find the designer of new bronze doors for the baptistry of Florence Cathedral. After a hard-fought contest, the artist Lorenzo Ghiberti beat the architect Filippo Brunelleschi to the prize and in the process, so the theory goes, introduced a culture of competition to the awarding of commissions to the artists of Florence, who from then on attempted to outdo each other in order to find rich patrons for their work. The problem with this theory, and the other two mentioned above, is that they all concentrate on the creativity of individual artists and almost completely ignore the wider social context in which they worked. By the fifteenth century, Florence had developed into a major European commercial and financial center, home to some of the wealthiest merchants and bankers in Italy as well as to a large aristocratic class of landowners. One way of expressing this wealth, both for the aristocracy and for social-climbing businessmen, was through the patronage of the arts. The leading family in Florence through much of this period was the Medici, who had made enormous amounts of money through their banking business and other trading activities, and while it would be exaggerating the case to claim that their money kick-started the Renaissance, it is nevertheless fair to say that their patronage of the arts helped to create the conditions in which it could flourish. And it all began in 1397 when Giovanni di Bicci de' Medici (ca. 1360–1429), the head of a reasonably well-off but by no means rich Florentine family, decided to use the money he had saved while working for a bank in Rome to start up in business for himself in his home city.

Giovanni di Bicci was one of the judges of the competition between Ghiberti and Brunelleschi, indicating that, just four years after opening his own bank in Florence, he had become one of its more notable citizens. This may also have been the moment when the Medici family first became aware of the potential advantages that could be gained from the patronage of art in Florentine society, which could be used as a means of advertising the wealth and success of the bank, leading to more people wanting to use its services. Giovanni certainly gives the impression of being an astute businessman, capable of spotting such an opportunity and exploiting it. He had already diversified his business interests by using the profits from his bank to buy land in the Mugello region of Tuscany, where his family had originally come from, and had also invested heavily in the highly lucrative wool trade, which is how he became involved with the Cloth Importers Guild. But he was by no means a gambler, unlike many of today's merchant bankers, relying instead on good business practices and the development of an extensive network of business contacts throughout Italy and in the major trading cities around Europe.

The success of the bank prompted Giovanni to expand, opening branches in a number of other cities, the most prominent and what would prove to be the most important one being in Rome. By far the richest institution of that period was the Catholic Church, and, more specifically, the Papacy in Rome, which commanded huge revenues from remittances submitted by its churches throughout Europe and beyond and through such practices as selling clerical positions and indulgences, a controversial practice that allowed sinners to buy the Pope's pardon. The papacy was undergoing a period of turmoil at this time, in which at least four different people were claiming to be the legitimate Pope. In an uncharacteristically daring move in 1402, Giovanni lent a huge sum of money to one of the claimants, a colorful character with little apparent religious conviction called Baldassare Cossa, who had made a fortune through piracy and used it to buy a

THE MEDICI BANK

cardinalship. The loan effectively bank-rolled Baldassare's bid and, in 1410, Giovanni's massive gamble paid off when Baldassare was elected as the Pope, taking the name of John XXIII and appointing the Medici Bank as the papal bankers.

COSIMO   The appointment catapulted the Medici Bank into the forefront of European banking and, as the bank was paid a commission on all the business it did for the Pope, it made Giovanni a very wealthy man. He gave his oldest son Cosimo the job of looking after the papal account and, even though only in his early 20s at the time, he proved to be at least as able as his father. The prestige accompanying the position of bankers to the Pope, and the papal endorsement of the Medici Bank that it implied, brought a flood of new custom, including from royal households around Europe and, even though the aristocracy were notorious for not repaying their debts, the huge increase in business, together with the family's numerous other commercial interests and investments, combined to make the Medici the wealthiest family in Europe. Even after John XXIII was forced to resign his position as Pope in 1415 at the Council of Constance, and was then declared to be an antipope, the Medici's reputation as loyal and trustworthy bankers ensured that they continued to hold the papal account.

COSIMO
Detail from a portrait of Cosimo de' Medici by the Florentine artist Jacopo Pontormo, painted about 50 years after his death.

Despite his wealth, Giovanni remained a prudent man throughout his life, not given to ostentatious displays or profligate spending. Cosimo followed in his father's footsteps until Giovanni died in 1429, at which point he began to pursue his own personal interests as well as the wider ones of the bank. Giovanni had treated the patronage of the arts as if it were a business transaction, while Cosimo appears to have held a much deeper appreciation of art for its own sake. As well as putting together his own private collection of art and becoming the patron of a number of struggling young artists, notably Donatello and Fra Angelico, Cosimo began to spend large amounts of money collecting manuscripts from around Europe and beyond, bringing together Classical and humanist learning in the library he established in Florence. He also became fascinated by architecture, constructing numerous buildings, including the Palazzo Medici as a home for himself, and was involved in the commissioning of Brunelleschi to build the dome of Florence Cathedral, widely regarded today as being the greatest example of Renaissance architecture.

On his deathbed, Giovanni is said to have warned Cosimo not to become involved in the fractious world of Florentine politics, but Cosimo ignored his father's advice, beginning a political dynasty that would rule over Florence and the Grand Duchy of Tuscany for most of the next 300 years.

Patronage of the arts would also continue to be a Medici family obsession long after Cosimo's death in 1464, most famously through his grandson Lorenzo the Magnificent (1449–1492), who became patron to both Leonardo and Botticelli, as well as providing the teenage Michelangelo with lodgings in his own house while he was an apprentice in the workshop of a Florentine sculptor. The Medici Bank had been in decline for some years by the time of Lorenzo's death in 1492 and ceased trading completely when the family were expelled from Florence two years later. According to Niccolò Machiavelli, who served in the Florentine Government during the Medicis' exile and is now best known for his writings on political science, the bank failed because the Medici had begun to behave more like princes than merchants, neglecting their business so that it collapsed as soon as it faced a crisis.

© Patrick A. Rodgers | Creative Commons

DONATELLO'S DAVID
This androgynous sculpture of David was commissioned by Cosimo de' Medici and now stands in the Bargello Museum in Florence.

The extraordinary wealth of the Medici family meant that they were largely unaffected by the failure of the banking business. Over the course of the sixteenth century, the family would go on to provide four Popes and two queens of France, but whatever political and social heights they would go on to achieve, they are now best remembered for their patronage of the arts during the Florentine Renaissance. During that period artists almost always worked to commissions and most of those came from one member of the Medici family or another. So the decision taken by Giovanni di Bicci in 1397 to start out in business for himself must surely be regarded as a great one not only in commercial terms, but also because of the enormous consequences it would have for the history of art. The Medici family did not start or inspire the Florentine Renaissance, but, in large part, their money paid for it.

DECISION

Social Change

Science and Innovation

Culture

Politics

Diplomacy

Military

Religion

GUTENBERG PRINTS A BIBLE

ca. 1450

Circumstances: A struggling entrepeneur comes up with another scheme to make some money

Protagonists: Johannes Gutenberg and his colleagues and creditors in Mainz and Strasburg

Consequences: The beginning of the printed book

We should note the force, effect, and consequences of inventions which are nowhere more conspicuous than in those three which were unknown to the ancients, namely printing, gunpowder, and the compass. For these three have changed the appearance and state of the whole world.

Francis Bacon, *Novum Organum*

The invention of the movable-type printing press is widely held to have been one of the key technological advances in European history—a development so significant it has been called the Gutenberg Revolution, after Johannes Gutenberg (ca. 1400–1468), the man who first developed it. It is hard to overstate the contribution his invention has made to what has been called the "democratization of knowledge," a process in which access to learning and information has changed from being the exclusive privilege of a select few to being available to all. Before printed books began to appear in Europe, books and manuscripts were produced by the slow and laborious process of being hand-copied by scribes, making them very expensive and restricting ownership to the wealthy few and the Church. After Gutenberg developed the printing press, the technology spread rapidly throughout Europe and, as it allowed books to be mass-produced, made them much more affordable and more widely available. The radical new ideas of Renaissance humanism and the corresponding rediscovery of Classical learning spread quickly through Europe as a consequence, leading to great advances in knowledge and learning in such spheres as philosophy and science.

Unfortunately for us today, details of Gutenberg's life are, at best, sketchy. What little we do know about him comes almost exclusively from a few official documents and the records of a number of court cases he was involved in, so any reconstruction of his working methods has to rely on an interpretation of what little information we can gather about him from these sources. One thing we can say is that Gutenberg's invention of moveable type and the printing press must have involved numerous decisions, many of which would qualify as being among the greatest ever made because of the impact printing would go on to have. It is not possible to pinpoint exactly when and where these decisions were made because of the scarcity of information we have about Gutenberg, so what follows is a more general description of how we think he developed his printing method rather than a dissection of the decisions he made, together with an appreciation of a further great decision he made to produce what would become his most famous printed work: the *Gutenberg Bible*.

GUTENBERG   Gutenberg was born in around 1400, give or take a year or two, in Mainz, a city on the River Rhine in what was then the Holy Roman Empire and is now south-western Germany. It was a period of fierce rivalry in the city between those of the aristocratic patrician class, including the Gutenberg family, and the merchants and craftsmen of the trade guilds. This conflict would force the family to leave the city on several occasions, when they would go to Eltville am Rhein, where Gutenberg's mother owned an estate. As a young man, Gutenberg is thought to have learned goldsmithing and the minting business, and may have also studied at the University of Erfut. Enrolment records from 1418 include a student named Johannes de Altavilla, which could be him because Altavilla is the Latin name for Eltville, but, then again, Johannes was a common enough name at the time so it is impossible to say for sure.

Nothing is known about what he did for the next 15 years, but in 1434, by then in his mid-30s, he turned up again in Strasbourg, in what is now eastern France. He was the subject of a court case in which a woman claimed that they were engaged to be married and that he had broken his promise to her, but we don't know the outcome of the proceedings, or whether he ever actually got married. Another court case a few years later sheds some light on what he was doing in Strasbourg. It would seem he was involved in developing a method of mass-producing magic mirrors—small sheets of polished metal with religious icons stamped on them, which were thought at the time to be able to capture the holy light given off by religious relics. Apparently he was intending to sell these magic mirrors at a huge profit to pilgrims attending a religious festival in the German city of Aachen, but the scheme floundered when the festival was cancelled. The court case involved a group of investors in the scheme who wanted their money back from Gutenberg. He appears to have been in charge of the manufacturing process, which may have involved some sort of press to stamp out the mirrors, enabling him to make thousands of them in a short space of time. During proceedings, Gutenberg promised to share a secret with the investors to make up for the money they had lost and, while we don't know what that secret was, he could have been referring to an early prototype of the printing press. At this vital moment in 1444, just when he may have made the decision to work on the development of the printing press using movable type, we lose touch with him completely and, for the next four years, we have no idea where he was or what he was doing.

By 1448 Gutenberg was back in Mainz and had borrowed money from Johann Fust, a wealthy citizen of the city, in order to set up a print shop. His great innovation was to put together several already existing technologies to make his press and then develop those parts of the printing process that were necessary for the whole thing to work. The press itself was much the same as those used in wine-making, in which juice was squeezed out of grapes by screwing a board down on top of them. The press was essential to ensure that a uniform pressure was applied over the whole page being printed, which would otherwise have been covered in smudges. Gutenberg must also have developed the required consistencies of paper and ink, presumably by trial and error, and the method of applying the ink to the typeface with soft leather dabbers. The typeface itself was composed of small individual blocks, known in the printing trade as sorts, made in a similar way to how coins were minted—using specially made punches, each carved in the shape of the required letters by highly skilled craftsmen called punch-cutters. The punches were used to stamp out molds, which were then filled with a metal alloy to make the sorts. These sorts had the raised profile of individual letters on their upper faces and could be arranged in a frame to make up the words and sentences of the page to be printed. This was the famous movable type, which, after it had been used once, could be broken up into individual sorts and used again to compose another page. It was the use of this movable type, together with the innovations Gutenberg introduced to make the press and the sorts, which would prove to be his major breakthrough and that would go on to revolutionize the book business. The techniques of printing were refined and developed over the centuries after Gutenberg first used them, but the essential elements of the process remained much the same right up until the middle of the nineteenth century, when the introduction of the steam-powered rotary press industrialized printing.

At first, Gutenberg used the press to produce individual sheets of text, before moving into books. None of his work was dated, making it difficult to ascertain the exact chronology, but it would appear that the first book he printed was a Latin grammar of the type he had most probably used himself at school and university. It does not appear that

THE PRINTING PRESS

the business was very lucrative, because Fust brought a court action against Gutenberg in 1451 for not paying the interest on his loan. Rather than collecting the money he was owed, Fust increased the size of the loan, perhaps having been convinced by Gutenberg that his next project would turn the business around. We don't know the circumstances of his hugely ambitious decision to print a Bible, but, in his book *The Gutenberg Revolution*, John Man speculates that Gutenberg may have been inspired by Nicholas of Cusa (1401–1464), a cardinal in the Holy Roman Empire, who was at the time engaged in a campaign to unify the text of the Bible across all Christian churches. Cusa also wanted to make the word of God much more widely available than it had previously been, and a printed Bible would have gone some way to achieving both of these aims. Needless to say, we don't know if Cusa ever met Gutenberg or was even aware of his printing press, so it is impossible to say if his ideas provided the inspiration or if he actually suggested the project in the first place. Wherever the original idea came from, one thing is certain: printing a Bible would be a massive undertaking. The Latin grammar book was 26 pages long, while the finished Bible ran to 1,275 pages in two volumes. Gutenberg used the money he had borrowed from Fust to set up a second print shop and take on more staff, possibly as many as 30. Over the course of the next three years, he printed about 180 copies of his Bible, of which 150 were on paper and 30 on vellum (treated calfskin).

GUTENBERG BIBLE
A detail of a page from an original Gutenberg Bible with illustrations added by hand after it had been printed.

© Mary Evans Picture Library

It was a staggering achievement, demonstrating the enormous potential of the printing press and producing a truly beautiful book. All 180 copies were sold, but even so, Gutenberg still could not repay his debts and he was sued again in 1455 by Fust, who won the case and took control of the entire business. Fust would go on to run the print shop in partnership with Peter Schöffer, his son-in-law and one of Gutenberg's former employees. It is hard not to come to the conclusion that Fust had waited until Gutenberg had done all the hard work in getting the business up and running and then, realizing its future value, seized it for himself. But, at the same time, while Gutenberg may have been a great innovator, he doesn't give the impression of being much of a businessman, forever borrowing more money than he could repay.

Fust and Schöffer went on to produce the second major printed book in 1457, an edition of the Psalms known as the *Mainz Psalter*, which included a publication date and the names of the two printers. Gutenberg was not mentioned; although he was involved in other printing ventures afterward, he still did not put his name on any of them and died in 1468 without receiving any recognition for the enormous contribution he had made to the development of the printed book. Today the situation is very different; even though we have no idea what he looked like, a statue of him has been erected in Mainz, also the location of the Johannes Gutenberg University (of Mainz). Among numerous other tributes, an asteroid and the first digital library, Project Gutenberg, have been named after him. All of the known 48 surviving copies of his Bible are held in major libraries around the world and, even though there is no chance of any of them being sold, they are considered to be the most valuable books ever printed. If we were to judge Gutenberg on his business career alone, then his decisions to develop a printing press and to produce a Bible can only be described as being disastrous ones, but if we judge him on the impact these same decisions would go on to have throughout the world, then they must surely rank as being some of the greatest ever made.

DECISION

Social Change

Science and Innovation

Culture

Politics

Diplomacy

Military

Religion

FERDINAND AND ISABELLA COMMISSION CHRISTOPHER COLUMBUS

1492

Circumstances: The dream of getting rich by opening a new trading route to the East Indies

Protagonists: A Genoese sailor and the Catholic monarchs of Spain

Consequences: The European discovery of the New World

Your Highnesses, as Catholic Christians, and princes who love and promote the holy Christian faith, determined to send me, Christopher Columbus, to the above-mentioned countries of India, to see the said princes, people, and territories, and to learn their disposition and the proper method of converting them to our holy faith; and furthermore directed that I should not proceed by land to the East, as is customary, but by a Westerly route, in which direction we have hitherto no certain evidence that any one has gone.

From Columbus' journal entry for August 3, 1492

© Dorling Kindersley

On October 12, 1492, Christopher Columbus (1451–1506) made landfall on an island that he named San Salvador after five weeks of sailing west from the Canary Islands. He was convinced that he had found an outlying island of the East Indies and, in doing so, had achieved his long-held ambition of opening up a commercial route from Europe to China and Japan, which, had he been right, would have made both him and the people who had invested in his expedition very wealthy indeed. We now know, of course, that his navigational calculations were wildly inaccurate and he had actually landed on one of the many small islands that make up the Bahamas, even if we don't know for certain which one. Columbus had spent the previous seven years lobbying royal courts in order to secure the backing he needed for the expedition — turning first to King João II of Portugal and then to the joint Catholic monarchs of Spain, King Ferdinand II of Aragon and Queen Isabella I of Castile — and, after so much effort, he was reluctant to admit he had been wrong all along. Despite mounting evidence to the contrary, he would maintain the conviction for the rest of his life that he had sailed from Europe to Asia rather than stumbling across the New World, as the landmass of the Americas was soon to be called. So, as disastrous as the subsequent colonization of the New World would prove to be for its indigenous inhabitants, both the initial decision by Columbus to pursue his ambitions and that of Ferdinand and Isabella to back him, even though they must have been aware how unlikely he was to succeed, must be regarded now as being among the greatest in history.

In his writings, one of the few things Columbus tells us about his early life is that he first went to sea at the age of ten. He was the son of a weaver, born in 1451 in the Italian city-state of Genoa, known for its large navy and extensive maritime trading networks throughout the Mediterranean and beyond, and he traveled extensively throughout this region as a young man. In some accounts of his life, he is said to have got as far as Iceland, where it has been suggested that he could have heard the sagas told about Leif Erikson, the Viking who sailed west 500 years before Columbus' day and established a colony called Vinland, now thought to be on the coast of Newfoundland in Canada. By 1476, Columbus was living in Lisbon, Portugal, where he had established a successful trading business with two of his younger brothers, and married Filipa Moniz Perestrello, the daughter of the nobleman and

COLUMBUS

CHRISTOPHER COLUMBUS
A portrait by Sebastiano del Piombo from 1519, thirteen years after Columbus's death. No portraits from life are known to exist.

explorer Bartolomeu Perestrello, who was also of Genoese descent and had connections to the court of King João II.

We don't know if Columbus was really inspired by the Icelandic sagas he may have heard or if the idea of sailing west had come to him from an entirely different source, but in 1485 he approached João II with a proposal to mount an expedition to search for a trading route to the East Indies by heading west out into the Atlantic Ocean. At that time in the late fifteenth century the overland trade routes from China, collectively known now as the Silk Road, had become difficult and dangerous, limiting the enormous commercial potential of importing spices, fabrics, including silk, and other commodities from the Far East. An alternative route by sea would have allowed whoever controlled it to monopolize the highly valuable trade in these goods, making the ambitious proposal put forward by Columbus lucrative enough to be taken seriously by the Portuguese king, who appointed a committee of his advisers to assess its potential. Accounts suggesting that João turned Columbus down because the prevailing opinion at the time was that the Earth was flat are very wide of the mark; the real reason he decided not to back Columbus was, in fact, almost the complete opposite. Portugal was one of the leading maritime nations, with advanced knowledge of geography and navigation, which led João's advisers to conclude, correctly as it would turn out, that the calculations made by Columbus were a huge underestimate of the actual distance from Portugal to China if measured in a westerly direction. In their opinion, it was far too great a distance for ships to sail between provisioning stops to be at all feasible, so, on their advice, João turned the scheme down. At the time, the Portuguese were more interested in establishing a route to the Far East around the African continent and appear to have decided to concentrate on this practical and achievable solution rather than back a scheme that appeared to be based on fantasy.

THE CATHOLIC MONARCHS

Columbus does not give the impression of having been a man lacking in self-belief and, rather than accept the sensible decision taken by João, instead took his proposal to the two Catholic monarchs of Spain. Ferdinand and Isabella had married in 1469, the beginning of the process of bringing the modern country of Spain into existence, and were engaged in a long-running program of converting their realm into an entirely Christian country. They initiated the Spanish Inquisition, a tribunal charged with maintaining the orthodox beliefs of the Catholic Church and, when Columbus approached them in 1485, were engaged in a war in Granada against the remnants of the Islamic state of the Moors in Andalusia. Initially, they took the same approach to the proposal as the Portuguese had done, appointing a committee to assess its merits and turning it down once that committee had established it was highly unlikely to succeed. But they did not dismiss Columbus entirely, giving him a grant and permission to stay anywhere he chose within Aragon and Castile at no cost, perhaps as a means of preventing him from taking his plan, as unpromising as it was, to any of the neighboring countries.

Columbus had not helped himself by making the outrageous demands in his proposal that he be appointed governor of any lands he discovered and be made Admiral of the Ocean Seas—titles that would make him one of the highest-ranking members of the Spanish royal court. Over the course of the following few years he began to adopt a more subtle approach, building up support among Ferdinand and Isabella's advisers by persuading them of the merits of his proposal, and how cheaply it could be put into action, and emphasizing the opportunity it would present for spreading the Christian message overseas, a tactic almost guaranteed to appeal to Ferdinand and Isabella's missionary zeal. Even so, it would take another seven years before the proposals were accepted, and even then, according to contemporary sources, only because Columbus required just three ships and a hundred men, and perhaps also because the likelihood of him returning to claim his titles were considered so slim as to be negligible.

THE SPANISH COURT
The Return of Columbus to the Spanish Court by Raimundo de Madrazo y Garreta (1841–1920).

In early 1492, Ferdinand and Isabella had also finally succeeded in defeating the last Moorish outpost in Granada, so were perhaps in a more amenable mood than when Columbus had first approached them and might have been looking toward the future expansion of their realm having finally made it secure within Spain. According to some accounts, Isabella was still reluctant to agree and had dismissed Columbus from her court, only for Ferdinand to send a detachment of his royal guards after him to bring him back. But, however it came about, the Catholic monarchs had finally decided to support Columbus and he entered into a protracted series of negotiations with their advisers over the exact terms of the contract. In April 1492, an agreement was finally reached, resulting in the Capitulations of Santa Fe, a document setting out the highly favorable terms awarded to Columbus by the Spanish Crown.

After his first successful expedition, Columbus made three further voyages to the Indies, as he referred to the New World, and served as governor of the Spanish territories in the region until being dismissed in 1500, accused of running a regime considered too brutal even by the standards of the monarchs who had initiated the Spanish Inquisition. After he died, a long series of lawsuits were brought against the Spanish Crown by his heirs, who were claiming 10% of the profits made by Spain from the New World colonies awarded to Columbus under the terms of the Capitulations of Sante Fe. The Crown successfully argued that Columbus had forfeited his right to his share of the profits after being sacked as governor, leading to a settlement in 1536 in which the heirs were awarded a title and land in the New World. In the meantime, the continents he had discovered without realizing it had come to be known as the Americas, a name most probably derived from that of Amerigo Vespucci, a Florentine explorer who, in the early sixteenth century, established that the New World really was a separate landmass of continental size and not part of Asia.

The decision taken by Columbus was, then, one of great courage and some foolhardiness, because he set sail into the unknown on the basis of calculations already proved incorrect. The Catholic monarchs, meanwhile, had made their decision because it had not cost them much and, in the unlikely case of it paying off, would bring enormous returns. Neither party could have had any idea of the consequences of these decisions, which would actually be the first steps in the future European colonization of North and South America rather than the discovery of a new trading route to China and Japan.

THE SIEGE OF VIENNA

1529

DECISION

Social Change

Science and Innovation

Culture

Politics

Diplomacy

Military

Religion

Circumstances: A huge Ottoman army arrives at the gates of Vienna

Protagonists: Suleiman the Magnificent, Archduke Ferdinand I of Austria, Count Nicholas of Salm, the Ottoman army, and the defenders of Vienna

Consequences: The gates of Vienna marked the furthest extent of the Ottoman expansion into Europe

Suleiman's boast was that he would not lay down his arms before he had erected a monument to his victory on the banks of the Rhine.

Lord Kinross, *The Ottoman Centuries*

OTTOMAN SULTAN
A portrait of Suleiman the
Magnificent attributed to
the Italian master Titian (ca.
1490–1576) and painted in
the late 1530s.

The great Ottoman sultan Suleiman the Magnificent arrived at the gates of Vienna in late September 1529 at the head of an army estimated to have been at least 100,000 strong (some have put the figure at an unlikely 300,000). The city was the de facto capital of the Habsburg territory ruled by Archduke Ferdinand I of Austria, the brother of the Holy Roman Emperor Charles V, and it occupied a vital strategic position on the River Danube. If the city fell to the Islamic forces of the Ottoman Empire, the way would be open for Suleiman to advance right into the heart of Christian Europe. Faced with the danger of the city falling to Suleiman, Ferdinand fled the scene, escaping north to Prague and leaving the defense of the city to its citizens and a small force of Spanish and German mercenaries under the command of the 70-year-old Count Nicholas of Salm. Altogether, the Viennese forces totalled about 20,000 and, in the circumstances, the most sensible course of action would have been to surrender to Suleiman. But the Viennese were not about to give up their city so easily and, instead, decided to fight.

CLASH OF EMPIRES

The Ottoman Empire arose out of the westward movement of Turkic tribes from Central Asia into Anatolia, challenging the supremacy of the Orthodox Christian Byzantine Empire, the remnants of the Eastern Roman Empire, which, by the early fourteenth century, had weakened to the point of total collapse. The Ottomans had already expanded into the European part of the Byzantine Empire before Constantinople, its capital, finally fell in 1453 to the Ottoman emperor Mehmet the Conqueror. From then on the Ottomans consolidated and expanded their empire into one of the largest and most powerful of the period, controlling much of the Middle East and North Africa as well as the eastern Mediterranean, and taking the important Balkan cities of Belgrade and Buda (the city that would later unite with Pest on the opposite bank of the Danube to form Budapest, the modern capital of Hungary). This brought them right up to the borders of the territory under the control of the Habsburg family and, as Suleiman was well aware, beyond the territory of the old Byzantine Empire of Orthodox Christianity and into the domain of western European Catholicism. It would lead to centuries of tension between the Ottomans and

Habsburgs, which lasted into the nineteenth century and only really came to an end with the dissolution of both empires after the end of the First World War.

The Habsburgs themselves were an aristocratic family originally from what is now Switzerland, who provided numerous kings across Europe through a series of dynastic marriages, including, from 1273, in the Holy Roman Empire, which at its height extended across much of central Europe, from the Low Countries and northern France, through Germany, northern Italy, and up to Poland and Austria. As well as holding the title of Holy Roman Emperor, Charles V was the King of Spain, giving him an extensive empire in the New World and the Far East as well as in Europe. In 1519, when Charles was elected Holy Roman Emperor, he gave control of the Habsburg's ancestral lands in Austria to his brother Ferdinand, which, together with the independent Kingdom of Hungary, became a buffer zone between his empire and the Ottoman Empire of Suleiman.

The Ottomans were not the only challenge facing the Habsburgs during this period. Charles was continually fighting with King Francis II of France, a battle that was as much personal as it was territorial. At that time, France was surrounded by enemies: the Habsburgs in Spain, Italy, and the Low Countries; and the English to the north-west. These threats led Francis to form an alliance with Suleiman that, in 1526, saw them both attacking Habsburg territory at the same time—Francis initiated a war in northern Italy and Suleiman began a campaign to push Ferdinand out of Hungary. The decisive victory for the Ottoman forces at the Battle of Mohács in August 1526 allowed Suleiman to create a vassal state in the south of Hungary and opened up the way for him to capture Buda, the Hungarian capital, three years later. From there, he turned his attention to the even bigger prize of capturing Vienna, thereby nullifying any further potential threat from Ferdinand and directly challenging Charles and the whole of the Holy Roman Empire.

THE SIEGE

The Ottoman campaign of 1529 was dogged by problems from the moment Suleiman led his army out of Constantinople in May of that year. The most serious difficulties were caused by the weather, heavy rainfall making progress across Bulgaria and Hungary painfully slow so that, even though the resistance the Ottoman army met was light and Buda had fallen quickly, they did not start out toward Vienna until the middle of September. By then, the state of the roads meant that it had become impossible for them to transport their heavy siege guns, which, had they been available, would easily have breached the relatively weak defensive walls of the city. Even so, Vienna appeared to be there for the taking; Charles was preoccupied with fighting the French and, despite Ferdinand's appeals for help, had left his brother to fend for himself. But if Suleiman had expected the Viennese garrison to submit as quickly as the one in Buda, he was set to be disappointed. Ferdinand himself may have departed the scene, but Nicholas of Salm was made of sterner stuff. Although getting on in years, he was a highly experienced military commander who had taken seriously Suleiman's boast of his intention to erect a monument to his victories on the banks of the Rhine, right in the heart of the Holy Roman Empire. His defending force was small in comparison to the besieging Ottoman army, but it included professional soldiers who were not intimidated by facing the Ottomans, however many of them there were, and included a detachment of German Landsknechte, mercenary pikemen with a fearsome reputation who could be counted upon no matter what the situation.

> **ALTHOUGH GETTING ON IN YEARS, NICHOLAS OF SALM WAS A HIGHLY EXPERIENCED MILITARY COMMANDER**

In the short time available before the siege began, Salm did what he could to strengthen the defenses of the city, reinforcing the walls and burning the buildings that lay outside them to create clear fields of fire. In the absence of heavy artillery, Suleiman had to rely on mining under the walls in an attempt to breach them, but the defenders detected where the digging was taking place from the vibrations it caused and easily repulsed every attempt to get into the city. Salm also managed to convince the Ottomans that his garrison was much larger than it actually was and that he was expecting the arrival of a relieving army led by Ferdinand. In reality, no such force existed, but this, together with the lack of success and the constant driving rain, weakened Ottoman resolve and, after only two weeks of the seige, Suleiman decided to try one final all-out assault, which, if unsuccessful, would mark the end of the attack. During that final encounter the Viennese inflicted heavy casualties on the demoralized Ottomans before Suleiman finally called his forces off and began the long retreat back to Constantinople.

The Ottomans would make further unsuccessful attempts to capture Vienna in the future, notably in 1683 in what is sometimes referred to as the Battle of Vienna (to distinguish it from the siege of 1529). But none of the later attempts were any more successful in capturing the city and its gates would ultimately mark the maximum extent of the Ottoman empire in Europe. Ferdinand was the most immediate beneficiary of the decision to stand and fight at Vienna, even though he took no part in the defense himself. The man who actually made that decision to fight and deserved to gain the most credit from it, Nicholas of Salm, was wounded during the siege and died of his injuries in May of the following year. It cost him his life, but Salm's decison would have a huge impact on European history. It allowed the Habsburg monarchy to survive in Austria, which it did for more than four centuries, and prevented Suleiman from establishing a base in the heart of Europe, from where he may well have achieved his ambition to get to the Rhine. It is difficult to imagine now, but if the Ottoman Empire had prevailed over the Holy Roman Empire, it could have resulted in the conversion of much of the population of central Europe to the Islamic faith.

THE SIEGE
An Ottoman depiction of the Siege of Vienna dating to the sixteenth century, with the Sultan's tent in the foreground.

DECISION

Social Change

Science and Innovation

Culture

Politics

Diplomacy

Military

Religion

COPERNICUS PUBLISHES *ON THE REVOLUTIONS OF CELESTIAL SPHERES*

1543

Circumstances: A lone astronomer makes a great advance in the field, but is reluctant to publish it

Protagonists: Nicholas Copernicus and Georg Joachim Rheticus

Consequences: A revolutionary change in our understanding of the universe

All the spheres revolve around the sun at their midpoint,
and therefore the sun is at the center of the universe.

Nicholas Copernicus,
Commentariolis

In approximately 1510, when Nicholas Copernicus (1473–1543) was in his late 30s, he wrote a short paper setting out the model he had worked out for the solar system, which placed the sun at the center with the planets, including the Earth, orbiting around it. This heliocentric model, as it came to be known, challenged the prevailing view, of the Earth being at the center of the universe, which dated back more than 1,300 years to the work of the Greek astronomer Ptolemy (ca. AD 90–168). Copernicus sent his paper to a very limited number of people, claiming that he was working on a longer version that would include a mathematical proof of his heliocentric model. Over the course of the next 20 years, he worked on this longer version, although, despite the encouragement of those people who had heard about what he was doing, he refused to publish it. In 1539, a 25-year-old mathematician named Georg Joachim Rheticus came to visit him and apparently talked him into changing his mind. The resulting book, *On the Revolutions of Celestial Spheres*, was published shortly before he died in 1543 and went on to become a landmark in the history of science. It signaled the start of the Scientific Revolution, a period in the sixteenth and seventeenth centuries when the basic principles of modern science were first established and when great advances were made by such people as Kepler, Galileo, and Newton. Copernicus's decision to publish his book, then, not only revolutionized our understanding of astronomy, but would also lead to the transformation of science as a whole.

NICHOLAS COPERNICUS
A portrait of Copernicus by an unknown artist dating to ca.1580.

THE REVOLUTIONARY

Copernicus does not, at first sight, give the impression of being a revolutionary in any sphere, let alone in science. For 40 years, he held the position of canon in the Catholic Church and lived for most of that time in Frombock, a town in north-east Poland that in the sixteenth century was a cathedral city in Warmia, a semiautonomous region governed by its bishop. He was born in 1473 in the Polish city of Toruń into a German-speaking family of wealthy merchants and, after the death of his father when he was about 10 years old, he was supported by his maternal uncle, Lucas Watzenrode, who went on to become the Bishop of Warmia and gave Copernicus the position of canon, which would provide him with a very good income throughout his adult life. Watzenrode also paid for his nephew's education, which continued at a number of universities around Europe, including at Kraców, Bologna and Padua, variously studying law, medicine, and a range of other subjects without gaining a degree in any. He gives the impression of being what we would now call a perennial student, flitting from one thing to another while avoiding getting a job in the real world. But while he was moving from university to university, he was meeting some of the most eminent mathematicians and astronomers of the day and appears to have engaged in extensive private study of both subjects.

FROMBOCK CATHEDRAL
Copernicus used one of the towers in the grounds of the cathedral as an observatory after he moved to Frombock in 1512.

Finally, at the age of 30, Copernicus was granted a doctorate in canon law and returned to Poland, where he became secretary and physician to his uncle in Warmia. Watzenrode appears to have expected his nephew to follow him as Bishop of Warmia, but Copernicus showed little inclination to do so. As far as we can tell, he was never ordained as a priest, the first step he would have had to take before he could hope to progress in the Church hierarchy. Then, after his uncle died in 1512, he moved back to the relatively remote and quiet city of Frombock, where, in his capacity as canon, he was provided with a house and servants. He also bought a tower in the grounds of the cathedral, which he converted into an observatory, although, as he was working in a period before the invention of the telescope, the astronomical equipment he had at his disposal was rudimentary. It was at about this time that he wrote his first short paper on heliocentricism, suggesting that he may have decided on the move to Frombock in order to concentrate more fully on his astronomical work and devote more time to his studies.

ON THE REVOLUTIONS

Over the next 20 years he would perform his duties as a canon, make astronomical observations and write the manuscript that would eventually be published as *On the Revolutions of Celestial Spheres*. He seemingly led a quiet and comfortable life, only occasionally disturbed by a brush with Church authorities over a number of affairs he had with women in Frombock, including with one of his housekeepers, which apparently continued after she got married. He maintained regular contact with a number of the astronomers and mathematicians he had met in the universities he had attended and, by this means, the nature of his work became known in academic circles. This is presumably how the young Rheticus, who studied at Wittenberg University, came to hear about Copernicus and, being sufficiently intrigued by what he had learned, made the journey to Frombock to meet the amateur astronomer who was proposing such a revolutionary idea.

Traveling from Wittenberg to Frombock was no small undertaking for Rheticus at that time because, as he was a Lutheran, and was coming from the university where Martin Luther himself worked, he was banned from entering the Catholic Kingdom of Poland. Nevertheless he arrived in the town in 1539 and must have made a favorable impression with Copernicus because he was taken on as a pupil—the first and only pupil Copernicus would ever have. Rheticus wrote a short summary of the heliocentric model and had it published in 1540. It was favorably received in academic circles, and this may have encouraged Copernicus to consider publishing his own work for the first time. He claimed that his reticence was a consequence of apprehension over how his work would be viewed by other astronomers, but he may also have been worried about his position as a canon in the Catholic Church, an institution that did not always react well to radical new scientific theories. But, whatever the cause of the delay and however Rheticus went about convincing Copernicus that the time was right for his book, he finally made the decision to publish it and together they prepared a manuscript to be sent to a printer.

Copernicus did not live long enough to see for himself the reception his book received after publication. He suffered from some form of seizure in late 1552 and, according to some accounts, died immediately after being given the first printed copy of his book. In truth, first reactions were muted among all except the Church, which predictably criticized it for going against the Bible, and those few astrologers who had known what Copernicus had been working on and now welcomed the mathematical proof they had waited 20 years to see. But it would be more than 50 years before his work really began to receive the attention it deserved, when the research carried out by Johannes Kepler (1571–1630) on planetary motion and the astronomical discoveries made by Galileo Galilei (1564–1642) brought the Copernican system, as the heliocentric model is sometimes called, to the attention of a much wider audience.

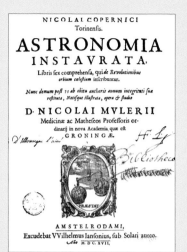

ON THE REVOLUTIONS
Title page of the third edition of *On the Revolutions of Celestial Spheres*, published in Amsterdam in 1617.

DECISION

Social Change

Science and Innovation

Culture

Politics

Diplomacy

Military

Religion

MICHEL DE MONTAIGNE RETIRES FROM PUBLIC LIFE
1571

Circumstances: A magistrate in Bordeaux has had enough of his job and wants to do something else

Protagonists: Michel de Montaigne and his cat

Consequences: Montaigne begins to write essays

I want to be seen here as myself, without ostentation or artifice, because it is myself that I am painting. My defects are here, true to life, along with my innate form, at least as far as decorum has allowed. If I was in those nations that are said to still live in the freedom of the first laws of nature, I would have portrayed myself as whole, and wholly naked. So, reader, I am myself the subject of my book, but it is not right that you should waste your leisure on such a frivolous and vain subject. So farewell then, from Montaigne; this first of March, one thousand, five hundred and eighty.

From "To the Reader," the introduction to the first volume of Montaigne's essays

In 1571, at the age of 37, Michel de Montaigne decided to give up his job as a magistrate in Bordeaux, having become, in his own words, "long weary of the servitude of the courts and of public employments," and retire to his estate in the country. He intended to devote himself to a life of the mind: to thinking, reading, and writing. To that end, he converted the top floor of one of the towers adjoining his château into a library where he could retreat from all those things that might otherwise have disturbed his peace and tranquillity. At first he found that having nothing in particular to do had the opposite effect than the one he had expected; rather than allowing him to settle down to write, idleness caused him to become anxious, for his mind to "bolt like a runaway horse." Fortunately for him and for the rest of us, Montaigne was not put off by such early setbacks and, over the course of the next 20 years, wrote a body of work that remains one of the great achievements in literature.

© Stefano Bianchetti | Corbis

MONTAIGNE
A seventeenth-century portrait of the great French writer and essayist Michel de Montaigne by an unknown artist.

Montaigne's work is as unclassifiable today as it was when he first wrote it; he had to coin a new word himself to describe the literary form he had invented, calling his pieces "*essais*," a word coming from the French verb *essayer*, "to try," and giving us the English word, "essay." He was attempting to find a way of expressing his thoughts, and, he tells us, his purpose in doing so was to write about himself, about what was on his mind, as well as to give his impressions on how to live a good life. What he doesn't tell us, beyond saying that he was tired of the public life he was leading in Bordeaux, are the circumstances that prompted him to retire in the first place so that he could take on such a huge writing project, which, as much as he made light of it himself, was no less than an attempt to describe what it is like to be a human being.

ON RETIREMENT

One reason why Montaigne was able to retire at such an early age was that he could afford to. His great-grandfather made a fortune as a merchant in Bordeaux and bought the Montaigne estate, which was roughly 30 miles (50 km) from the city and came with the hereditary title of Seigneur (roughly equivalent to the British title of Lord). After the death of his father in 1568, Montaigne inherited the estate and the title, and from then on preferred to go by that name rather than his given surname of Eyquem. If his wealth is taken together with his own statement of how tired he had grown with his work in the Bordeaux

MONTAIGNE'S TOWER
After he retired, Montaigne converted the top floor of this tower next to his château into a library.

court, words that he had inscribed on the wall of a small side-chamber to his library, then it could be argued that we already have enough reasons to explain his decision. He packed in his job because he'd had enough of it and decided to go back home to manage his estate instead. The problem with this explanation is that Montaigne tells us on a number of occasions how little concerned he is with the estate and how hopeless he is at managing it. Converting his tower into a library was, in part at least, a way of getting away from all the duties he had taken on as Seigneur of the estate, so it would appear unlikely that he would voluntarily come back to something he regarded more as an obligation and a burden than as a better alternative to his role as a magistrate.

Montaigne lived through a traumatic period of French history in which the country was ripped apart by sporadic outbreaks of civil war and mob violence between French Catholics and Protestant Huguenots. He was a Catholic, but refused to get involved in the fractious politics of the Bordeaux court or in the wider religious conflict. This stance may well have been the reason why he failed to gain a position in the higher chamber of the court, which he applied for shortly before he resigned and appears to have been prevented from getting by his political opponents. His decision to retire, then, could have been an emotional response to being overlooked for a promotion, combined with a wish to get away from the factional in-fighting of the court, but, by returning to his estate, in reality he was moving from the relative safety of the city to Perigord, where his estate was situated, one of the regions where the fighting between Catholics and Huguenots was at its most intense.

ON DYING

In the years leading up to Montaigne's retirement, he suffered a string of personal tragedies that left him contemplating his own mortality and the transitory nature of life. In 1563, his closest friend, Étienne de La Boétie, the man who inspired him to begin writing, died at the age of 33 during an outbreak of the plague. This was followed by the death of his father in 1568 from complications brought on by kidney stones, a condition that would also lead to Montaigne's own death in 1592. A few months after his father died, Montaigne's 27-year-old brother Arnaud died in a freak accident in which he was hit in the head by a hard tennis ball and, several hours after the event, suffered a fatal brain haemorrhage. In such circumstances, it is hardly surprising that he was left thinking about the fragile nature of existence and, in his early essays, he is clearly preoccupied with a fear of death, writing of his brother in "To Philosophize is to Learn How to Die":

> With such frequent and ordinary examples before our eyes, how can we rid ourselves of the thought of death and the idea that at any moment it is gripping us by the throat?

Such thoughts can only have been compounded by a serious horse-riding accident Montaigne experienced early in 1570, shortly before he retired, in which, while out riding with some of his estate workers, one of them suddenly spurred his horse into a gallop and rode straight into the back of Montaigne's horse, sending him flying to the ground and causing him to be knocked unconscious. At first his companions thought he was dead and, when he gradually began to regain his senses, they would later tell him, he became highly agitated, clawing at his chest as if he were having convulsions, yet when his own memory of the accident returned to him, he recalled experiencing nothing more than a feeling of peace and inner calm.

The account of the riding accident is one of the few passages to relate an extended autobiographical incident in all of Montaigne's essays, which otherwise concentrated on what he was thinking and not on his past life. It gives the impression that he attached a great importance to the accident, or, at least, of how he came to view it after he had thought about what had happened. He came to the conclusion that his excessive fear of death was an unjustified response to the tragic events that he had experienced and it was preventing him from enjoying however much of his life he had left to live. The near-death experience of the accident, and the calmness he had felt within himself while it was happening, had convinced him that, when his own time came, there would be nothing for him to be afraid of. This realization appears to have freed him from his preoccupation with morbid thoughts, allowing him to think, and then write, about life rather than about death.

The first writing projects Montaigne took on after he retired involved preparing the works of Étienne de La Boétie for publication and then finishing a long piece he had promised to write for his father before he died, which would be published years later under the title of *An Apology for Raymond Sebond*. After finishing these two projects, he appears to have felt as if he had fulfilled his commitments to other people and could begin to write for himself. His great ability as a writer was to seamlessly mix serious philosophy with apparently casual anecdotes and his own observations, enabling him to engage his readers effortlessly in the discussion he was having with himself. In one famous example, he tells us that while he was working through a serious philosophical point his cat jumped onto his desk and dabbed her paw on the end of his quill pen. Rather than shooing her away so he could get on with his work, he swept the quill across his desk for her to chase, asking himself the question, "When I'm playing with my cat, how do I know she is not playing with me?" He then digresses from his point to consider the impossibility of knowing what is in the mind of an animal, or in the mind of another person for that matter, and then makes this the central theme of the essay, which, apparently, had only occurred to him after his cat had jumped onto his desk.

"WHEN I'M PLAYING WITH MY CAT, HOW DO I KNOW SHE IS NOT PLAYING WITH ME?"

Montaigne is now acclaimed as being the greatest writer of the French Renaissance because, in taking himself as his subject, he was able to write with both humanity and humility not only about himself, but about all the rest of us as well. Just as it is impossible to know what his cat was thinking when she was chasing his quill pen, we cannot know for certain exactly what was on Montaigne's mind when he decided to retire, even if the circumstances tend to suggest that he needed to take some time to recover from the tragedies he had experienced and, once he had recovered, he found the peace of mind that enabled him to begin his great writing project. In this essay I have made my own attempt to unravel the nature of these circumstances that led to his decision, but in the end it is only my opinion and I can't pretend to have all the answers. After all, to quote one of Montaigne's favorite phrases, which he used repeatedly to qualify his own essays, *"Que sçais-je?"*—what do I know?

DESCARTES FINDS HIS REASON

1619

DECISION

Social Change

Science and Innovation

Culture

Politics

Diplomacy

Military

Religion

Circumstances: Descartes spends a day and a night in a stove-heated room

Protagonists: Descartes on his own

Consequences: The beginning of a new way of thinking about the world

I decided to review the various opportunities that are open to people in this life and to try to choose the best one. I thought I could do no better than to persevere in the very same occupation that I already had, that is, to use my whole life to develop my reason and to make as much progress as I could in discovering the truth in accordance with the method I had prescribed for myself.

René Descartes, *Discourse on Method*

René Descartes (1596–1650), who has been called the father of modern philosophy, produced a body of work that is still widely studied and debated after almost 400 years. In it he attempted to begin the study of philosophy anew, starting from its foundations and separating it from the restrictions imposed on thought by religious scholasticism and moving away from a strict adherence to the works of Aristotle and other Classical Greek philosophers. In doing so, he established a fundamental method of enquiry based solely on the application of reason and observation, one that did not rely on a supernatural explanation for any part of the human experience. He took as his starting point that most quoted of philosophical phrases, *cogito ergo sum* (I think, therefore I am)—the proposition that, if a person is capable of thinking about whether they exist or not, then that act of thinking in itself provides a proof that they do exist. This principle provided Descartes with an absolute certainty on which he began to build a way of thinking based on what can actually be known and, in doing so, provided a philosophical underpinning of the sciences that were beginning to develop at that time.

RENÉ DESCARTES
A portrait of the great French philosopher by the Dutch artist Franz Hals, now in the Louvre in Paris.

Before beginning his philosophical enquiries, Descartes had already made important contributions to the sciences and mathematics, including establishing the law of refraction in optics and laying the foundations for analytic geometry using a system of coordinates to plot three-dimensional shapes on a two-dimensional axis, familiar to all students of mathematics as the x and y axis of graphs, and that would later prove crucial in the invention of infinitesimal calculus by Isaac Newton and Gottfried Leibniz. Even if Descartes had stopped there, before he began his philosophical enquiries, he would now be considered an important figure in the Scientific Revolution of the seventeenth century, which goes some way to indicating the overall scale of his achievement. But, rather than considering the work itself, here we are concerned with what led him to take on such a vast project in the first place and, in particular, his decision to devote his life to the pursuit of knowledge, which, if the fragments of autobiography he wrote are to be believed, arose as a consequence of the sort of visionary experience his entire philosophy disavowed.

Descartes was born in the small French town of La Haye, which was renamed Descartes in his honor in 1967, into a wealthy land- and property-owning family. He was educated at a Jesuit college and then studied law at the University of Poitiers, intending to follow his father into the legal profession. In 1618, a year after he left university, he traveled to the city of Breda in the Dutch Republic to join the army of Maurice of Nassau, the prince of Orange. The reason why a Jesuit-educated Catholic Frenchman chose to enlist in the army of a Protestant prince of the Dutch Republic remains a mystery, leading some of Descartes's biographers to suggest that he may have been engaged in some kind of espionage work. No evidence has ever been found to back up such claims and it may well have been that Descartes chose the highly regarded Dutch army because he wanted to study military engineering in the best possible place. But, whatever his motive, it remains a strange decision, not least because at that time Europe was on the verge of the Thirty Years War, a bitter and destructive religious conflict fought in the main between the Catholic Holy Roman Empire and an alliance of Protestant states.

While in Breda, Descartes met the mathematician and teacher Isaac Beeckman (1588–1637), who would have a lasting influence on his thinking and who encouraged him to study mathematics, leading to his first serious written work on the subject the following year. By 1619, Descartes had left the Dutch army and joined up with the forces of Duke Maximilian of Bavaria in the Holy Roman Empire, the leading Catholic power of the day, leading to more speculation over Descartes' intentions. On the night of November 10, 1619, Descartes experienced a series of vivid dreams, which, he later wrote, profoundly affected the direction of his life and would lead to a major breakthrough in his philosophical enquiries. In *Discourse on Method*, published 17 years after the event, he tells us that he was traveling from Frankfurt to Vienna, having attended the coronation of the Holy Roman Emperor Ferdinand II in Frankfurt Cathedral, when he was delayed by a period of bad weather in Bavaria. On the day in question, he says, he was, "shut up alone in a stove-heated room, where I was completely free to converse with myself about my own thoughts." These "meditations," as he called them, concerned how he proposed to go about working on his philosophical enquiries; these thoughts appear to have spilled over into the extraordinary dreams he

DESCARTES' DREAMS

© Stapleton Collection | Corbis

WORKING PHILOSOPHER
A ca.1790 engraving of René Descartes working at his desk by the French artist Jean Baptiste Morret.

was to have that night in which he saw how he could find the solutions to the problems he had posed himself.

Descartes woke on two occasions during the night and wrote down the details of what he had been dreaming in a notebook, before having one last dream that he noted down as well in the morning. He is said to have kept the notebook with him for the rest of his life, but unfortunately it has not survived, its contents known to us only from the writing of other people who had either seen it themselves or had heard what was in it from others. His interpretation of these dreams, taken together with the meditations of that day, left him feeling as if he had experienced some form of awakening in which he could suddenly see the way forward to achieving his aims in philosophy. Without specifying the exact time and place, Descartes goes on to tell us that, in the aftermath of that extraordinary day, he decided to commit himself to philosophical enquiry for the rest of his life and, in particular, to answering the question, "What can be known for certain?" by means of the application of reason and logic.

The *cogito ergo sum* argument apparently came to Descartes not long after his decision to commit himself to philosophy, but it would take many years for him to find a way of articulating it fully in writing. In 1620, he left the army and spent the following nine years traveling in Europe, before finally settling in the Dutch Republic, where he would live for almost all of the remaining 20 years of his life. The reason he chose the Netherlands is not known, but the Dutch Republic had a reputation for tolerance at that time, so perhaps Descartes felt that he would encounter less opposition to his radical new ideas there. Whatever the reason, it was during this period that *Discourse on Method* and *Meditations on First Philosophy* were first published—the major works on which his fame now rests. He died in February 1650, at the age of 54, after contracting pneumonia while he was in Stockholm. His work had been controversial during his lifetime, particularly in Catholic countries, but was nevertheless widely recognized as being of fundamental importance in the history of philosophy, as it remains today.

NEWTON GOES BACK TO SCHOOL

1659

DECISION

Social Change

Science and Innovation

Culture

Politics

Diplomacy

Military

Religion

Circumstances: Isaac Newton's mother considers what the future holds for her son

Protagonists: A scientific genius in the making, his mother, his uncle, and his former schoolmaster

Consequences: A farmer's son from Lincolnshire, England, revolutionizes the natural sciences

The alteration of motion is ever proportional to the motive force impressed; and is made in the direction of the straight line in which that force is impressed.

Newton's Second Law of Motion, first published in *Philosophiæ Naturalis Principia Mathematica*

ISAAC NEWTON
A portrait of Newton at the age of 46, painted in 1689 when he was Lucasian Professor of Mathematics at Cambridge University.

The list of the achievements of Sir Isaac Newton (1645–1727) is a long and impressive one. He is most famous for his work on gravity and for the three laws of motion, all published at the same time in the monumental *Philosophiæ Naturalis Principia Mathematica* (Mathematical Principle of Natural Philosophy), but made numerous other important contributions to mathematics, optics, physics, astronomy, and a range of other subjects. He is still widely regarded as being one of, if not the, greatest of all scientists and, during his lifetime, held the positions of Lucasian Professor of Mathematics at Cambridge University, President of the Royal Society, Member of Parliament, and Master of the Royal Mint, together with being knighted by Queen Anne.

But, as accomplished as he was in the natural sciences and mathematics, there were other fields in which he did not excel, namely the management of his family's farm in Woolsthorpe, a small village in the English county of Lincolnshire. Unlike many of the great scientists and thinkers of that period, Newton came from a relatively modest background and, at the age of 16, having finished his schooling in the nearby market town of Grantham, returned home to work on the farm. Young Isaac proved himself to be such a hopeless farmer that his mother soon realized that there was no future in it for him. She talked the matter over with his uncle, William Ayscough, and John Stokes, his former schoolmaster in Grantham, and between them they reached the decision that he should return to school for a course of special tuition aimed at gaining entry to Cambridge University. Rather than struggling with a life on the land, they pointed him in the direction of a life of the mind, even if they could not possibly have predicted the extraordinary outcome of their decision.

YOUNG ISAAC

The stone farmhouse where Newton was born is now protected by the National Trust, restored to something like how it would have looked in the seventeenth century. It is a beautiful old house, but despite being called Woolsthorpe Manor, it is very obviously the sort of property lived in by a successful farmer rather than that of a member of the landed gentry. Newton's father, also called Isaac, died three months before he was born, and his mother, Hannah, married again when he was three. Her new husband, Barnabas Smith, was, at 63, almost 40

years older than her and, as well as being the rector
of a neighboring parish, had a substantial private
income. Hannah moved to the rectory, leaving
young Isaac with his grandparents in Woolsthorpe
and inadvertently causing future speculation as
to the psychological impact on Newton of being
abandoned by his mother; he never married and
is not known to have had a physical relationship
in his life. Amateur psychologists have also made
a great deal of a list Newton wrote at the age of 19 in which he set
out what he considered to be the sins he had committed in his life;
these included threatening to burn down his stepfather's house. This
has been taken to indicate that Newton had a difficult relationship with
his stepfather, but, as Smith died when Newton was ten, this is again
reading a great deal into not very much.

© Xander89 | Creative Commons

**WOOLSTHORPE
MANOR**
The farmhouse in
Lincolnshire where Newton
was born, now owned by
the National Trust and open
to the public.

Hannah had three children with Smith and, after she was widowed
for a second time, she brought them back to Woolsthorpe with her.
She had inherited much of Smith's wealth and, together with a good
income from the farm, was now a relatively wealthy woman. Newton
was sent to the grammar school in Grantham at the age of 12, where he
did well in his studies despite preferring to work on his own projects
rather than those set out in the school curriculum—a preference he
would display throughout his life. He certainly did enough to suggest to
John Stokes that he had the potential to attend Cambridge University;
after the experiment with farming had failed, Stokes was the one who
recommended he apply. Before returning to school, Newton spent
almost a year on the farm, where he appeared intent on demonstrating
that farming was not for him. He would leave all the work to the farm's
laborers while he read a book and, on one occasion, managed to return
from the market in Grantham carrying the bridle of the horse he had
ridden to town on in his hand, having absent-mindedly left the horse
itself behind. If his plan had been to impress on his mother that he
would be better off back at school than wasting his time in a half-
hearted effort at farming, it certainly worked.

Newton was successful in his attempt to gain entry to Cambridge
University and, in 1661, at the age of 19, he was admitted to Trinity
College as a sizar, which meant that he had to work to pay for his board

**NEWTON'S
APPLE**

and lodgings, most likely as a drudge for one of the fellows. In a college dominated by the wealthy upper classes, Newton initially appears to have struggled to fit in, keeping himself much to himself and embarking on his own program of study rather than following the college syllabus. He was by no means an outstanding student, even if the often repeated story that he failed his Bachelor's degree is probably apocryphal. He would later return to the college to take a Master's degree and then become a fellow himself—an unlikely outcome for somebody who had failed their first degree. It appears that he was beginning to conduct his own experiments as an undergraduate and he spent more time working and reading in the fields he was investigating himself than he did in studying for exams.

Shortly after Newton finished his degree in 1665, the university closed down for a period as a precautionary measure due to the outbreak of the Great Plague in London. He returned to Woolsthorpe, where he stayed for much of the next two years, continuing to conduct his own experiments. He was particularly interested in examining Kepler's work on planetary motion and, finding that the type of calculations he needed to do to continue his studies were not possible using the available mathematical techniques, he invented his own method, which he called "fluxions" and which would later form the basis for the development of infinitesimal calculus. The famous incident of Newton finding the inspiration for his theory of gravity after seeing an apple falling from a tree in the orchard at Woolsthorpe also occurred at this time and, as it was a story that Newton told himself, probably had some basis in truth, even if its importance may have been exaggerated in the telling. Newton was certainly thinking about the question of why the Moon continued in its orbit around the Earth during this period and arrived at the solution of it being the result of the pull of the same force, gravity, which caused an apple to fall from the tree to the ground. It would be 20 years before he was finally persuaded to publish his law of universal gravitation in the *Principia*, thereby providing the foundation stone of classical mechanics for over 300 years, until it was finally replaced in 1916 by Einstein's general theory of relativity. Quite an achievement for a man who, but for his mother's decision to send him back to school, might otherwise have spent his life as a farmer in Lincolnshire.

PETER THE GREAT REFORMS RUSSIA

1697

DECISION

Social Change

Science and Innovation

Culture

Politics

Diplomacy

Military

Religion

Circumstances: A country that had been left behind by the political, social, and technological advances made in Western Europe

Protagonists: Peter the Great, his Russian and European advisers, and the Russian people

Consequences: Russia becomes a major player in European affairs for the first time

The Great Embassy was one of the two or three overwhelming events in Peter's life. The project amazed his fellow countrymen. Never before had a Russian tsar traveled peacefully abroad; a few had ventured across the border in wartime to besiege a city or pursue an enemy army, but not in time of peace.

Robert K. Massie, *Peter the Great: His Life and World*

© Roman Samokhin | Shutterstock

PETER THE GREAT
A portrait of the Emperor of All the Russias, the title adopted by Peter in 1721, painted in 1838 by Paul Delaroche.

Toward the end of the seventeenth century, the Petrine Revolution, as the reforms initiated by the Romanov tsar Peter the Great (1672–1725) are sometimes called, began the process of transforming Russia from what had remained up until then an essentially medieval kingdom into a modern state capable of competing both militarily and economically with the more advanced Western European countries and the Ottoman Empire. The first major obstacle to Peter's ambitions was geographical; at that time Russia had no western sea ports to give it access to the Baltic Sea or Black Sea, preventing the country from fully exploiting its vast natural resources through commercial links with Europe, where more developed countries had built their prosperity on maritime trade. The eastern Baltic was largely controlled by Sweden, while the Black Sea was entirely within the sphere of the Ottoman Empire. The latter was controlled either directly from the Ottoman territory on the southern shore or through the creation of vassal states in the Crimean and along the northern bank of the sea in the territory of the Tartar Khanates, a collection of small states made up of the settled remnants of the Golden Horde, whose rulers claimed descent from Genghis Khan and that is now part of Ukraine. As a consequence, the first step in Peter's plan to modernize Russia had to involve the expansion of the territory he controlled to include a sea port in one, or preferably both, of these locations.

THE GREAT EMBASSY

In 1695, Peter attempted to take the fort of Azov on the northern coast of the Black Sea, which was under Ottoman rule and controlled access to the Sea of Azov, an inlet of the Black Sea. An initial attack by land was unsuccessful, causing Peter to rethink his tactics and begin to build ships to form a Russian navy for the first time. The combination of land attack and bombardment from the Black Sea led to the capture of Azov, but, with the Ottomans controlling the rest of the Black Sea, it still did not lead to Russia having possession of a suitable trading port. Peter realized that to stand any chance of gaining the necessary territory, the army would have to be modernized and a navy developed from almost nothing. The expertise required to achieve these goals did not exist in Russia at that time, so Peter began to look to those countries that had already developed advanced military technology and naval engineering.

He decided to send out a huge diplomatic mission, known as the Great Embassy, to travel extensively through Europe with the expressed intention of developing relations with those Christian countries of Europe that opposed the Ottoman Empire, but also in an attempt to learn as much as he could about European military and naval methods. The embassy was nominally led by some of his closest advisers, but Peter also traveled with the mission himself, remaining incognito to avoid spending all his time in ceremonial duties in the countries he visited.

It was an unprecedented move by a Russian tsar, not least because Peter was leaving his country, which had a volatile political history, for 18 months. The diplomatic mission failed to achieve its aims of forming alliances against the Ottomans because the major European powers were involved in various disputes between themselves, which would lead to the War of the Spanish Succession in 1701. While

SIEGE OF NÖTEBORG
A painting by Alexander von Kotzebue showing Peter directing his army during the Great Northern War.

they were preparing to fight each other, they had no wish to antagonize the Ottoman Empire as well by siding against it with the relatively insignificant Russians. But while this largely unsuccessful diplomacy was going on, Peter spent his time visiting shipyards, armament factories, and military bases, together with learning as much as he could about how different European countries organized their affairs in general. In the Dutch Republic, for instance, Peter was given access to the shipyard of the Dutch East India Company, the largest and most advanced of its time, where he worked for four months on the construction of a ship.

By the summer of 1698, Peter was forced to return to Russia after an uprising in one part of the army. The uprising was quickly and, in typically Russian fashion, brutally repressed before Peter had even arrived back in the country, leaving him free to implement the many reforms he had been planning while he had been away. An extensive shipbuilding program was undertaken and the new Russian navy was modeled on those of the British and Dutch Republics, while the army was reorganized along the lines of the Prussian and Swedish military, then widely recognized as being the best armed forces of the day. Peter had employed numerous experts in various different fields during his travels, who arrived in Moscow to begin work on modernizing the country as a whole as well as its armed forces. As well as military advisers, there were engineers, scientists, architects, and a whole range of others. As part of the overall plan, Muscovites were encouraged to adopt Western dress and customs, a practice that would famously result in Peter instituting a tax on beards in an effort to get those who were resisting change to at least take on the appearance of clean-shaven Westerners.

ST. PETERSBURG

In what would prove to be the only diplomatic success of the Great Embassy, Peter formed an alliance with Poland and other countries with interests in the Baltic against the dominance of Sweden in the region, resulting in 1700 in the outbreak of the Great Northen War in which Russia gained territory for the first time on the Gulf of Finland, an eastern extension of the Baltic. To ensure that Russia could maintain this territory and to exploit the maritime access this opened up, Peter ordered the founding of a new city on a stretch of unpromising marshland next to the River Neva, about 3 miles (5 km) inland from the gulf, using the foreign engineers, architects, and city planners he had employed while abroad to make the bogland habitable, and then constructing the first buildings of what would become St. Petersburg. In 1712, Peter made a decisive break with the past by moving his capital city from Moscow to St. Petersburg, which became known as the Window on the West, both because of its geographical position and the Western-leaning attitude of its people. The city would also become famous for its beautiful buildings, many designed by the Italian architect Domenico Trezzini in what has been called the style of the Petrine Baroque.

Peter's decision to reform Russia and instigate a policy of engagement with Western Europe had far-reaching consequences for Russian society and would lead to it becoming a major power in the region. He also initiated a huge expansion in the territory under his control, forming what would from 1721 be known as the Russian Empire. In this respect, he is now remembered as one of Russia's greatest leaders, even if he was capable of great brutality against his own people if they opposed his rule. But there was one institution that Peter did not attempt to reform or modernize in any way—the Russian tsardom would remain an absolute monarchy of Romanov tsars for the next 200 years, until it was finally overthrown in 1917 by the Bolsheviks during the Russian Revolution.

THE DECLARATION OF INDEPENDENCE

1776

DECISION

Social Change

Science and Innovation

Culture

Politics

Diplomacy

Military

Religion

Circumstances: Colonists who were not represented in the British Parliament objecting to being taxed without consultation

Protagonists: Thomas Jefferson, John Adams, Benjamin Franklin, and all the other delegates attending the Second Continental Congress

Consequences: The United States of America

We, therefore, the Representatives of the United States of America, in General Congress, Assembled, appealing to the Supreme Judge of the world for the rectitude of our intentions, do, in the Name, and by Authority of the good People of these Colonies, solemnly publish and declare, That these united Colonies are, and of Right ought to be Free and Independent States; that they are Absolved from all Allegiance to the British Crown, and that all political connection between them and the State of Great Britain, is and ought to be totally dissolved.

From the conclusion to the US Declaration of Independence

On July 2, 1776, the Second Continental Congress, an assembly of representatives from all 13 American colonies, decided by a vote of 12 in favor and one abstention to declare independence from the British Empire. At the time of the vote, the delegates from New York did not possess the constitutional authority from their state legislature to vote for independence, so were forced to abstain. A week later, they obtained the required authority and voted in favor, making the decision in favor of independence for what would soon become known as the United States of America a unanimous one. Two days after the vote, and after some alterations to the document as it was first written by Thomas Jefferson, the formal statement, the Declaration of Independence, was adopted by the Congress and sent to the printer for publication. It is this date, July 4, that is celebrated in America as Independence Day. Although fighting in the American Revolutionary War started at the Battles of Lexington and Concord on April 19, 1775, its roots can be traced back to the aftermath of the French and Indian War, also known as the Seven Years War.

THE REBELLION

The French and Indian War (1756–1763) was fought primarily between Britain and France over disputed colonial interests and had been vastly expensive for both countries. In France, the military defeat to Britain and the financial strain it placed on the economy was a contributory factor to the French Revolution in 1789, while in Britain, despite accomplishing most of its war aims, the national debt doubled. The cost of defending the British Empire remained a huge burden on public spending, leading the government to attempt to raise more revenue in the colonies by introducing new systems of taxation. In the 13 colonies of the British Empire on the eastern seaboard of North America, the first direct tax, the Stamp Act of 1765, caused widespread protests, including a boycott of British goods. As they were not represented in the British Parliament, the colonists argued that the consent of their colonial legislatures was required before direct taxes could be raised, leading to the slogan, "No taxation without representation." The Stamp Act was repealed, but, in 1767, the duty imposed on a number of commodities, such as paper and tea, was increased, leading to further organized protests and outbreaks of mob violence. The British responded by increasing the number of troops garrisoned in the colonies, inevitably leading to a number of ugly incidents and the deaths of some protestors.

The British Parliament again repealed the tax increases on everything except tea and when, in 1773, the East India Company was granted the monopoly to supply tea to the colonies, it provoked a furious response, most famously in what became known as the Boston Tea Party of December 16, 1773, in which all the tea in the holds of three East India Company ships was thrown into Boston harbor by a protest group calling themselves the Sons of Liberty. Rather than recognize the legitimate grievances of the protestors, the British Government instead decided to impose its authority on the colonies by closing Boston harbor until compensation had been paid for the destroyed tea. This was followed by a number of further punitive measures taken against Massachusetts, collectively known as the Coercive or Intolerable Acts, which were intended to quash colonial resistance to the authority of the British Parliament. The actual effect was the direct opposite, causing widespread outrage among many people throughout the 13 colonies at what was seen as an arbitrary violation of their rights and, rather than intimidating people into accepting British rule, it actually encouraged them to escalate their protests into outright rebellion.

THE CONTINENTAL CONGRESSES

The First Continental Congress was called in direct response to the Coercive Acts and met on September 5, 1774, in Philadelphia. It was composed of 56 delegates sent from the legislatures of 12 of the 13 colonies, the exception being Georgia, which at that time did not want to antagonize the British because it wanted their help in a frontier war it was engaged in with Native American tribes. Over the course of the next few months, the delegates decided to implement a ban on the import of British goods if the conditions imposed by the Coercive Acts were not removed and to petition King George III in an effort to find a solution to the grievances held in the colonies. Whatever the personal opinions of the delegates may have been, there was no suggestion at this stage of a movement toward independence from Britain. The intention was to reach an agreement through negotiation whereby the colonies could become more self-governing but remain within the British Empire.

THE FIRST DRAFT
In John Trumbull's *The Declaration of Independence*, Thomas Jefferson is shown handing the first draft to the seated John Hancock.

One further decision reached by the First Continental Conference was to set a date for a second meeting, May 10, 1775, at which the delegates intended to consider the results of their actions, in particular the petition sent to the king. By the time the Congress reconvened, events on the ground had moved beyond petitioning George III because fighting in a revolutionary war had already broken out. The American forces were made up of numerous separate militias and, in an effort to coordinate them into an effective fighting force, one of the first decisions made by the Congress was to form the Continental Army and appoint George Washington as its Commander-in-Chief. The prospect of a return to negotiations was ended after the British issued a Proclamation of Rebellion in August 1775, decreeing that the American rebels, including the delegates at the Second Continental Conference, were traitors. As a consequence, rather than attempting to find a resolution to the conflict, the Second Continental Congress ended up managing the war effort, making it the de facto government of the 13 colonies.

MUCH OF THE DEBATE SURROUNDING INDEPENDENCE WAS HELD IN THE BACK ROOMS OF TAVERNS AND COFFEE HOUSES AROUND PHILADELPHIA

The Congress included a faction of delegates with loyalist sympathies — those who wanted the colonies to remain a part of the British Empire — so the path toward the Declaration of Independence was by no means a straightforward one. Much of the debate surrounding independence was not held in the formal setting of the Congress but went on instead in the back rooms of taverns and coffee houses around Philadelphia, making it difficult to reconstruct the exact sequence of events that led to the Declaration. But before anything could be debated, the delegates had to get authorization from their own legislatures, which, in effect, meant that each of the 13 colonies had to come out in favor of independence before their delegates could vote for it at the Continental Congress. The Boston lawyer John Adams, who had long been in favor of independence, played a key role in the political maneuvering that paved the way for this to happen. On June 7, 1776, a resolution was brought before Congress by Richard Henry Lee of the Virginian delegation, which proposed:

> ... that these United Colonies are, and of right ought to be, free and independent States, that they are absolved from all allegiance to the British Crown, and that all political connection between them and the State of Great Britain is, and ought to be, totally dissolved.

Loyalists, led by John Dickinson of the Pennsylvanian delegation, argued vigorously against the resolution, but were defeated in the ensuing vote. A committee, including Adams and Benjamin Franklin of Pennsylvania, was established to draft a formal declaration, although the job of actually writing the document was given to another of the committee members, Thomas Jefferson of Virginia.

Over the course of the next few weeks, Jefferson wrote a first draft and, in consultation with Adams, made numerous changes before the committee was happy with it. It was ready by June 28, at which point Congress decided to let it "lie on the table" for a few days to give everybody a chance to consider their responses. In the vote on July 2, a number of key opponents of independence, including Dickinson, abstained, allowing the resolution for independence to be adopted. The main body of the finished document published on July 4 was composed of a long list of grievances against George III, some of which were what had led to the rebellion in the first place, such as, "For imposing Taxes on us without our Consent," and "For depriving us in many cases of the benefit of Trial by Jury." One or two others were a little more fanciful, seemingly thrown in to increase the volume of charges leveled against the king. One part of the finished document that received little attention at the time was its preamble, the first sentence of which read:

THOMAS JEFFERSON
The Continental Congress delegate from Virginia was given the task of writing the Declaration of Independence by the drafting committee.

> We hold these truths to be self-evident, that all men are created equal, that they are endowed by their Creator with certain unalienable Rights, that among these are Life, Liberty, and the pursuit of Happiness.

These words would become some of the most quoted in the English language and, in a single sentence, managed to sum up the entire ethos of the country that would become the United States of America. The fact that the sentence provoked almost no response at the time, however, suggests that people were far more concerned with the main aim of the document—to declare independence from Britain—than with the stating of lofty ideals.

Critics of the declaration immediately picked up on the lack of attention it paid to the rights of both women and Native Americans, a major oversight in a document of this nature. Any mention of slavery was also removed from the final draft before it was published, leaving the Founding Fathers, as the men who signed it came to be called, open to accusations of hypocrisy because their declaration promoted equality and the liberty of the individual, yet a sizable number of its signatories, including Thomas Jefferson, were slave owners. It could be argued that the failure to deal with the issue of slavery at this early stage in the history of the new nation laid the foundations for the catastrophic civil war that erupted 85 years later and all but ripped the country apart. If these criticisms can be left aside, however, the significance of the event is abundantly clear. In the Declaration of Independence, the American colonies set out their intention to separate from Britain and gave their reasons for doing so, thereby formally changing what had started out as a rebellion against the way authority had been imposed on the colonies to an all-out revolution aimed at getting rid of the British from America for good. It would take another eight years for this aim to be realized, until the decisive victory at Yorktown and the subsequent peace treaty in which Britain officially recognized the United States of America as a free and independent nation. The success of the revolution and the creation of a new independent state must surely mean that the vote in favor of independence was the single most important decision taken in American political history.

THE STORMING OF THE BASTILLE

1789

DECISION

Social Change

Science and Innovation

Culture

Politics

Diplomacy

Military

Religion

Circumstances: The volatile atmosphere of Paris in the summer of 1789

Protagonists: A Parisian mob, the defenders of the Bastille, King Louis XVI of France

Consequences: The start of the French Revolution

The people rushed against the place, and almost in an instant were in possession of a fortification, defended by 100 men, of infinite strength, which in other times had stood several regular sieges & had never been taken. How they got in, has as yet been impossible to discover. Those who pretend to have been of the party tell so many different stories as to destroy the credit of them all. They took all the arms, discharged the prisoners & such of the garrison as were not killed in the first moment of fury, carried the Governor and Lieutenant Governor to the Greve (the place of public execution) cut off their heads & sent them through the city in triumph to the Palais royal.

From a letter written by Thomas Jefferson, the US Ambassador to France at the time and an eyewitness to the event

The French public holiday of Bastille Day on July 14 was instituted in 1880 to mark the moment when the French Revolution began in 1789 with the storming of the Bastille, which would lead to the fall of the despised Ancien Régime (the Old Order) and the eventual establishment of a republic. Today, nothing much is left of the Bastille, a huge fortress and prison that had originally been built in the fourteenth century to guard the eastern approach to Paris. After the building was stormed, it was demolished and the stone was either used again in new construction work or made into souvenirs of the revolution. In overcoming the garrison of troops stationed within the building, the Parisian mob that took part in the attack actually achieved very little in practical terms; the Bastille had long since ceased to have any military role and, at the time, held only seven prisoners in its cells. The significance of its capture had much more to do with what it represented than what it really was. It had become a symbol of the power of the king and in storming what was supposed to be an impregnable fortress, the mob not only demonstrated that it was possible to take the building, but also that it was possible to take on the monarchy and win.

News of the fall of the Bastille quickly spread throughout France, prompting similar outbreaks of insurrection and, even though the king quickly backed down from any further confrontation with the people of Paris, the scene was now set for a full-scale revolution. It is not possible to identify a single individual who was responsible for making the decision to attack the Bastille; instead, we must look at the actions of a mob, within which spontaneous decisions arose in the heat of the moment and pushed people into undertaking an extremely dangerous and, had it been considered rationally, seemingly impossible venture. Ultimately, however, regardless of how the decision was reached, the consequences, both for France and more widely around the world, would prove to be enormous and, as the Bastille Day celebrations in France show, ones that remain with us today.

THE PATH TO REVOLUTION

The political commentator Alexis de Tocqueville, writing with the benefit of hindsight in the 1850s, said of the French Revolution that, "Never was any such event so inevitable yet so completely unforeseen," making the point that France was heading in the direction of some form of major social upheaval in the late eighteenth century and that, if the revolution had not been ignited by the storming of the Bastille, then it would probably have begun in some other way. The Enlightenment ideas of republicanism and the liberty of the individual as expressed by such French writers as Voltaire and Rousseau had been influential in the political philosophy of the American Revolution, which had successfully expelled the British only six years previously, and were widely known and much discussed. Taken together with the disastrous state of the French economy at the time and a widespread dissatisfaction with the rule of King Louis XVI, this created a great desire for change across much of French society, which, despite numerous promises of reform by the king and his government, had found little outlet for its expression.

The Seven Years War (1756–1763) fought against Britain, and then France's support for the American Revolution, had effectively bankrupted what had previously been one of Europe's wealthiest countries. In an effort to raise money, taxes were increased and, as so often happens, the burden fell disproportionately on those less able to pay. The French aristocracy used their influence with the king's government to ensure that they remained untouched by the economic problems of the country, while the king himself continued to live a life of extravagance and excess. In an effort to placate the French people, the government called a general assembly, known as the Estate Generals, with the aim of finding a solution to the financial disaster. It was made up of representatives of the three estates of French society: the clergy (the First Estate), the nobility (the Second Estate), and everybody else (the Third Estate), made up of the middle-class bourgeoisie, together with common people and peasants, who in reality played almost no part in proceedings.

LOUIS XVI
The King of France in the painting by Jean-François Garneray (1755–1837), *Louis XVI at the Tour du Temple.*

The Estate Generals first convened on May 5, 1789, and it immediately became apparent that the nobles intended to dominate the assembly, shattering any illusions the delegates representing the Third Estate may have had about finding a more equitable solution to France's economic problems. The Third Estate began to meet separately and, in June, declared itself to be the National Assembly. The king attempted to bypass the newly established assembly and, when that did not work, on June 20, locked the doors of the room they were using and posted soldiers there to prevent the delegates from gaining access. They met instead in the nearby royal indoor tennis court, where they swore an oath to continue with the assembly until a new constitution had been implemented that limited the power of the king. The Tennis Court Oath, as it came to be called, was a pivotal moment in the beginning of the revolution as it was the first occasion in which the power of the king had been directly challenged by a group of citizens.

While this was going on, the situation in Paris steadily deteriorated, exacerbated by rapidly increasing food prices. To add to the economic difficulties, the previous two years had seen very poor harvests, pushing the price of bread, the staple food of the poor, up in the summer of 1789 to a higher level than at any other time during the whole of the eighteenth century. With unrest growing daily, the king ordered an increasing presence of the army in the city, including regiments made up of soldiers from Switzerland and Germany. The Gardes Françaises, the regiment usually stationed in Paris, was thought to be largely sympathetic to the views of the people, while foreign mercenaries were considered more reliable and would, if ordered, not hesitate to open fire on the French people. The presence of these troops, widely distrusted in Paris for exactly the same reason, only inflamed the situation even further, as did the king's decision on July 11 to sack his finance minister Jaques Necker, the only member of the government who had shown any support for the Third Estate and the new National Assembly.

JULY 14 | The situation in Paris in the middle of July had become highly volatile. A widespread desire for reform and the convergence of the political and economic factors outlined above, together with the inflammatory actions of an already widely despised and out-of-touch king, combined to create an atmosphere that was ready to explode. Rumors were circulating that the king intended to use his foreign mercenaries to restore order by force and, on the morning of July 14, a large crowd gathered outside Les Invalides, a hospital and retirement home for wounded soldiers, where an arsenal of weapons was known to be stored, with the intention of arming themselves against the threat posed by the king's troops. The unit of Gardes Françaises stationed there did not make any effort to stop the crowd from forcing their way into the cellars, where they found about 30,000 muskets and several cannons, but very little gunpowder or shot. It was at this point that people in the crowd began to turn their attention to the Bastille, perhaps following a prearranged plan to gather as many weapons as possible, but more likely through a mob reaction to a shout from a single individual or from an accumulation of rumors that had spread through the crowd that caused a spontaneous movement in the direction of the fortress.

The Bastille held a huge stockpile of gunpowder and was guarded by about 80 old soldiers from Les Invalides, reinforced in the days leading up to July 14 with a detachment of 32 Swiss grenadiers. A regiment of 5,000 regular French Army troops were also stationed on the Champs de Mars, a short walk away, and could easily have dispersed the crowd, which is thought to have numbered no more than 1,000, had they chosen to. Instead, they opted not to intervene at any stage during the day. The Governor of the Bastille, the Marquis de Launay, admitted two representatives into the fortress for talks, which dragged on into the afternoon. The crowd outside was rapidly growing impatient with the apparent lack of progress and had been reinforced by soldiers from the Gardes Françaises. Early in the afternoon, people surged forward into the outer courtyard of the building, where an exchange of musket fire began between the attackers and defenders. It is not clear which side began the shooting, but it continued intermittently through the afternoon until, at five o'clock, the governor ordered a ceasefire and, in a note pushed out through a crack in the inner gate, offered terms for his surrender. The terms were refused, but the governor surrendered anyway, perhaps fearing that if the situation deteriorated any further, it would lead to a bloodbath. He ordered the inner gates to be opened and the mob surged into the fortress.

As a consequence of the attack, a total of 98 of the attackers had been killed, compared to only one of the defenders. In the aftermath, eight of the garrison were killed by the mob, including de Launay, who was dragged out of the Bastille into the street, where he was beaten, stabbed, and then beheaded. The officer in charge of the Swiss troops, Lieutenant Louis de Flue, survived and later wrote a report highly critical of de Launay, blaming his indecision and prevarication for the loss of the supposedly impregnable fortress. In the days following

BASTILLE DAY
The Storming of the Bastille and Arrest of the Governor M. de Launay by an unknown artist, now in the National Museum at Versailles.

FRENCH REVOLUTION
An engraving of the execution of Louis XVI on January 21, 1793, three and a half years after the storming of the Bastille.

the fall of the Bastille, the king, finally realizing how dangerous the situation had become, backed down. He sent out an order for the troops in and around Paris to go back to their barracks, reinstated Necker, and then returned to Paris himself, where he wore a tricolor cockade, the red, white, and blue ribbon that had become the symbol of the people. The National Assembly then began the process of writing a new constitution, in which the king was to have almost all of his powers removed and become the figurehead of a constitutional monarchy. A period of relative calm returned to Paris, but it could only be a matter of time before the more radical revolutionaries, who were advocating a republic, not a constitutional monarchy, returned to the streets to continue the struggle. So, even if the intention of the mob who stormed the Bastille had primarily been to capture its arsenal of weapons and gunpowder, the outcome was to spark one of the great turning points in European history, and, once the absolute power of the monarch had been successfully challenged in this way, the scene was set for a full-scale revolution.

THE LOUISIANA PURCHASE

1803

Circumstances: The American government makes France an offer to buy the port of New Orleans

Protagonists: Thomas Jefferson, Robert Livingston, James Madison, and Napoleon Bonaparte

Consequences: A doubling in the size of America for a knockdown price

We have lived long but this is the noblest work of our whole lives ... The United States take rank this day among the first powers of the earth.

Words spoken by Robert Livingston on April 30, 1803, after signing the agreement with France to purchase the Louisiana Territory

The acquisition of the Louisiana Territory by the United States of America was formalized on April 30, 1803, by the signing of an agreement between the US envoys Robert Livingston and James Monroe and the French Treasury Minister François Barbé-Marbois. The price was $15 million, made up of $11.75 million in cash, raised through the sale of bonds, and the cancellation of $3.25 million of France's debt to America. The exact expanse of the territory was not known at the time because most of the region had not been mapped, but it would encompass approximately 825,000 sq. miles (about 2.1 million sq. km), an area almost four times the size of France and one that would double the size of America. Livingston and Monroe had been authorized by US President Thomas Jefferson to offer up to $10 million for the port of New Orleans on its own and had no instructions what they should do when the whole of the territory was put on the table. Between them, they decided to accept the price asked by the French, coming to the conclusion that it was too good an offer to turn down, and, in doing so on their own initiative, struck what must rank as the best real-estate deal of all time.

WEST OF THE MISSISSIPPI

After victory in the Revolutionary War over Britain, achieved in 1783 after eight years of fighting, America began to expand westward from its original 13 states, beyond the Appalachian Mountains and into the valleys of the Ohio and Mississippi rivers, which provided vital transport links for the import and export of goods by river transport through the port of New Orleans. Up until 1800, the land west of the Mississippi had been in the possession of Spain, which had then ceded the entire region between the river and the Rocky Mountains, the Louisiana Territory, to Napoleon Bonaparte's France in a secret treaty, even though some of the land on the western bank of the Mississippi had already been settled by Americans. When Thomas Jefferson became US president in 1801, he immediately became concerned that Napoleon intended to incorporate the territory into the French Empire, preventing further westward expansion of America and controlling access to the Mississippi through New Orleans. The Spanish, who were nominally still in control of the city, had closed it to American traffic on a number of occasions in the past and Jefferson was looking for a permanent solution to the problem. One option was to take New Orleans by force, risking a war with both Spain and France, or, alternatively, America could enter into an alliance with Britain to make it difficult for

Napoleon to take up his possession. Jefferson did not like either of these options, so, despite being concerned about the constitutional legality of purchasing territory, decided to make Napoleon a cash offer for New Orleans and, if that failed, approach the British about an alliance. To that end, in March 1803, Jefferson dispatched James Madison, a future US president, to assist the American ambassador to France, Robert Livingston, in the ensuing negotiations.

Before Napoleon could make any use of his new American possessions, he had to make peace with the British, who possessed the naval power to prevent him from establishing a French Empire on the American continent. The Treaty of Amiens accomplished that aim in March 1802, even if it was to prove a short-lived peace settlement, and by that time Napoleon was already attempting to establish a base on the Caribbean island of Saint-Domingue, now Haiti, having despatched an army there to put down a slave revolt so that he could then use the island as a staging post to America. The French forces met much stiffer resistance from the Haitian rebels than had been expected and their numbers were decimated by disease, leading to a military defeat that appears to have persuaded Napoleon to give up his ambitions in the New World. Without a base in the Caribbean, and with Florida remaining a Spanish possession, Napoleon knew that a colony in Louisiana would have proved impossible to defend against either the Americans or the British. By the spring of 1803, hostilities with the British were on the brink of reigniting and Napoleon was making plans for an invasion of Britain, which he would later abandon. In order to pay for the build-up of an invasion force, he needed money quickly and, with his attention now firmly back on Europe, he decided to make the Americans an offer they could not refuse.

ROBERT LIVINGSTON
The American ambassador to France, who, together with James Monroe, was responsible for negotiating the Louisiana Purchase.

It would have taken several months to receive an answer from Jefferson if the two American negotiators had attempted to convey to him Napoleon's offer to sell the whole of the Louisiana Territory for $15 million, and Napoleon was well known for his tendency to change his mind. Rather than give him the opportunity to do so, Livingston and Madison made the decision to accept the offer themselves and on April 30, 1803, as quickly as it could be arranged, signed the treaty with Barbé-Marbois to make the agreement official. On July 4, Jefferson

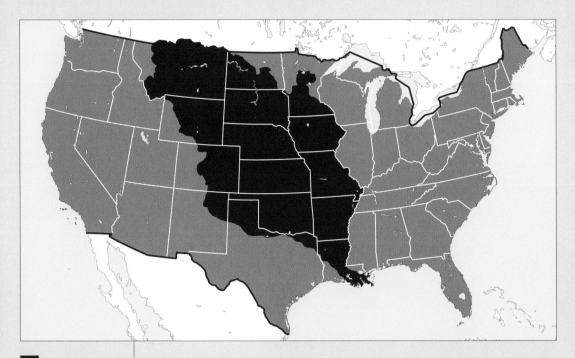

■ Louisiana Purchase

LOUISIANA PURCHASE
The extent of the area sold to America by Napoleon was unknown at the time, but it would double the size of the country.

announced the extraordinary deal, which doubled the size of the country of which he was president at a cost of less than 4 cents an acre (about 9 cents per hectare) and without a shot being fired. The deal was not universally welcomed in America at the time, particularly after doubts about its legality began to emerge. Napoleon, it turned out, had no more constitutional authority to sell the territory than Jefferson had to buy it and, at the time when the treaty had been signed, Spain had not actually formally transferred the title of the land to France anyway. And, of course, nobody at the time stopped to consider that the Native American tribes who were then living all across the region could, had they been consulted and given legal advice, have actually claimed that it belonged to them in the first place through right of possession, making the geopolitical horse-trading between Spain, France, and America over the territory redundant.

LEWIS AND CLARK

Before the Louisiana Purchase, Jefferson had always insisted on adhering to the US constitution, but he was a landowner himself and could appreciate just how good a deal it was for America, so on this occasion he was prepared to let the matter rest and, legal or otherwise, accept it as it stood. The Spanish were not so accommodating, challenging the extent of the territory being claimed by the United States and insisting that the deal had only been for New Orleans and the land on the western bank of the Mississippi, not for all the territory right up to the Rocky Mountains. Jefferson had already been considering sending out expeditions into the territory before the purchase and now commissioned the first of several, dispatched with the primary aim of assessing the economic and commercial potential of the new territory, but also under the premise that the country with the best maps would have the better claim to the territory. In May 1804, the expedition, which was led by Meriwether Lewis and William Clark, embarked west along the Missouri River, making, for the most part, friendly contact with the Native American tribes they encountered, and then headed further to the west through the disputed Oregon Country and on to the Pacific Ocean.

The Lewis and Clark Expedition into the Louisiana Territory was followed by several further expeditions, which explored the Red River Basin and the area further south. The maps drawn up by these expeditions would subsequently play a part in negotiations between America and Spain to establish the western boundary of the territory. In the Adams–Onís Treaty, signed in 1819, the American negotiator John Quincey Adams not only achieved almost all of what the US had wanted in setting the border between American and Spanish territories, but also secured the purchase of Florida from Spain as well, making it one of America's greatest diplomatic successes. In the 1840s, the territory west of the Rockies came into American possession through a process of annexation and negotiation with Mexico, which had become independent from Spain in 1821, and by treaty with Britain over the Oregon Country, establishing the border between America and Canada on the 49th parallel. The Alaska Purchase of 1867, in which America paid Russia $7.2 million for a huge area of what was then considered a barren arctic wilderness added almost as much territory to the United States as the Louisiana Purchase had done. The addition of Hawaii in 1959, after Hawaiians voted in favor of accepting statehood rather than remaining as a US territory, completed the 50 states of America as they are today.

DECISION

Social Change

Science and Innovation

Culture

Politics

Diplomacy

Military

Religion

THE CONGRESS OF VIENNA

1814–15

Circumstances: The end of the Napoleonic Wars

Protagonists: Diplomatic representatives from the Great Powers

Consequences: The reorganization of European states and the establishment of the Concert of Europe to maintain peace through the balance of power

The reconstruction of Europe at the Congress of Vienna is probably the most seminal episode in modern history. Not only did the congress redraw the map entirely, it determined which nations were to have a political existence over the next hundred years and which were not.

Adam Zamoyski, *Rites of Passage*

After more than 20 years of almost constant war, the Great Powers of Europe came together at the Congress of Vienna, beginning in November 1814, with the dual objectives of negotiating a peace settlement and establishing a system of diplomacy to try to avoid further wars in the future. The French Revolutionary Wars, beginning in 1792, had been followed by the Napoleonic Wars, which had led to the dissolution of the Holy Roman Empire and left much of the Continent in disarray. Napoleon was defeated at the Battle of Leipzig in October 1813 and subsequently exiled to the island of Elba, off the coast of Italy, after which France formally surrendered to the Sixth Alliance, a coalition of forces primarily made up of the other four Great Powers: Britain, Russia, Austria, and Prussia. In the immediate aftermath of the French surrender, the members of the alliance decided to state formally in a treaty that they would remain as allies for at least the next 20 years and to convene the Congress of Vienna to sort out all the outstanding issues arising from years of war.

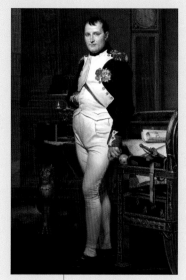

NAPOLEON BONAPARTE
The Congress of Vienna was convened after the defeat of Napoleon at the Battle of Leipzig and the subsequent surrender of the French.

The outcome of the negotiations led to the reorganization of much of Europe, affecting almost every continental European state, and established a system of maintaining the balance of power by diplomatic means—known as the Concert of Europe—in which the Great Powers could settle disputes by negotiation rather than war. The congress has attracted a great deal of criticism over the years, largely because of the Great Powers' preference for reinstating dynastic monarchies over the more liberal and enlightened systems of governance that had begun to develop as a consequence of the French Revolution. Nevertheless, the negotiated settlements achieved through the Concert of Europe helped to limit the extent of future conflicts, preventing the occurrence of another major European war for almost 50 years and not one involving all of the Great Powers until the outbreak of the First World War 100 years later. Overall, the decisions taken at the Congress of Vienna, although motivated by self-interest, were nevertheless effective in their aims of maintaining peace in Europe and they established a precedent for the conduct of future diplomatic meetings between the Great Powers.

THE CONGRESS

The Congress was convened in Vienna under the chairmanship of the Austrian Foreign Minister Prince Klemens von Metternich, an accomplished diplomat and statesman who would remain highly influential in both Austrian politics and European diplomacy for several decades afterward. The subsequent meetings held between the Great Powers in order to maintain the balance of power are now widely known as the Concert of Europe, but at the time were often referred to as being part of the Metternich System because he was acknowledged as being the man behind the development of this approach. He was also known for the conservatism of his position on the future of Europe, whereby he favored the continuance of rule by monarchies and aristocratic families, a stance that fitted in well with the main negotiators from the other three Great Powers. The Russian delegation, although nominally led by Foreign Minister Count Karl Nesselrode, was directed by Tsar Alexander I, who remained in Vienna for the entire period, while the Prussians were led by their chancellor, Prince Karl von Hardenberg. Lord Castlereagh initially led the British delegation until he returned to Britain after a few months because of ill health and was replaced by the Duke of Wellington. The duke in turn had to leave the Congress in order to lead the campaign against Napoleon, who had escaped from exile on Elba and returned to France, beginning a period known as the Hundred Days. While Wellington was away from Vienna, the British delegation was led by the diplomat Richard Trench, the Earl of Clancarty, who had been involved in the formal negotiations throughout the course of the Congress and would remain in Vienna until its conclusion.

METTERNICH
The Austrian foreign minister chaired the Congress of Vienna, which established the Concert of Europe, also known as the Metternich System.

At first, the French were excluded from the Congress because they were held responsible for the wars that had made it necessary in the first place. They were admitted later, however, after astute diplomatic maneuvering from their foreign minister, Charles Talleyrand, who was known as a great schemer and manipulator—despite being from an aristocratic background, he had come through both the French Revolution and Napoleonic era unscathed. One of the early decisions taken by the Congress was to restore the Bourbon dynasty, in the shape of King Louis XVIII, to the throne of France in succession to Napoleon.

Although delegations from every other European state, of which there were almost 200 at the time, were involved in the formal discussions, they had little influence on the decisions taken because most of the real negotiations occurred in numerous informal meetings held in private between the representatives of the Great Powers. While the serious business of negotiating the settlement was being conducted behind closed doors, an almost constant round of balls and dinner parties was held to entertain the huge number of aristocratic delegates who had arrived in Vienna for the Congress, many of whom are said to have done more dancing than talking.

The final settlement was signed by all participants on June 9, 1815, nine days before the Battle of Waterloo. One of the principal intentions of the reorganization of European states was to create a buffer zone of independent states around France, itself forced to revert to borders as they had been before the start of the French Revolutionary Wars. Prussia, one of the main beneficiaries of the Congress, was given territory in the Rhineland, on its north-west border with France, while the neutrality of Switzerland was guaranteed and the Kingdom of Piedmont-Sardinia was restored as a constitutional monarchy and given territory on the eastern border of France. To the north, the Kingdom of the Netherlands was created out of the Dutch Republic and those adjacent parts of the French Empire that would later split away to form Belgium.

The other major decisions included giving Finland and part of Poland to Russia, with the rest of Poland going to Prussia, together with several of the smaller German states of the former Holy Roman Empire. All the remaining German states, principalities, and grand duchies, of which there were more than a hundred, were assimilated into about 30 states and united as the German Confederation, while Italy was also reorganized into seven states, and Norway, which had previously been governed by Denmark, was given to Sweden without the Norwegian people being consulted about their fate. By the end of this process, the map of Europe had been almost completely redrawn, with most of the new states both large and small being placed under the rule of either an absolute or a constitutional monarchy. The only one of the Great Powers to remain the same after the settlement had been reached was Britain, which was more interested in its overseas empire than in

THE SETTLEMENT

any particular territories in Europe other than where its maritime and commercial interests were concerned.

The complete lack of concern showed by the delegates from the Great Powers for the wishes of the people in those countries that were being reorganized would lead to problems in the future, as would the failure to acknowledge the desire for reform felt in many parts of Europe — something that would lead to the revolution in Belgium in 1830 and a series of revolutions and uprisings in 1848 that again began in France and then spread across much of the Continent. But these revolutionary struggles did not develop into wider wars and for the most part the conflicting interests of the five Great Powers continued to be managed through the Concert of Europe. The main area of contention during much of the remainder of the nineteenth century concerned the decline of the Ottoman Empire, in which some of the Great Powers, particularly Britain and Russia, competed with each other to gain the most benefit for themselves as Ottoman influence in Europe, the Middle East, and North Africa gradually eroded.

THE MAIN AREA OF CONTENTION DURING MUCH OF THE REMAINDER OF THE NINETEENTH CENTURY CONCERNED THE DECLINE OF THE OTTOMAN EMPIRE

The Eastern Question, as the decline of the Ottoman Empire became known, was behind the Crimean War, fought between 1853 and 1856 by the Russian Empire and a coalition of European states led by Britain and France. The failure of the Great Powers to find a negotiated solution to this conflict before hostilities began can be seen as the beginning of the end for the Concert system established by the Congress of Vienna. It was further undermined by the Austro–Prussian War of 1866 and the Franco–Prussian War of 1870–71, both fought, it could be argued, at the instigation of the Prussian chancellor Otto von Bismarck as a means of facilitating the unification of Germany under Prussian control. The creation of a unified Germany, with the industrial and military capacity to dominate Europe, disrupted the balance of power, putting an end to the Concert system once and for all as the Great Powers sought to form individual alliances between each other rather than to maintain strong diplomatic relations across the Continent. Germany viewed the alliance between Russia and France as a threat to its security and so formed a counter-alliance with Austria, while, for the most part, Britain maintained a policy of "splendid isolation" as it continued to concentrate on its empire rather than become involved in European affairs. These alliances were by no means the only cause of the First World War, but when put together with the breakdown of diplomacy, they certainly played a major part in the failure of the Great Powers to negotiate a solution to the crisis that developed in July 1914 after the assassination of Archduke Franz Ferdinand in Sarajevo.

The peace settlement reached after the end of the First World War provides an illustration of how successfully the Congress of Vienna had dealt with the issues arising out of the Napoleonic Wars. The punitive measures taken against Germany in 1919 as part of the Treaty of Versailles were one of the direct causes of the Second World War, so much so that some historians have described the 20-year gap between the wars as being nothing more than a break in hostilities. The decisions taken at Vienna did not pay heed to the more liberal atmosphere that had developed in Europe by that time, nor did they anticipate the later rise of nationalism in many European countries, but even the left-wing historian Eric Hobsbawm, no friend of dynastic monarchies, commented about the settlement achieved at the Congress, "given the entirely antiliberal and antinational purpose of its makers, it was reasonable and sensible." It is hardly a ringing endorsement, but, considering the circumstances, being "reasonable and sensible" was not a terrible way of settling differences either.

DECISION

Social Change

Science and Innovation

Culture

Politics

Diplomacy

Military

Religion

KARL DRAIS AND THE LAUFMASCHINE
1817

Circumstances: The rising price of oats in Baden

Protagonists: An inventor trying to find a way of replacing the horse

Consequences: The first two-wheeled self-propelled mode of transport, the forerunner of the modern bicycle

These machines move at the rate of from 6 to 10 or 12 miles an hour, according to the peculiarities of the road traveled and the dexterity of the rider. The agreeable and moderate exercise they afford, help to promote digestion, invigorate the corporeal system, insure health to those who are indisposed: and thus save the doctor's, druggist's, and housekeeper's bills.

From an advertisement offering velocipedes to rent in the
***Connecticut Herald* on June 15, 1819**

The largest volcanic eruption in the last 2,000 years began on April 10, 1815, on the island of Sumbawa in the Dutch East Indies, now Indonesia, when the build-up of magma underneath Mount Tambora caused an immense explosion, throwing a huge amount of debris out into the atmosphere. The German historian Hans-Erhard Lessing has proposed a connection between this devastating event and the invention of the laufmaschine, the earliest form of the bicycle. Other than the fact that the invention occurred only two years after the eruption, this connection might appear to be a little tenuous, but Lessing's theory makes more sense than initial appearances might suggest. The ash and dust thrown high into the Earth's atmosphere by the eruption caused a rapid cooling in the climate across the Northern Hemisphere, leading in Europe to what became known as the Year Without a Summer. The poor harvest experienced that year resulted in famine in some European countries and caused a spike in food prices across much of the rest of the continent, including in the city of Mannheim in what was then the Grand Duchy of Baden, where the forestry official and inventor Karl Drais lived. A dramatic increase in the price of oats made feeding horses an expensive business and, at least according to Lessing, this led to Drais's decision to revisit an unsuccessful project he had worked on a few years previously to develop a horseless carriage, only this time, rather than the four-wheel contraption he had originally envisaged, he decided to concentrate on a simpler version with only two wheels; he called this the laufmaschine, literally the "running machine."

THE MECHANICAL HORSE

Drais was born on April 29, 1785, in the city of Karlsruhe, the capital of Baden. His father was a senior civil servant with the title of baron in the government of the Grand Duke of Baden, working as the chief administrator of the forestry department, an important role in Baden because of the extent of the Black Forest, which covered a large part of the Grand Duchy. The grand duke became Karl's godfather and as a result of both family connections and the duke's patronage, he joined the forestry service himself in 1803, but then had to wait for several years before a suitable position opened up. In the meantime, he studied sciences at the University of Heidelberg and, if he had not already developed a fascination for mechanical devices beforehand, certainly appears to have done so while at the university. After finishing his studies, and while still waiting for a position in the forestry service, he

KARL DRAIS
A portrait of the inventor from about 1820, a few years after he had constructed the first laufmaschine.

taught for a few years at the school run by his uncle, which specialized in forest administration. After two more years of waiting, finally a position opened up, but by this time he appears to have become much more interested in mechanical engineering than forestry.

In 1812 he was granted indefinite leave from the forestry service on a full salary, allowing him to concentrate on making mechanical devices. A string of inventions followed, including in 1814 his first attempt at a horseless carriage, which was driven by a crank handle turned by its passengers. Drais demonstrated the carriage to some of the nobles who had gathered for the Congress of Vienna later in that year, but it provoked little interest in them or, in truth, in anybody much else either. He shelved the idea, concentrating on other projects, like the stenotype machine he had invented for recording musical notation by punching holes in paper. Drais did not explain the reasons behind his decision to return to the idea of a self-propelled mechanical vehicle, but the scarcity of animal feed during the winter of 1816 certainly provides a reasonably convincing one. German newspapers from that time carried reports of the rising price of oats and of horses having to be put down because they could not be fed, so it is entirely possible that this was a motivating factor behind his decision, even if this can only be regarded as, at best, circumstantial evidence.

The complete lack of interest in his horseless carriage most likely caused Drais to rethink and was perhaps also behind his decision to concentrate on developing a mechanical horse to be ridden by a single rider. By the summer of 1817, Drais had constructed his first laufmaschine, consisting of two small wooden coach wheels with metal rims, connected in line by a beam with a seat on it and with a pivot and handlebars above the front wheel so that it could be steered. On June 12, he took it out for a demonstration ride, sitting on the laufmaschine and propelling it with his feet as if he were walking or running, and in a little over an hour he had covered 9 miles (15 km). In the following month, and having made a few adjustments, he traveled from Gernsbach to Baden-Baden, a distance of 32 miles (50 km), in four hours, more than twice as quickly as anybody could reasonably walk the distance.

The two demonstrations received extensive coverage in German newspapers, leading to an instant demand for the laufmaschine. Drais was awarded a grand ducal privilege to enable him to exploit his invention, but although this protected his invention in Baden, he did not have a wider patent so there was nothing to stop anybody else from outside the region copying his invention. Lots of other people began to make their own versions of the laufmaschine and a craze began throughout Germany and in other parts of Europe, even if the original name did not catch on. Different versions of Drais's invention were known as the velocipede and the draisine, while in Britain, where it attracted its fair share of ridicule, it was called the dandy horse because, according to its critics, it was mostly ridden by dandies showing off in front of everybody else. But, like all crazes, once the initial excitement of something new had begun to die down, the laufmaschine gradually became less and less popular, until it remained in use only by a few die-hard enthusiasts.

In truth, riders on their velocipedes and draisines did look faintly ridiculous and its popularity was not helped by the state of most roads at the time, which were often deeply rutted and uneven from the passage of carriages and carts, or by the amount of scorn it attracted from the newspapers. The adverse publicity may account, at least in part, for why it took 50 years for somebody to think of adding pedals to their velocipede so that it could be propelled without having to run along the ground, an innovation that, with the benefit of hindsight, might appear to be a little obvious. The first person usually credited with making a bicycle in this way is Pierre Michaux, a blacksmith and carriage maker from Paris, who attached pedals directly to the front wheel of his velocipede in 1868, allowing him to move forward by turning the wheels with the pedals even if it made steering difficult. The problem was solved by the addition of a chain drive to propel the back wheel rather than the front, allowing the rider to steer much more easily and improving the weight distribution and balance of the resulting bicycle as well. The first of these to be produced commercially, the Rover Safety Bicycle, was made in Coventry, UK, in 1885 by the English inventor and industrialist John Kemp Starley. It was the first recognizably modern bike and began a second craze for individual mechanical horses that, with a few adjustments and modifications over the years, continues to this day.

THE PEDALS

DECISION

Social Change

Science and Innovation

Culture

Politics

Diplomacy

Military

Religion

THE MONROE DOCTRINE

1823

Circumstances: The possibility of a resurgence of European colonization in the New World

Protagonists: President James Monroe and Secretary of State John Quincy Adams

Consequences: The establishment of a principle of US Government policy that continues to this day

The American continents, by free and independent condition which they have assumed and maintain, are henceforward not to be considered as subjects for future colonization by any European powers.

From the address given to Congress by President James Monroe on December 2, 1823, setting out the principle that would later be known as the Monroe Doctrine

The tradition of the US president giving an annual message to a joint session of Congress, now known as the State of the Union Address, was initiated by George Washington in 1790 during his first term in the office and only two years after independence. President James Monroe (1758–1831) used the occasion on December 2, 1823, to set out the American position on a particular point of foreign policy, a stance that would become known as the Monroe Doctrine, the principle that European powers should no longer consider any of the states of either North or South America as being potential colonies. He went further to say that the US would respect those European colonies on the two continents already in existence and that America would not intervene in the internal affairs of any European country, but would regard European interference anywhere in the Americas as an act of aggression against the United States. This robust statement was the result of a decision reached over the course of several cabinet meetings held that November in which the Secretary of State John Quincy Adams (1767–1848), the son of the second US president John Adams, who would succeed Monroe to the presidency two years later, argued forcibly against a proposal to issue a joint declaration with the British that contained much the same content. In deciding to go it alone, the US Government was both asserting its independence on the world stage and establishing a principle of foreign policy that remains today. The way in which the Monroe Doctrine has been interpreted over the years has sometimes been controversial, being used, for instance, as a justification for US intervention in Central and South American states, but the original decision to formulate the doctrine must surely rank as a great one in US diplomatic history because it has formed the basis of its foreign policy for almost 200 years.

JAMES MONROE
A portrait of the fifth president of the United States of America by Samuel Morse, the man who invented Morse code.

One of the reasons why the Monroe Doctrine has lasted for so long is because it was stated in language that did not make it specific to an individual set of circumstances, even if the decision to make the statement in the first place arose as a consequence of the state of world affairs at that particular moment in history. By the summer of 1823, America had formally recognized those Latin American countries that had won their independence from Spain after the end of the Napoleonic Wars

THE SUMMER OF 1823

in Europe. The Peninsular War, the theater of the Napoleonic Wars fought across Iberia, had left Spain in political turmoil, all but bankrupt and incapable of maintaining its colonies in the New World when challenged by the development of independence movements. Earlier in the year, a French army had intervened in Spain to restore the Bourbon king Ferdinand VII as the absolute monarch of the country and, after that successful campaign, rumors in diplomatic circles suggested that an alliance of Spain, France, and Russia was now planning to restore the Spanish Crown's former colonies in the Americas by force as well.

At the same time, the Russian Tsar Nicholas II had been making statements about extending Russian territory in North America. The Americans and British had yet to agree a border between their own territories in the northern regions and the last thing either country wanted was a third party like the Russians becoming involved and complicating matters even further. The British held a dominant position over much maritime trade, and ships following commercial routes came under the protection of the Royal Navy, which, at that time, really did rule the waves. It was not in Britain's interests for other European powers to become any more established in the New World than they already were, so, as well as opposing Russian expansion in the north, Britain was firmly against the restoration of Spanish rule in the south, particularly if that rule was imposed with the help of France, which would then surely use the opportunity to regain a foothold in the region itself. Relations between Britain and America had been improving in the previous few years, even if the War of 1812 was still fresh in the memory, and in August 1823, the British Foreign Secretary George Canning proposed that the two countries issue a joint statement disapproving of any outside intervention in the former colonies of Spanish America. The statement was to be worded in the usual diplomatic language, which did not actually mention the names of the countries it concerned, while, at the same time, it was obvious to everybody that its purpose was to warn off both France and Russia.

Before discussing the British proposal with his Cabinet, Monroe consulted with two of his predecessors, Thomas Jefferson and James Madison, both of whom expressed the opinion that it would be wise to go along with Canning. The first Cabinet debate on November 7 appeared to be heading for a decision in line with the advice given by

THE BRITISH HELD A DOMINANT POSITION OVER MUCH MARITIME TRADE AND SHIPS FOLLOWING COMMERCIAL ROUTES CAME UNDER THE PROTECTION OF THE ROYAL NAVY

Jefferson and Madison, until Quincy Adams spoke, putting forward his view that:

> It would be more candid as well as more dignified to avow our principles explicitly to Russia and France than to come in as a cockboat in the wake of the British man-of-war.

Adams thought that America would look stronger as a nation if it issued a statement on its own behalf rather than doing so with the British and then relying on the Royal Navy to police the ensuing policy. He was also certain that the threat from France and Russia had been exaggerated in the diplomatic rumors and in his opinion neither had any intention of intervening in the New World on behalf of Spain. This being the case, the United States had the opportunity to make its position clear without risk to itself and without having to enter into an alliance with the British, who, nevertheless, would still want to protect their interests in the region whether or not they issued a joint statement. In formulating this view Quincy Adams may have had an eye on his own interests as well as those of America. If, by this time, he had already decided to run in the presidential election of 1825 himself, which appears likely, then being seen by the American people to be both refusing a British request and enhancing America's reputation on the world stage would certainly do his chances of success no harm.

QUINCY ADAMS
The Monroe Doctrine was named after the president, but was principally the work of the Secretary of State, John Quincy Adams.

In the weeks that followed, Quincy Adams's views were accepted by Monroe, who asked him to write a statement that could be incorporated in the presidential address to Congress. So, even though the resulting declaration was named after Monroe, it was largely the work of Quincy Adams. Critics of the doctrine immediately picked up on the point that, in reality, there was little America alone could have done if any European country had chosen to ignore it. Despite this, the Monroe Doctrine came to be seen as a defining statement of the separation of the Old World and the New, together with expressing the difference in values espoused by them, from Europe's continuing attachment to monarchism to the republicanism of America. It also pointed to a new-found confidence in what was then still a relatively young country, in which America was beginning to assert itself on the world stage.

DECISION

Social Change

Science and Innovation

Culture

Politics

Diplomacy

Military

Religion

DARWIN JOINS THE VOYAGE OF HMS *BEAGLE*

1831

Circumstances: A young naturalist is presented with a great opportunity

Protagonists: Charles Darwin, Robert Darwin, and Josiah Wedgwood II

Consequences: A revolutionary change in our understanding of the natural world and our place within it

Considering how fiercely I have been attacked by the orthodox it seems ludicrous that I once intended to be a clergyman. Nor was this intention and my father's wish ever formally given up, but died a natural death when on leaving Cambridge I joined the Beagle as Naturalist.

From an autobiographical sketch written by Darwin in 1876

On August 30, 1831, the 22-year-old Charles Darwin returned from a geological study tour of North Wales to his family home in Shrewsbury, England, to find a letter waiting for him from John Henslow, one of his tutors at Cambridge University. In the letter Henslow explained that an opportunity had come up for a naturalist to join the Royal Navy ship HMS *Beagle* on its next voyage, beginning in a month, which was planned to last for two years and was primarily concerned with surveying the coast of South America. The position on offer was not as the official Royal Navy naturalist on the voyage, duties that would normally be undertaken by the ship's surgeon, but as what was called a "gentleman companion" to the captain, Robert FitzRoy, meaning that whoever took up the position would not be financed by the navy and would have to pay his own way. Nevertheless, it offered the chance to undertake a study of the natural history of the places visited by the *Beagle*, which, in the course of its voyage, would circumnavigate the globe. At that moment, Darwin was about to return to Cambridge to begin the study of divinity with a view to becoming an Anglican clergyman, but, as soon as he read Henslow's letter, he decided on the spot that he wanted to be considered for the position. The only problem he now faced was to convince the man who would have to foot the bill if he was accepted, his father Robert Darwin, that delaying his studies for two years while he sailed round the world was in any way a sensible thing to do.

CHARLES DARWIN
A photograph taken in 1854 when Darwin was 45, more than 20 years after he had embarked on the voyage of the *Beagle*.

As it would turn out, the voyage of the *Beagle* would last for five years rather than the two initially planned and, as well as making Darwin's name as a naturalist, it would set him not only on course to becoming the most famous naturalist of his day, but also the most celebrated figure in the history of the biological sciences. But, as a young man, it was by no means apparent that he would go on to become so successful in his chosen field. After leaving school, he first went to the University of Edinburgh at the age of 16 to study medicine, following in the footsteps of his older brother Erasmus and his father, who ran a successful medical practice in Shrewsbury and had become very wealthy through a series of shrewd financial investments. Once at Edinburgh, Darwin found the lectures dull and the practical demonstrations nauseating, leading him to the conclusion that the medical profession was not the

THE NATURALIST EMERGES

right one for him. Rather than studying medicine, he spent most of his time going out with friends and indulging his enthusiasms for shooting and fishing, while at the same time also keeping up his childhood interest in natural history.

After two years studying medicine, Darwin left Edinburgh and, again on the advice of his father, moved to Cambridge University to take a Bachelor of Arts degree, the necessary first step to becoming an Anglican clergyman. It is hard to imagine now, given the reaction of the Church to his later work, that anybody could think this would be a suitable career choice for Darwin, but he agreed to the plan even though he had never expressed any great interest in religion. He appears to have been quite taken with the idea of becoming the vicar of a country parish, where he could continue his interest in natural history and perhaps follow in the footsteps of Gilbert White, the author of one of his favorite books, *The Natural History of Selborne*, who famously studied the birdlife in and around a Hampshire village in the late eighteenth century.

At first Darwin carried on at Cambridge much as he had done at Edinburgh, enjoying the social side of being a student more than the academic one, but over the course of the next three years he gradually became more serious and studious, an attitude that brought him to the attention of a number of his tutors, including the geologist Adam Sedgewick and John Henslow. Country sports were replaced by beetle collecting and walking tours to study geology, and he not only began to attend lectures but also to read around the subjects that he was studying. One of the books that left a lasting impression on him was *Personal Narrative of a Journey to the Equinoctial Regions of the New Continent* by the German scientist and explorer Alexander von Humboldt, who traveled through the New World between 1799 and 1804. The book would influence Darwin's account of his own journey, known today as *The Voyage of the Beagle*. It began by describing an extended stay Humboldt had made on Tenerife in the Canary Islands in which he made observations of its unusual geology and natural history. At the end of his three-year degree course, Darwin planned to mount his own expedition to Tenerife, but before setting out for the island he accompanied Adam Sedgewick on his annual summer geological tour of North Wales to learn more about the practical and technical aspects of geological investigation.

On returning home after this trip to find Henslow's letter waiting for him, Darwin was suddenly presented with a much greater opportunity to study natural history overseas than his planned trip to Tenerife. Henslow knew about Darwin's desire to travel and considered that he had the potential to make a fine naturalist. Joining the *Beagle* would be the perfect way to extend his knowledge and it would also bring him to the attention of the wider scientific community. Robert Darwin, on the other hand, was far from convinced and initially refused to provide his son with the necessary funds, no doubt thinking that Darwin was in the process of throwing away a respectable career in the clergy just as he had done with medicine. But he did not completely rule out the idea either, telling his son that he would reconsider if Charles could find a man of common sense who would support the scheme. The inference was clear; Robert Darwin had often said that his brother-in-law Josiah Wedgwood II was the most sensible man he had ever met, so if Charles could persuade Uncle Jos, as he was known, of the merits of the scheme then his father would agree to it as well.

HMS *BEAGLE*
An engraving of the Royal Navy brig on which Darwin set sail in December 1831 for a five-year voyage around the world.

© Getty Images

Darwin made a list of his father's objections, of throwing away his career before it had even started and of it being a "wild scheme," and went to see Uncle Jos at his country estate 30 miles (50 km) away in Staffordshire. Wedgwood immediately supported his nephew and wrote a letter to Robert Darwin addressing all of his objections, but then, after posting it, changed his mind about the best way of dealing with the matter and immediately drove over to Shrewsbury in his carriage to see his brother-in-law in person. By the time Wedgwood arrived in Shrewsbury, Robert Darwin had already changed his mind, probably knowing all along what his brother-in-law's opinion would be. With his father now supporting him, and prepared to pay for everything, Darwin's decision was finalized and, after gaining the approval of the Admiralty and of Captain FitzRoy himself, he spent a frantic few weeks gathering all the equipment he would need for the voyage.

As it would transpire, the *Beagle* did not actually leave Britain until the end of December, setting sail on the first leg of its voyage to cross the Atlantic to South America via the Cape Verde Islands. Darwin turned

NATURAL SELECTION

out to be a terrible sailor, becoming seasick almost as soon as the ship left port, and he spent as much time as he could on land whenever the opportunity presented itself. But the voyage would prove to be the major formative experience of his life, giving him the opportunity to study the geology and natural history of a wide variety of habitats, from the Amazon rainforest of Brazil to tiny coral atolls in the Pacific Ocean. On the Galapagos Islands, 600 miles (1,000 km) off the coast of Ecuador, Darwin could not fail to be struck by the remarkable geological formations and diversity of animals and plants he encountered, which, he noted in his journal, were very different from what he had seen on the South American continent, even if he did not begin to formulate his theory of evolution through natural selection, which would explain these differences, until after he had returned to Britain.

In the introduction to *On the Origin of Species*, published in 1859, Darwin would reflect on this period of his life, saying:

> When on board HMS *Beagle*, as naturalist, I was struck with certain facts in the distribution of the inhabitants of South America, and in geological relations of the present to the past inhabitants of the continent. Those facts seemed to me to throw light on the origin of species—that mystery of mysteries, as it has been called by one of our greatest philosophers. On my return home, it occurred to me, in 1837, that something might perhaps be made out of this question by patiently accumulating and reflecting on all sorts of facts which would have any bearing on it.

Darwin embarked on an intense period of study once he got back to Britain, together with sorting out the various collections he had made during the five-year voyage and writing up his account of it for publication. He kept a series of notebooks on his study of the "transmutation of life," or evolution as we call it now, detailing the direction of his thinking at this time; this would in October 1838 crystallize into the theory of natural selection after he read *An Essay on the Principle of Population* by Thomas Malthus. In the book, first published in 1798, Malthus set out his thoughts on the likelihood of human population growth outstripping the availability of resources and the ensuing struggle for existence that this would cause. By combining Malthus's theory together with his own work and observations made during the *Beagle* voyage, Darwin arrived at what he described as "a theory by which to work," natural selection, in which he envisaged species of animals and plants changing over time as a consequence of the competition for resources between individuals of the same species. Those individuals that were best adapted to their environment would be the ones most likely to survive and reproduce, thereby passing on their characteristics to their offspring.

It would be another 20 years before Darwin was prepared to publish his theory, and even then he only did so because another naturalist, Alfred Russell Wallace, had come to much the same conclusion from his own studies. In *On the Origin of Species*, he presented the evidence he had accumulated over the years to support his theory, some of which went back to the work he had done as a naturalist on board the *Beagle*. The book proved to be a turning point in the biological sciences and was highly controversial at the time among those who considered that it challenged the biblical account of creation. Despite the overwhelming quantity of evidence that now supports the theory, it remains controversial in some circles today. But the decision taken by Darwin, with the help of his father and Uncle Jos, to join the voyage of the *Beagle* would lead to him dedicating his life to his work, which he described as being "one long argument" in favor of evolution. In doing so, he did more than anybody else before or since to further our understanding of the natural world, in the process changing the way we think about ourselves and the world in which we live.

DECISION

Social Change

Science and Innovation

Culture

Politics

Diplomacy

Military

Religion

LINCOLN AND EMANCIPATION

1862

Circumstances: The US president considers what can be done about a series of reverses in the Civil War

Protagonists: President Abraham Lincoln and his Cabinet of Ministers

Consequences: The end of slavery in the United States of America

While Washington sweltered through the long, hot summer [of 1862], Lincoln made the momentous decision on emancipation that would define both his presidency and the Civil War.

Doris Kearns Goodwin, *Team of Rivals*

President Abraham Lincoln made the decision to issue a proclamation to free the slaves of the 13 states of the Confederacy on July 12, 1862, and first mentioned it the following day to two members of his cabinet, Secretary of State William H. Seward and the Secretary of the Navy Gideon Welles, who noted in his diary that Lincoln had said the issue had, "occupied his mind and thoughts day and night" for several weeks. By that time the Civil War had been raging for more than a year and it had not been going well for the Union. Lincoln intended issuing the proclamation as a war measure, which he was entitled to do under the US Constitution as commander-in-chief of the armed forces, citing the use of slaves by the Confederacy in their war effort. At a Cabinet meeting on July 22, Lincoln discussed his intention with his colleagues and accepted the advice of Seward not to issue the proclamation until the Union had achieved a significant victory on the battlefield, otherwise it would look like a desperate measure adopted by the side losing the war.

ABRAHAM LINCOLN
A portrait taken on November 8, 1863, by which time the Emancipation Proclamation had been in force for ten months.

It took two months for a suitable occasion to arise and, in the aftermath of the Battle of Antietam, the president made public his intention of issuing the Emancipation Proclamation, stating that it would come into force in all those Confederate states that had not rejoined the Union by January 1 of the following year. In doing so, Lincoln officially broadened the war aims of the Federal Government, from countering the rebellion in the southern states and preserving the Union to include the liberation of the slaves of the Confederacy. It was, by any standards, a momentous decision and a defining moment in both the Civil War and in the history of America as a whole—even if its immediate effect was limited and it did not actually apply to those slaves held in the border states that had not joined the Confederacy, but in which slavery was still legal.

There can be no doubt that slavery was a major issue during the Civil War, but the extent to which it actually caused the war in the first place has become one of those intractable historical debates that is set to continue because the answer is a matter of opinion. But the division of the states fighting on either side of the war essentially came down to those in the north, where slavery had either been abolished or had never been legal in the first place, and the southern slave states, which

SLAVERY AND THE CIVIL WAR

formed the Confederacy after Lincoln, the candidate of the anti-slavery Republican Party, won the 1860 presidential election. Unlike in the rapidly industrializing north, the economy of the southern states largely remained an agricultural one, primarily based on the lucrative cotton trade. It relied on the plantation system and slavery, and, even though the majority of white people in the south had never owned a slave, most of their political representatives came from the slave-owning class who were not prepared to risk their positions and wealth by allowing what they considered to be interference in a state issue by a federal government dominated by northern abolitionists.

EVEN THOUGH THE MAJORITY OF WHITE PEOPLE IN THE SOUTH HAD NEVER OWNED A SLAVE, MOST OF THEIR POLITICAL REPRESENTATIVES CAME FROM THE SLAVE-OWNING CLASS

The crux of the matter was in whether the newly emerging states created as a result of the westward expansion of America should be slave states or free states. The opinion at the time was that, if these new states were free, then the institution of slavery would gradually wither away throughout America because the slave states would become an increasingly small minority in Congress and would eventually have to ascent to abolition even if they did not agree with the moral arguments against slavery. This split had already led to violent confrontations in the 1850s during what is known as the Bleeding Kansas era, in which immigrants from both sides, slave-owning southerners and northern free-staters, fought over the status of the territory in the Midwest. This would become the free state of Kansas in January 1861, three months before the Confederate attack on Fort Sumpter in South Carolina that started the Civil War. So it would be possible to argue that the Confederacy went to war to maintain the right of individual states to determine their own laws and that the North went to war to preserve the Union, as Lincoln said himself on numerous occasions. However, the poisonous issue underpinning everything was slavery.

The extent to which Lincoln was genuinely committed to the abolitionist cause rather than using it as a political tool to help the Union win the war has been the cause of almost as much speculation as the role slavery played in the start of the war. He has been characterized by some as being no more than a political manipulator, employing any means at his disposal to achieve his aims, and by others as an idealist whose main purpose in seeking election as president and then in fighting the Civil War was to abolish slavery. The truth of the matter probably lies somewhere between these two extremes and, at least according to the current trends in historical research, now tends toward the latter argument. The major obstacle facing Lincoln was that, under the US constitution at the time, the president did not possess the power required to abolish slavery on his own. To make any proposed constitutional change legal it had to be ratified by both houses of Congress and by the legislatures of each state of the Union. The Republican Party may have been in a majority in Congress, but Lincoln was well aware that at least some of the states, particularly those border states where slavery was still legal, were not going to support any abolitionist legislation, making it impossible for him to push a constitutional change through by this method.

One strategy Lincoln adopted in an attempt to overcome this impasse was to persuade the Congressional representatives of the border states to accept a deal he called "compensated emancipation," in which the states would enact laws to put an end to slavery in return for slave owners receiving compensation for the loss of their property, the slaves they owned. He held several meetings in the White House to discuss this proposal, but could not reach an agreement with the representatives of the border states, and after one particularly fruitless encounter that took place on July 12, 1862, the day of his momentous decision, came to the conclusion that, no matter what he did, it was never going to happen. A few weeks before this meeting, the Union had suffered a major setback in the war. The Union Army of the Potomac had attempted to capture Richmond, the Confederate capital in Virginia, but were defeated in a series of encounters with a Confederate army under the command of Robert E. Lee, which became known as the Seven Days Battles, and had been forced to retreat. Lee's successes on the battlefield prompted rumors that both Britain and France were considering recognizing the Confederacy as the legitimate government of the southern states, which, if it happened, could have forced Lincoln into a settlement, putting an end to his hopes of preserving the Union.

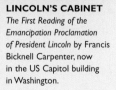

LINCOLN'S CABINET
The First Reading of the Emancipation Proclamation of President Lincoln by Francis Bicknell Carpenter, now in the US Capitol building in Washington.

One consequence of the reverses suffered by the Union army in Virginia was Lincoln's decision to prosecute the war more vigorously. After concluding that he was never going to get anywhere with the border states, he also changed his approach to abolition, making the decision to emancipate the slaves held in Confederate states first because he

THE PROCLAMATION
A reproduction of the Emancipation Proclamation issued by Lincoln on January 1, 1863, freeing the slaves in the Confederate states.

could do so without the approval of Congress or the state legislatures. It was, Lincoln said, "a military necessity absolutely essential for the salvation of the Union," and he countered Confederate claims that it was unconstitutional by stating, "The rebels could not simultaneously throw off the Constitution and evoke its aid." Over the course of the following two months, the war continued to go badly for the Union; Lee advanced through north Virginia until his army was only 20 miles (30 km) from Washington, but then turned north and crossed the Potomac River into the Union state of Maryland, before finally being stopped on September 17 at the Battle of Antietam.

The battle was the most costly single day in the entire war, with a combined total of 23,000 casualties, of which 3,500 were killed. In reality it was fought to a stalemate, even if it was treated like a victory by the Union forces because it prevented Lee advancing further into Maryland. Lincoln also claimed it as a victory and used the occasion to publicly issue his provisional proclamation. None of the Confederate states complied with the terms of this proclamation by returning to the Union before January 1, 1863, leading to the Emancipation Proclamation entering into law on that date. Approximately 4 million slaves in the Confederacy became technically free that day, even if almost half a million more in the border states remained in bondage. Over the course of two and a half years, the advancing Union army gradually freed those slaves in the Confederate territory that they captured. As the war was drawing to a close, Lincoln, knowing that the Emancipation Proclamation could be construed as being only a temporary war measure, proposed an amendment to the US constitution to make slavery illegal throughout America. It read, "Neither slavery nor involuntary servitude, except as a punishment for crime whereof the party shall have been duly convicted, shall exist within the United States, or any place subject to their jurisdiction." By December 6, 1865, it had been ratified by Congress and all the states of the Union, thereby coming into law as the Thirteenth Amendment nine months after Lincoln had been assassinated by the Confederate sympathizer John Wilkes Booth.

DECISION

Social Change

Science and Innovation

Culture

Politics

Diplomacy

Military

Religion

THE WRIGHT BROTHERS BUILD AN AIRPLANE

1903

Circumstances: Two brothers indulge their childhood fascination with flying

Protagonists: Wilbur and Orville Wright

Consequences: The beginning of the age of the airplane

There are only two ways of learning to ride a fractious horse; one is to get on him and learn by actual practice how each motion and trick may be best met; the other is to sit on a fence and watch the beast awhile, and then retire to the house and at leisure figure out the way of overcoming his jumps and kicks. The latter system is the safer, but the former, on the whole, turns out the larger proportion of good riders. It is very much the same in learning to ride a flying machine; if you are looking for perfect safety, you will do as well to sit on the fence and watch the birds; but if you really wish to learn, you must mount a machine and become acquainted with its tricks by actual trial.

From a speech given by Wilbur Wright to the Western Society of Engineers in Chicago on September 18, 1901

ORVILLE WRIGHT
The younger of the Wright
Brothers piloted the first
powered flight on
December 17, 1903, near
Kitty Hawk, North Carolina.

On December 17, 1903, Orville Wright flew the Wright Flyer 1 for a distance of 120 ft (37 m), which took him about 12 seconds. It was the first in a series of four successful flights that day, with Wilbur and his brother Orville alternating as pilot. It was Wilbur who was at the controls for the longest flight of the day, which lasted for almost a minute and on which he traveled 852 ft (260 m). It might not have been very far, but according to the Smithsonian Institute, the Flyer was, "the first powered, heavier-than-air machine to achieve controlled, sustained flight with a pilot aboard," or, to the rest of us, the first proper airplane. Before becoming aviation pioneers, the Wright Brothers had opened a bicycle shop together in their home town of Dayton, Ohio, where they constructed and repaired their own version of the safety bike, and both had been fascinated by the idea of flight since childhood. The inspiration behind their decision to attempt to build their own airplane came from reading a newspaper report of the death of the German flyer Otto Lilienthal on August 10, 1896; he had made more than 2,000 gliding flights before losing control of his hanggglider, as we would now call it, and breaking his neck in the subsequent crash. Many people would have been put off the idea of flying by such a report rather than inspired by it, but apparently not Wilbur and Orville, who differed from all the other early pioneers of flight by adopting a much more rigorous and methodological approach to the design and testing of their machines. Flying was clearly a dangerous business and, while it was not possible to eliminate all the risks, the Wright Brothers intended to leave as little to chance as possible.

CONTROL

The fundamental problem preventing all the pioneers of flying from making a sustained flight was not so much staying in the air, the aerodynamics of lift having already been worked out, but in keeping control of the airplane when it was in flight. Lilienthal's system of control had simply involved moving his body to both maintain the balance of his glider and to change direction, in the process making adjustments to what is known in aviation as its pitch, roll, and yaw, the ability of an airplane to move in three dimensions around its point of balance. While this worked up to a point, as Lilienthal and various other pilots of the day had found out to their cost, it made their gliders difficult to handle in the changing wind conditions encountered in the air. This problem would only be worse for powered flight, the holy grail of early aviation, in which airplanes would be much heavier as a consequence of having engines and propellors, so for anybody to successfully achieve it, and survive the attempt, they would first have to find a solution that allowed them to control all three potential ways for the airplane to move.

The earliest evidence we have that the Wright Brothers were working on finding a solution to the control problem comes from 1899, three years after they first began to investigate powered flight. Wilbur, acknowledged as the innovator of the two brothers, wrote to the Smithsonian Institute to request any material the institute might have on the subject of mechanical flight, suggesting that the brothers were only just beginning the serious study of aerodynamics three years after Lilienthal's death or, alternatively, Wilbur had already arrived at the solution to the problem and wanted to be sure nobody else had beaten him to it. He would later say that his first inspiration for the mechanical control system that he devised had come from his observations of birds in flight, in which he noticed how a pigeon leaned into a turn in a similar way to how a person shifted their weight to take a corner on a bicycle. The pigeon achieved this by moving the long feathers on both its wing tips; this altered the angle of air flow over its wings, allowing it to turn without losing control of its flight. But, even if this was the way a bird maneuvered in the air, it was far from obvious how that could be transferred to an airplane, which would have to have wings flexible enough to move while, at the same time, being both strong enough to cope with the pressure being placed on them and light enough to allow the plane to fly. Wilbur worked out how to design wings combining all of these features after he picked up a long thin box that had previously contained the inner tube of a bicycle tire and twisted it at either end. When he released the pressure he had applied to the box, it naturally sprang back into its original shape, leading him to envisage a biplane in which the two wings, separated by struts, formed the shape of a box and could be twisted to alter the air flow over them by means of wires attached near their tips and pulled by the pilot from the cockpit.

WILBUR WRIGHT
Four years older than Orville, Wilbur is acknowledged as being the innovator of the control system used in the Wright Flyer.

THE WRIGHT FLYER

Before risking their lives with a full-scale version of the biplane, the Wright Brothers tested their idea on a series of kites and unmanned gliders that made use of the so-called wing-warping technology Wilbur had developed. In the autumn of 1900 they began to travel to Kitty Hawk on the coast of North Carolina, where wind conditions were suitable for conducting tests and where they could work in privacy. Over the course of the next few years they conducted experiments with larger manned gliders in which they both developed their skills as pilots, learning to keep the glider balanced in a similar way to how people learn to ride a bike. Over the course of these experiments, they increased the size of the wings to gain more lift and, as well as the wing-warping to control roll, added a forward elevator and rear rudder to control pitch and yaw. When they were satisfied that everything worked, they decided the time had come to add an engine. With nothing suitable available to buy, the brothers had to design and build both it and the propellor themselves, helped by Charlie Taylor, a mechanic in their bicycle shop, who put a lightweight engine together from their plans in only six weeks.

WRIGHT FLYER
The Wright Model A, a two-seater version of the Wright Flyer III and the first airplane to be commercially produced.

From start to finish, the Wright Flyer I took seven years to design and build—a truly remarkable achievement considering they had no outside investment and had done all of the required design and construction either in the back of their bicycle shop or from a camp on the sand dunes near Kitty Hawk. At first their achievements received little attention in the press, in part because of the secrecy they had adopted to prevent anybody stealing their ideas, but also because few people believed that two brothers who ran a bicycle shop could really have built a working airplane. Over the next few years they worked on improving the design of their plane to make it more stable. In 1905 they built the first truly practical airplane, the Wright Flyer III, which Wilbur flew for 40 minutes, covering 24 miles (39 km) and demonstrating beyond doubt that the brothers had overcome all the problems involved in powered flight, combining lift and propulsion with control. Their major breakthrough was undoubtedly their system of control, the basic idea of which remains in use in fixed-wing airplanes today.

D. W. GRIFFITH MAKES A MOVIE IN HOLLYWOOD

1910

DECISION

Social Change

Science and Innovation

Culture

Politics

Diplomacy

Military

Religion

Circumstances: A director looks for an outdoor location for his next movie

Protagonists: D. W. Griffith and the early pioneers of American film

Consequences: The establishment of Hollywood as the center of the movie industry

Griffith did everything. He preceded Hollywood in everything that has been done since. It is an abiding mystery and a scandal to me that an ungrateful industry has not raised a statue to him ninety feet tall at the intersection of Hollywood Boulevard and Vine Street.

Lionel Barrymore,
We Barrymores

© Getty Images

D. W. GRIFFITH
The pioneer of early film directed more than 500 movies and was the first to shoot a movie in Hollywood.

The first movie shot in Hollywood was made in 1910 by D. W. Griffith, one of the great innovators of early cinema, who was working for the Biograph Company at the time and decided to use a location in the Hollywood Hills for the outdoor scenes of one of his movies. Like most movie companies in those early days, Biograph was actually based in New York, initially using a studio built on the roof of what is now the Roosevelt Building on Broadway, before moving to an indoor studio in 1906 on East 14th Street. Griffith joined the company in 1908, first as an actor and then, within a matter of months, as its principal director. He had come to New York from Kentucky hoping to make his name as a playwright and, after achieving little success in that field, switched to acting and then, after the previous principal director at Biograph had been forced to retire through illness, to making movies rather than being in them. The role of director appeared to suit Griffith, who was something of a workaholic, regularly churning out movies at the rate of three a week. All of them were shot on single reels of film, the industry standard at the time, making them under 20 minutes in length, but it was nevertheless an incredible achievement, not least because of the high quality of the movies he made. Griffith employed the latest techniques in movie-making, which he either devised himself or adapted from the work of others, moving film away from being made solely with a fixed camera pointed at a stage and establishing it for the first time as an art form in its own right.

HOLLYWOOD

In January 1910, Biograph sent Griffith and his company of actors, which included Mary Pickford and Lilian Gish, out to Los Angeles to take advantage of the sunny weather of southern California in order to shoot outdoor locations rather than being limited to the indoor studio in New York. Independent filmmakers had been working in Los Angeles for a number of years by that time, having moved out of New York to get as far away as possible from the Motion Picture Patents Company, an organization started by Thomas Edison in order to protect the patents he and several other film companies held over almost all of the equipment and film stock used in movie-making. The methods employed by the MPPC to prevent illegal filming could be brutal, on occasion resorting to hiring groups of thugs to break up film sets by force, and it is no coincidence that the independents picked southern California not only because it was far away from New York, but also because the California authorities had a relaxed attitude to patent laws and because of its proximity to Mexico in case they had to skip the country in a hurry.

Biograph had no such concerns. They were members of the MPPC and had come to Los Angeles because of the weather and to assess the potential for a permanent move to California. Griffith maintained his extraordinary work rate, shooting in an outdoor studio erected on a vacant lot in Los Angeles and, on the odd occasion when he wasn't actually shooting a film, he was scouting locations for a future project. For the film *In Old California*, set in early nineteenth-century Spanish America, he needed rural locations and, having chosen the Hollywood Hills, decided to establish a base at a hotel in the small town of Hollywood itself, which was conveniently near to the locations and only a few miles outside the city of Los Angeles. The resulting movie, in truth, has little to distinguish it other than being the first to be shot in Hollywood. It was thought to have been lost completely until 2004, when it was rediscovered and shown for the first time in more than 90 years. It proved to be a 17-minute melodrama concerning a Spanish woman who has to choose between two suitors for her hand in marriage, picking the one who turns out to be a worthless drunk rather than the one who goes on to become the governor of California. It is only really notable for Griffith's camera work in photographing the scenery of the Hollywood Hills.

In the following year the first studio, the Nestor Motion Picture Company, opened in Hollywood, which by this time had become incorporated as a suburb of Los Angeles. In 1914 Cecil B. DeMille shot the feature-length film *The Squaw Man* there, which really put it on the map. Over the next few years Paramount, Warner Brothers, and RKO all opened studios in Hollywood, while Universal moved to a huge new studio nearby. By this time D. W. Griffith had left Biograph, wanting to make features of over an hour himself rather than continue to be restricted to the single-reel films still favored by the company. In 1915 he released what is considered to be his masterpiece, *The Birth of a Nation*, an epic story set in the Civil War and the following period of reconstruction. It was controversial at the time, as it remains today,

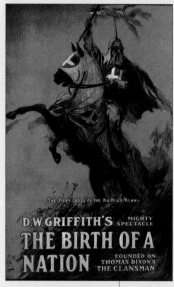

THE FIERY CROSS OF THE KU KLUX KLAN—

D.W.GRIFFITH'S MIGHTY SPECTACLE

THE BIRTH OF A NATION FOUNDED ON THOMAS DIXON'S "THE CLANSMAN"

GRIFFITH'S MASTERPIECE
The movie was technically brilliant but highly controversial because of the racist nature of the material.

for its overtly racist content. It set a new standard as far as technical filmmaking goes and while it can still be appreciated from this perspective, the appalling characterization of black people and the depiction of the Ku Klux Klan as heroes are now so offensive as to be laughable, giving the impression that it was actually intended to be a parody rather than a work of serious drama.

Screenings of the movie provoked riots in several American cities and the controversy it provoked no doubt boosted its audience, people going to see it to find out for themselves what all the fuss was about. Griffith's next movie, *Intolerance*, was an even grander and more expensive affair, intercutting four separate stories and lasting well over three hours. It was a commercial failure and, although Griffith continued to make movies into the 1930s, he would not have another success. He may have been the first to make a movie in Hollywood, but he died in 1946, at the age of 73, without receiving the recognition that his achievements in the history of film in America deserved. This was partly, no doubt, as a consequence of the controversial nature of *The Birth of a Nation*, but also because Hollywood had simply moved on, leaving many of its early pioneers behind. It would be stretching the truth to suggest that Griffith founded Hollywood; his decision to shoot one of his movies in the Hollywood Hills may have opened up the way for others to follow his lead, but it was the big movie studios buying up real estate on the outskirts of Los Angeles, where land was available and relatively cheap, that really resulted in the town becoming the center of the film world. Nevertheless, Griffith pioneered the way, as he did for so much of the industry, and deserves to be recognized for that and for all the other contributions he made to early film. Charlie Chaplin summed it up after Griffith died, saying, "He was the teacher of us all."

DECISION

Social Change

Science and Innovation

Culture

Politics

Diplomacy

Military

Religion

GANDHI AND CIVIL DISOBEDIENCE

1917

Circumstances: The struggle against British imperial rule in India

Protagonists: Mahatma Gandhi and the people of India

Consequences: The independence of India

This was my first act of civil disobedience against the British. My desire was to establish the principle that no Englishman had the right to tell me to leave any part of my country where I had gone for a peaceful pursuit. The Government begged me repeatedly to drop my plea of guilty. Finally the magistrate closed the case. Civil disobedience had won. It became the method by which India could be made free.

From an interview conducted with Gandhi by Louis Fisher on June 9, 1942, concerning the indigo protests in Champaran

By the time 46-year-old Mohandas K. Gandhi returned to India in January 1915, he was already an internationally recognized figure for his work campaigning for the civil rights of the Indian community in South Africa, where he had worked as a lawyer for the previous 21 years. He was widely known by the name Mahatma, an honorific title in India meaning "Great Soul," and as Bapu (Father) to his followers in the communities, or ashrams, he founded in South Africa and then near Ahmedabad in his home province of Gujarat. It was a natural progression for him to become involved in the civil rights movement in India and the struggle for its independence from Britain, leading to him joining the Indian National Congress, the leading political party campaigning for an end to British rule. While still living in South Africa, he had been advised by the leader of the Congress Party, Gopal Krishna Gokhale, who died shortly after Gandhi returned to India, to take at least a year to acquaint himself with the complicated political situation in India before taking on any active role himself, advice that Gandhi accepted, later describing the moderate and sensible Gokhale as being his mentor and guide.

At a Congress meeting in December 1916 Gandhi was approached by Rajkumar Shukla, a farmer from Champaran in the Himalayan foothills of the sate of Bihar, who asked him to come to the region to help with a dispute indigo farmers were having with their British landlords. Gandhi was initially reluctant to get involved, having never heard of Champaran and with no knowledge of indigo farming, but Shukla persisted, turning up at every meeting Gandhi attended until he agreed to come. On arriving in Champaran, he found the farmers to be in a desperate situation, which, if nothing was done, could escalate into a famine. As part of their rental agreements, the farmers were forced to plant a proportion of their land with indigo, which was used in an industrial process to make dye, rather than food crops. They were also obliged to sell the indigo at a fixed price to their landlords, who, despite refusing to pay more for the crop, were in the process of raising rents beyond what the farmers could afford to pay. When they attempted to take their grievances to the local authorities, the farmers were dismissed out of hand because the Bihar government was in the pockets of the landlords. It was a straightforward case of rich and powerful colonialists using their position and influence to exploit the poor and powerless. In the light of what he had seen in Champaran, Gandhi decided that the time had come to test the methods of civil disobedience he had developed in South Africa against British rule in his homeland.

SATYAGRAHA

Gandhi trained as a lawyer in London and then worked for a shipping company run by wealthy Indian Muslims in Durban, South Africa. He would later say that he experienced a personal "awakening" in May 1893 after being thrown off a train in Pietermaritzburg because of the color of his skin, writing, "I discovered that as a man and as an Indian I had no rights." He was traveling from Durban to Pretoria on company business and had been given a first-class ticket, when a white man got on at Pietermaritzburg and objected to his presence in the first-class compartment. The conductor on the train told him to move to third-class seating but, as he had the correct ticket, he refused. A police officer was called and he was forcibly removed from the train. Over the course of the next few hours, as he waited for another train at the station in the freezing cold, he came to the decision not to ignore this relatively minor incident and, from then on, resolved not only to stand up for his own rights, but also to do so for the rights of the wider Indian community in South Africa, many of whom were indentured laborers who were routinely treated much more severely than he had been. From then on he began to campaign for social reform, developing the concept of *satyagraha*, which literally means "truth-force," as a means of nonviolent resistance to oppression. This philosophical stance put forward the belief that people who are oppressed but have the force of being morally right on their side can ultimately defeat a stronger oppressor by accepting the need for personal suffering and sacrifice in order to achieve their aims.

MAHATMA GANDHI
A portrait of Gandhi from 1918, shortly after the Champaran *satyagraha*, the first protest he led after he returned to India.

Gandhi had developed his method of protest into active civil disobedience rather than passive resistance by the time he became involved in the dispute between the indigo farmers and their landlords. He was joined in Champaran by a number of his followers, who helped him to hold meetings in which evidence from the farmers of the mistreatment they had endured was collected and protests and strikes organized. The British authorities in Bihar arrested Gandhi and ordered him to leave the region, creating in the process a news story that had already been reported nationally but was now attracting international interest because it involved such a well-known figure. Gandhi refused to comply and was put on trial, charged with disobeying the order to leave. The national government intervened, no doubt aware that the actions of the British landlords and the corrupt nature of their relationship with the officials in the local government would not stand up to the scrutiny Gandhi's involvement had attracted. The charges against him were dropped and an official enquiry convened, with Gandhi on the committee, to examine the causes of the dispute. This would eventually lead to a change in the law to prevent British landlords from forcing Indian farmers to grow indigo and to place limits on the rent increases they were legally allowed to impose.

THE SALT MARCH

It was a victory for Gandhi and his method of *satyagraha*, which he would go on to use on numerous occasions in other disputes across India. The British had no idea how to deal with him, sometimes negotiating and at other times throwing him into jail, but never gaining the moral high ground and almost always giving in to his demands in the end. One of his most famous protests occurred in March 1930 when he began a *satyagraha* against the tax the British administration had imposed on salt, which effectively gave them a monopoly on the collection and sale of this naturally occurring commodity. A few months earlier the Congress Party had issued a Declaration of Independence, ignored by the British, and many of Gandhi's political associates were left baffled by his insistence on concentrating on what they perceived to be a relatively minor injustice compared to the much greater issue of independence.

Gandhi began the protest by walking with a group of his followers from his ashram to Dandi on the coast of Gujarat, a small village where salt was produced. It was a distance of 241 miles (390 km) and the walk, which became known as the Salt March, took 24 days and was extensively covered by newspapers and newsreels from around the world. Once at the coast and in front of thousands of people, Gandhi picked up a handful of salty mud and said, "With this, I am shaking the foundations of the British Empire," before going on to break the law by boiling the mud in seawater to make salt without paying the tax. Millions of Indians followed his example and at least 60,000 were arrested by the British authorities, including Gandhi himself, who was held in prison for almost a year before being released in early 1931 to enable him to negotiate a settlement to the dispute with Lord Irwin (later Lord Halifax), the Viceroy of India. The negotiations resulted in Gandhi agreeing to end the campaign of civil disobedience in exchange for the release of political prisoners and the promise of the British entering into talks to discuss constitutional reform in India. But perhaps the most significant outcome of the protest was to reinvigorate the independence movement among ordinary Indians and return the issue to prominence both in India and around the world.

SALT MARCH
In 1930 Gandhi and his followers walked to Dandi on the coast of Gujarat to protest about the British tax on salt.

It would take another 16 years before the British were eventually forced to accept the inevitable and agree to leave India, a period in which Gandhi initiated further campaigns of civil disobedience, most notably his Quit India Movement of 1942, which demanded that the British get out of the country without delay. On August 15, 1947, India became a Dominion within the British Empire, giving it the status of a separate country while the constitution of the Republic of India was drafted. But it was a bitter-sweet victory for Gandhi, who had promoted Hindu and Muslim unity throughout his life, because of the partition of British India along religious lines into India and Pakistan, a division that resulted in terrible sectarian violence and the deaths of up to a million people. Gandhi did not live to see India become a republic, which occurred on January 26, 1950; he died on January 30, 1948, at the age of 78, after being shot by a Hindu extremist as he was on his way to address a prayer meeting in New Delhi. But he left a legacy of tolerance and nonviolence that remains in India today, and his methods have been adopted by others in their struggle against oppression in different parts of the world, including by Martin Luther King in his campaign for civil rights in America and by the antiapartheid movement led by Nelson Mandela in South Africa. Gandhi is remembered today as the Father of India, a man who was prepared to stick to his principles throughout his life no matter what the consequences and succeeded because what he was fighting for, the right of the Indian people to self-determination and justice, was a just cause. In the end, even the British had to acknowledge that.

DECISION

Social Change

Science and Innovation

Culture

Politics

Diplomacy

Military

Religion

ROBERT JOHNSON AT THE CROSSROADS

1930s

Circumstances: A blues singer records some of his songs

Protagonists: Robert Johnson and other bluesmen of the Mississippi Delta

Consequences: A small but highly influential body of work

Robert Johnson has become the ultimate blues legend,
and it is easy to forget that he was once just
a man who sang beautifully and played expert guitar.

Elijah Wald, *Escaping the Delta*

© Thomas R. Machnitzki | Creative Commons

When a record company promotes one of their artists these days as being "authentic," it usually means that either nobody has ever heard of them or they write their own songs but don't have a very good singing voice. During the blues revival of the late 1950s and early 1960s, no such record company spin was required as a new audience, mostly made up of young white college boys, rediscovered the original blues singers of the 1930s and 1940s from the Mississippi Delta. Many of them had not actually disappeared in the first place, continuing to perform throughout their careers, even if most had followed their audience north to Chicago and to other industrial cities and were now playing the electric guitar rather than the acoustic ones most of them had started out with. John Lee Hooker, Muddy Waters, Howlin' Wolf, B. B. King, to name just a few of the best known, all had their roots in the Delta, which, just to be confusing, in this context refers to the flat agricultural plain between Vicksburg, Mississippi and Memphis, Tennessee, immediately to the north of the actual delta of the Mississippi River in Louisiana. Then in 1961 Columbia Records released *King of the Delta Blues Singers* by Robert Johnson, a man unknown to almost everybody, including many of the other artists from the Delta.

© Jean-Luc | Creative Commons

DELTA BLUESMAN
Like many of the great blues singers, including Robert Johnson, Muddy Waters was born and raised in rural Mississippi.

CROSSROADS

The release was the idea of the Columbia executive and record producer John Hammond, a blues enthusiast who had not only heard of Johnson, but in 1938 had traveled to Mississippi in an attempt to sign him up for a blues concert he was organizing at Carnegie Hall in New York, only to find when he got to the Delta that Johnson had recently died. The record contained 16 of Johnson's songs, recorded in two sessions in 1936 and 1937, and despite the scratchy nature of the recording, his fine guitar playing and the mournful quality of his voice, together with some truly great songs, would make it a landmark release, even if it took a number of years for it to be appreciated beyond a small circle of blues enthusiasts. Over the following ten years, both Eric Clapton and Keith Richards would acknowledge Johnson as a major influence on their own music and record a number of his songs, bringing him to the attention of a much wider audience and fuelling an interest in the man himself, about whom almost nothing was known. In the absence of any certain facts, stories began to circulate about him, in particular one that still attatches itself to his name today. Johnson, it was said, had gone to the crossroads at midnight where the devil offered to make him a great guitarist in exchange for his soul.

Now, let's be honest, none of us really believe that Robert Johnson actually decided to sell his soul to the devil. No doubt he became a great guitarist the same way as every other great musician has done, through long hours of practice, but the haunted nature of the lyrics to his songs and the spectral quality of his voice certainly suggests that he was deeply troubled by something. Without any biographical detail to shed some light on what that trouble might have been, it became possible for people who were listening to his music for the first time more than 30 years after he died to believe anything they wanted to believe about him, turning him into the archetypal bluesman, a tortured and misunderstood genius who died at that most rock 'n' roll age of 27. It was the same age that Jimi Hendrix, Jim Morrison, and Janis Joplin had all been when they died. Brian Jones, the original member of the Rolling Stones who first introduced Keith Richards to Johnson's music, was also 27 when he drowned in his swimming pool. Adding Johnson's name to this list of musical legends who died young was an easy enough jump to make, and the mythology that grew up around him only served to add another layer of intrigue to fascinate people who listened to his music.

A MAN EMERGES

It was inevitable, given the renewed interest in Delta blues and in the mysterious life of one of its greatest exponents, that people would begin to investigate the circumstances of Robert Johnson's life. From interviews conducted with other Delta blues musicians and with people living in the Delta who had known him personally, a picture of the man himself has gradually emerged, even if some of the stories told about him have not always proved to be very reliable. He was born in Hazelhurst, Mississippi in May 1911 and grew up in Memphis and various rural villages in the Delta. The noted blues musician Son House remembered him living in Robinsonville sometime in the 1920s, describing him as a "little boy" who could already play the harmonica but was a poor guitarist. By the time he was 20, he was earning a living as an itinerant musician, traveling around Mississippi playing on street corners, in juke joints, and for Saturday-night parties. Other musicians, like Johnny Shines and David "Honeyboy" Edwards, sometimes accompanied him on his travels, occasionally going to Memphis and cities in Texas as well as going further afield to Chicago and New York. Johnson apparently had girlfriends in numerous different towns, staying with them when he was passing through or picking up somebody else after one of his gigs. According to some accounts of his life, his promiscuity eventually got him into trouble with the husband of one of his girlfriends, who is said to have poisoned a bottle of whiskey and then offered him a drink. Despite claims by some researchers to have identified his murderer, no credible evidence has ever come to light. All we can say with any certainty is that he died on August 18, 1938, near Greenwood, Mississippi and could have been buried in an unmarked grave at the Mount Zion Missionary Baptist Church not far away.

© Getty Images

ELECTRIC BLUES
Robert Johnson's contemporary John Lee Hooker left the Delta in the 1940s for the northern industrial cities.

These biographical details are, it must be admitted, only the bare bones of a life, but one account of an incident involving Johnson, told by the family of the girl involved, could shed some light on the origins of the stories about him. In February 1928, at the age of 17, Johnson married the 16-year-old Virginia Travis, who was pregnant at the time and died in childbirth not long afterward. Johnson was not present during this terrible event, having left his heavily pregnant young wife to play a gig somewhere out of the district. By the time he returned, she was already dead and buried, a tragedy that some religious members of her family would later claim was divine retribution for his decision to leave her to play what they described as the "devil's music." We can only speculate now what Johnson's reaction to this may have been, but he never settled in any one place for long afterward and the "hellhound on his trail" could have been his own guilt over the death of his wife.

Whatever the truth of the matter, the great decision we are dealing with here is not really what Robert Johnson did or didn't do with his soul, but, in common with all great musicians and songwriters, it is simply his decision to learn to play the guitar and sing the blues in the first place. It may have taken a very long time for his music to be appreciated beyond the juke joints of the Mississippi Delta, but for anybody interested in the history of popular music, the fact that it emerged at all is a miracle enough on its own.

DECISION

Social Change

Science and Innovation

Culture

Politics

Diplomacy

Military

Religion

ROOSEVELT'S NEW DEAL

1933

Circumstances: The Wall Street Crash leads to the Great Depression

Protagonists: Franklin D. Roosevelt, the Brain Trust, and the American people

Consequences: America emerges from the Great Depression

I pledge you, I pledge myself, to a new deal for the American people. Let us all here assembled constitute ourselves prophets of a new order of competence and of courage. This is more than a political campaign; it is a call to arms. Give me your help, not to win votes alone, but to win in this crusade to restore America to its own people.

From a speech given by Franklin D. Roosevelt on July 2, 1932, accepting the presidential nomination of the Democratic Party

In his speech accepting the Democratic Party's nomination to run as their candidate for the presidential election to be held in November 1932, Franklin D. Roosevelt used the words "new deal" without laying any particular emphasis on the phrase and with no apparent intention to give it any greater significance than anything else he said. But the newspapers picked up on it in the days after the speech and it came to embody the American Government's policies aimed at dealing with the economic and social disasters created by the Great Depression of the early 1930s. In his election campaign, Roosevelt did not specify exactly what he intended to do once elected and on occasion issued contradictory statements, promising at one moment to cut public spending and, at the next, to fund huge programs to get people back to work. In truth, he could have said almost anything and still won; President Herbert Hoover had been keen to claim credit for the financial boom America had experienced immediately before the Wall Street Crash of October 1929 that had precipitated the depression and then had done his best to deflect blame for it on to everything and everybody else other than himself, so he hardly gave the impression of being the right man to lead America back to prosperity.

FDR
On becoming US president, Franklin D. Roosevelt initiated the New Deal, policies designed to drag America out of the Great Depression.

Roosevelt went on to win a landslide victory in the election and, in that strange period in American politics between the election of a new president and the inauguration ceremony, in this case between November 1932 and March 1933, he spent his time appointing members of his future government and doing his best to ignore Hoover, who wanted to find a way of working with Roosevelt to tackle the depression. He also brought together a group of advisers, later known as the Brain Trust, to help him devise his own plan, but what he didn't do in this period, just as he hadn't during the election campaign, was spell out what it was going to entail. He was no more forthcoming in his inaugural address, in which he blamed the depression on the irresponsibility and corruption of bankers and financiers and famously said, "the only thing we have to fear is fear itself." Many people were left wondering if Roosevelt really had any idea what he was going to do, but, as he also made clear in his inaugural speech, the time for talking had come to an end. The time had now come to make some big decisions and to put the New Deal, whatever it was, into action.

THE HUNDRED DAYS

There are as many different explanations for the onset of the Great Depression as there are economists attempting to explain it, much as there have been more recently over the financial crisis that began in 2008, and most of them have come to conclusions that have supported their own particular points of view in the first place, giving the impression that in reality they have little better idea about what happened than the rest of us have. At the time, some economists were making the case for massive state intervention in the economy, while others advocated the complete opposite; reduce public spending and the role of the government in the economy to allow the free market to correct itself. But if there was little agreement over the best way of dealing with the depression, the effects were obvious for everybody to see. The winter of 1932/3 had been a desperate one for many people; the unemployed and homeless were visible everywhere and what amounted to shanty towns, known as Hoovervilles, sprang up on the outskirts of many American towns and cities, and children all over America were not only going without shoes, but were not getting enough to eat. The unemployment rate was running at almost 25%, and there were 13 million people without work, while industrial production had dropped by 45% since the 1929 crash. As if that were not enough, the Dust Bowl in America's agricultural heartlands was just getting underway, in which unusually dry weather conditions combined with unsuitable farming practices to cause topsoil to be blown away in giant dust storms from huge areas of what had once been productive farmland.

DUST BOWL
A dust storm in Stratford, Texas, in April 1935, caused by dry weather, strong winds, and unsuitable farming practices.

The problems facing Roosevelt, then, as he first stepped into the White House, were immense. To his great credit, he did not pursue an ideological agenda in an attempt to find a solution (some have argued that he didn't have an ideology to pursue in the first place). Rather, he developed policies, from whatever source they came, on the basis of whether or not they were likely to work. Members of the Brain Trust, including Raymond Moley and Frances Perkins, the first woman to serve in the US Cabinet as Secretary of State for Labor, contributed ideas on reforming the banking system and the labor markets. In what became known as the Hundred Days, Roosevelt introduced numerous new bills into Congress and all of them passed, supported by Democrats and Republicans alike, and in the process beginning the tradition of the American media assessing how a new president has fared after their first hundred days in office.

One of the first measures Roosevelt took was to close every bank in the country while he introduced an emergency banking bill in an attempt to deal with one of the most pressing problems, the failure of banks, many of which had crashed as a result of bank runs (people removing all their savings from a bank because they thought it was about to go bust and, in doing so, actually causing the bankruptcy). Roosevelt explained what he was doing to the American people in the first of what became regular "fireside chats," in which he described the closures as being a "bank holiday." The banking act was passed on the same day as it was introduced to Congress, March 9, having only been read through once. It made unlimited loans available to accredited banks through the Federal Reserve, effectively guaranteeing all deposits. When the banks reopened four days later, people were queuing up outside many of them to deposit the money they had previously withdrawn because it would now be much safer in the bank than under the mattress. A blizzard of legislation followed the banking act, on farming, industry, housing, labor, and to repeal prohibition, a move that was enormously popular with the American people and increased the tax revenue of the government as well. Not all of the new legislation was as successful as the banking reform, but overall the program appeared to be working, gradually dragging the American economy out of the depression it had been in for the previous three years.

As it would turn out, March 1933 was the lowest point of the Great Depression in America. Roosevelt's greatest achievement in bringing in what became known as the First New Deal, the first two years of his program of legislation, was in restoring confidence, creating conditions in which ordinary Americans felt secure enough to carry on with their lives without worrying unduly about losing their jobs and homes. Where Hoover had given the impression of being defeated by the size of the problems the country faced, Roosevelt looked like a man of action, prepared to do whatever was necessary to get the American economy moving again and to get people back to work. Banks and businesses began to return to their normal modes of working, industry began to pick up and rehire some of the many employees who had been

THE FIRST NEW DEAL

laid off. The depression was by no means over, but many people could now foresee a brighter future than had previously been apparent. In what is sometimes called the Second New Deal, Roosevelt attempted to build on the success of his first raft of measures, introducing legislation between 1936 and 1938 to deal with a variety of pressing social issues. As has always been the case in America, federal government involvement in such social matters as health insurance and social security would prove much more controversial than the initial economic measures he had introduced, reopening splits between liberals who supported the reforms and conservatives who most definitely did not, not unlike the situation today over President Obama's health care reforms.

THE EFFECTS OF THE NEW DEAL CONTINUED TO BE FELT FOR DECADES AFTER IT WAS FIRST INTRODUCED

In the years since the New Deal was first introduced criticisms of it have followed a similar pattern, some arguing that Roosevelt went too far in allowing the state to become involved in people's lives to a much greater extent than had previously been the case, while others have argued that he did not go far enough and should have introduced the full range of social measures that have since been adopted in many European countries while he had the chance. But, however the outcome of the New Deal is assessed, Roosevelt's initial decision to take direct action to combat the deepest and most damaging depression in both American and world history must surely be regarded as being one of the greatest political decisions ever taken in America. The effects of the New Deal continued to be felt for decades after it was first introduced and some of the programs remain in place today. It also caused a fundamental realignment in American politics, known as the Fifth Party System, in which voters of a more liberal persuasion began to support the Democratic Party, while conservatives tended toward the Republicans, a situation that has largely stayed the same to this day. Roosevelt remained as US president until his death in 1945, serving into but not completing an unprecedented fourth term, so, as well as dealing with the Great Depression, he was responsible for taking America into the Second World War, giving him plenty more big decisions to make.

THE BRITISH CABINET RESOLVES TO FIGHT ON

1940

DECISION

Social Change

Science and Innovation

Culture

Politics

Diplomacy

Military

Religion

Circumstances: The desperate situation for Britain at the beginning of the Second World War

Protagonists: Winston Churchill, Neville Chamberlain, Lord Halifax, Clement Attlee, Arthur Greenwood

Consequences: No negotiation with Hitler

Even though large parts of Europe and many old and famous States have fallen or may fall into the grip of the Gestapo and all the odious apparatus of Nazi rule, we shall not flag or fail. We shall go on to the end, we shall fight in France, we shall fight on the seas and oceans, we shall fight with growing confidence and growing strength in the air, we shall defend our Island, whatever the cost may be, we shall fight on the beaches, we shall fight on the landing grounds, we shall fight in the fields and in the streets, we shall fight in the hills; we shall never surrender...

From the speech made in the House of Commons by Winston Churchill on June 4, 1940, and repeated on the radio that evening

Toward the end of May 1940, the war against Nazi Germany that had begun in September of the previous year was going very badly for Britain. Norway, Denmark, the Netherlands, and Belgium had either already surrendered over the course of the previous few weeks or were on the brink of doing so and, after a lightning invasion of France, beginning on May 13, the British Expeditionary Force was stranded on the beaches of Dunkirk, where a desperate attempt was being made to evacuate as many of them as possible before they were either destroyed or captured. The fall of France appeared to be only a matter of days away, leaving Britain on its own and facing the threat of an imminent German invasion. Winston Churchill had only been appointed to the position of prime minister on May 10, three days before the invasion of France began, and, on May 28, he called a meeting of his War Cabinet to discuss the disastrous situation Britain was facing.

THE WAR CABINET

On becoming prime minister, Churchill had formed a national government comprising a Cabinet of ministers from all three of the main political parties; he also appointed a much smaller War Cabinet to make the decision-making process relating to the war effort as efficient as possible. The War Cabinet had five members; as well as Churchill himself, it was composed of two Conservative ministers, Neville Chamberlain, his predecessor as prime minister, and the Foreign Secretary Lord Halifax, and two ministers from the Labour Party, Clement Attlee and Arthur Greenwood. The discussion held during the meeting on May 28, which would remain secret until 30 years after the end of the war, primarily revolved around a proposal received two days previously from Benito Mussolini, the dictator of Italy, who was offering to act as a mediator in negotiations aimed at reaching a peace settlement between Britain and Germany. Halifax was in favor of the offer, arguing that Britain would be able to achieve more favorable terms if a settlement could be reached at that moment rather than waiting until after the fall of France and, by doing so, would also avoid the threat of an invasion. Churchill was predictably enraged by such a suggestion and argued forcibly against any negotiations with Adolf Hitler, saying, "Nations which went down fighting rose again, but those who surrendered tamely were finished."

V FOR VICTORY
A characteristic pose from Churchill, who vigorously argued against negotiating with Hitler during a War Cabinet meeting in May 1940.

Churchill had the support of both Attlee and Greenwood, but Chamberlain was wavering, wondering if it would not be preferable to at least listen to the terms on offer. Before coming to a final decision, Churchill spoke to the full Cabinet of 25 ministers, telling them that he had been considering the proposal to enter into negotiations with "that man," as he called Hitler, and thought any deal achieved would lead to Britain becoming a "slave state" of the Nazi regime. He finished by saying:

> I am convinced that every man of you would rise up and tear me down from my place if I were for one moment to contemplate parley or surrender. If this long island story of ours is to end at last, let it end only when each one of us lies choking in his own blood upon the ground.

His short speech was greeted with cheers and applause, showing that the majority of the Cabinet was behind him and bringing Chamberlain firmly on to his side as well. Only Halifax remained unconvinced, writing in his diary for that day, "I thought Winston talked the most frightful rot." But the decision had been made; there would be no deals with Hitler and Britain would fight on alone no matter what happened at Dunkirk or in any other theater of the war.

When Churchill became prime minister three weeks beforehand, the only other serious contender for the position had been Halifax. We can only speculate now what could have happened if he had become prime minister rather than Churchill, but the most obvious conclusion, given his stance at the War Cabinet meeting, is that he would have entered into negotiations with Hitler. Even if any peace settlement offered had then been rejected out of hand, Churchill thought that it would have been interpreted as a sign of weakness by Hitler and could only have encouraged his plans to invade Britain. From that moment on, Churchill's already weak confidence in Halifax evaporated completely, even if he persuaded the Foreign Secretary not to resign immediately after the War Cabinet's decision had been reached because he did not want to show any sort of disunity in the government at such a critical moment in British history. Halifax remained in the War Cabinet for a further nine months, until Churchill found a suitable moment to remove him

LORD HALIFAX
After arguing in favor of negotiating with Hitler, Halifax lost the confidence of Churchill and was later removed from the War Cabinet.

by appointing him to the position of British ambassador to America, replacing him with Anthony Eden.

FINEST HOURS

Later that same night Churchill issued a memo to everybody in the Cabinet and to senior civil servants, saying:

> In these dark days the Prime Minister would be grateful if all of his colleagues in the Government, as well as high officials, would maintain a high morale in their circles; not minimizing the gravity of events, but showing confidence in our ability and inflexible resolve to continue the war till we have broken the will of the enemy to bring all Europe under his domination.

The message was clear. The decision to fight on had been taken and Churchill was not going to tolerate any public signs of defeatism. As a former soldier himself, he was well aware of the importance of maintaining morale under difficult circumstances and, with bombs falling on British cities and the situation at Dunkirk looking worse by the minute, the last thing he needed was to be undermined by his own government. Over the course of the next few days more than 300,000 troops were evacuated from Dunkirk and, although it was nothing short of miraculous, the overall extent of the defeat was obvious to all. With such thoughts on his mind, Churchill made one of the greatest speeches of his life in the House of Commons on June 4, quoted from at the beginning of this chapter, which he then repeated to the nation by a radio broadcast that evening. Further stirring words were required two weeks later in the aftermath of the French surrender on June 16, in which Churchill began by saying, "What General Weygand [the Commander-in Chief of the French army] has called the Battle for France is over. I suspect that the Battle of Britain is about to begin," and continued:

> ... if we fail, then the whole world, including the United States, including all that we have known and cared for, will sink into the abyss of a new dark age made more sinister, and perhaps more protracted, by the lights of perverted science. Let us therefore brace ourselves to our duties, and so bear ourselves, that if the British Empire and its Commonwealth last for a thousand years, men will still say, "This was their finest hour."

If further evidence of Churchill's resolve to fight were needed, his decision, taken on July 3 together with the War Cabinet, to issue an ultimatum to the commander of the French Navy ships stationed at the port of Mers-el-Kébir in Algeria made the British position crystal clear. The ultimatum demanded that the French ships be handed over to the British to prevent them from falling into the hands of the Germans and, when the French commander refused to comply, the Royal Navy opened fire, putting most of the French ships out of action and killing almost 1,300 French sailors. By any standards, it was a ruthless and cold-blooded attack on the armed forces of a country that had been an ally only weeks beforehand. If Hitler or anybody else had doubted the British will to fight, then this terrible event must surely have persuaded them to think again.

At the same time as the attack at Mers-el-Kébir, the Battle of the Atlantic was intensifying and the Battle of Britain was getting underway. In the ocean, German U-boats and surface warships were attempting to sever Britain's vital supply lines from North America, while in the skies over southern England the fighter pilots of the Royal Air Force (RAF) and German Luftwaffe engaged in aerial dogfights while the German bombing campaign of British cities continued. In order to mount an invasion of Britain, Hitler knew that he had first to achieve air superiority over the English Channel and the coast where any landings would take place. Without it, an invasion force crossing the channel from France would be sitting ducks for the RAF and Royal Navy, and throughout July and into August the aerial onslaught did not let up. On August 16, Churchill visited the headquarters of 11 Group Fighter Command in Uxbridge and sat in the gallery over the operations room watching as the positions of wave after wave of German planes crossing the Channel were marked out on the map table below. At one point during that day, every squadron in the group was in the air at the same time, prompting Churchill to say afterward, "Never in the field of human conflict has so much been owed by so many to so few." The remark echoed the St. Crispin's Day speech from Shakespeare's *Henry V*, in which the king rallied his army on the eve of the Battle of Agincourt; Churchill would include it in a later speech, demonstrating again his uncanny ability to sum up the mood of the nation in words.

THE FEW

HEINKEL HE 111s
In the summer of 1940, wave after wave of German bombers attacked Britain as the Luftwaffe attempted to gain air superiority.

After the war was over, captured German documents revealed that Hitler had earmarked September 15 as the day for the invasion and on that day, later known as Battle of Britain Day, some of the most intense aerial battles were fought. Losses had been mounting up on both sides, but were in favor of the the RAF by a factor of more than two to one. The Luftwaffe were at a disadvantage because the fighting mainly occurred over England, where the German fighter planes could only remain for a matter of minutes before having to return to France to refuel, while RAF pilots could spend longer in the air and refuel much more quickly. The RAF could also recover more pilots who had survived being shot down than the Luftwaffe could, contributing further to the disparity between the losses experienced on either side. After September 15, and as the Luftwaffe switched exclusively to night-time bombing raids, it became clear that the Battle of Britain had been won. The German advance across Western Europe had been halted at the coast of France, vindicating the decision taken by Churchill and the War Cabinet to fight on however bleak the prospects for Britain had looked at the time.

THE ATLANTIC CHARTER

1941

DECISION

Social Change

Science and Innovation

Culture

Politics

Diplomacy

Military

Religion

Circumstances: A diplomatic exchange between America and Britain four months before America entered the Second World War

Protagonists: President Franklin D. Roosevelt, Prime Minister Winston Churchill, together with military and diplomatic representatives from America and Britain

Consequences: The formation of a close working relationship between Roosevelt and Churchill and a charter that would lay the foundations for the formation of the United Nations

1. Their countries seek no aggrandizement, territorial or other.

2. They desire to see no territorial changes that do not accord with the freely expressed wishes of the peoples concerned.

3. They respect the right of all peoples to choose the form of government under which they will live; and they wish to see sovereign rights and self-government restored to those who have been forcibly deprived of them.

The first three clauses of the Atlantic Charter

On August 9, 1941, US President Franklin D. Roosevelt and British Prime Minister Winston Churchill met for what would be the first of many occasions during the Second World War on board the USS *Augusta*, anchored in Placentia Bay off Newfoundland and within sight of the recently constructed American naval base of Argentia. The base had been acquired from Britain six months previously as part of the land-lease agreement between the two countries in which America supplied Britain with war materials in exchange for, among other things, the lease of a number of military facilities in the Caribbean and North Atlantic. The two men had been in regular communication by telephone and telegraph since the outbreak of the war in September 1939, when Churchill had held the position of First Lord of the Admiralty in the British War Cabinet. Both set great store in face-to-face meetings in which they could assess the character of the person they were dealing with and establish personal relations, so they had been receptive to the suggestion of the American diplomat Harry Hopkins to arrange the meeting. While Churchill crossed the Atlantic aboard HMS *Prince of Wales*, Roosevelt sent a double on a trip on board the presidential yacht to cover his absence from Washington so that he could go to Newfoundland in secrecy.

THE ATLANTIC CONFERENCE

The main purpose of the Atlantic Conference, as the meeting was called, was to discuss the shared aims of Britain and America during the war and, assuming the defeat of the Axis powers, to decide on the organization of the postwar world. As well as these stated objectives, there can be little doubt that both sides were pursuing their own agendas at the conference. The British were hoping to extract a deeper commitment to engaging in the war from the Americans, going beyond supplying materials and support to actually becoming militarily involved. Churchill was aware of the political reasons preventing Roosevelt from announcing an American entry into the war at that moment, both because of a perceived lack of public support in America and the long-standing foreign policy of the American Government, going back to the Monroe Doctrine of 1823, of not becoming involved in European wars. With the US presidential election coming up that November, in which Roosevelt was hoping to be elected for a convention-busting third term, he could not be expected to take any action that would alienate a large proportion of the electorate, but nevertheless Churchill was hoping for a private commitment from him to enter the war when the time was right. The unstated aims of the American delegation were rather more subtle and long-term. They were looking for a way of reducing the long-standing British influence on world affairs and to promote republicanism around the world, preferably based on the American model, as a replacement for British imperialism, thereby initiating a new world order in which the wealth and strength of the American economy would allow them to take over Britain's former position as the dominant world power.

The conference began on August 11 and consisted of three separate sets of meetings. As well as the talks held personally between Roosevelt and Churchill, the chiefs of staff of both countries came together to discuss military strategy, having been instructed by the two leaders to find a way of working together so that they could manage areas where American and British interests overlapped without constantly having to request confirmation from the politicians. The third set of meetings were between American and British diplomatic staff, who had the job of preparing a joint statement to be released after the conference was over that set out the objectives agreed by Roosevelt and Churchill for postwar planning. After two days of talks, the conference broke up; the following day, August 14, the finished document was released to the press under the title, *Joint Statement by President Roosevelt and Prime Minister Churchill*, soon renamed in newspaper reports as the Atlantic Charter.

The purpose of the charter was not to set out the details of postwar planning, but to establish the general principles governing how it would be conducted. It was also not a binding document in the form of a treaty between Britain and America and, even though the press release stated that it had been signed by both Roosevelt and Churchill, in reality neither had done so; Churchill had been on his way back to Britain before the final draft was finished. Even so, it was an important document in a number of respects, not least because it sent a clear message to Hitler that America was firmly on Britain's side and expected Nazi Germany to lose the war. The first three of the eight clauses in the charter, quoted at the beginning of this chapter, concerned the territorial settlements that might be reached after the war was over, stating that any changes to boundaries must be done

ATLANTIC CONFERENCE
FDR and Churchill on board HMS *Prince of Wales*. Roosevelt's son Elliott, to the right, provides his father with support.

THE CHARTER

in consultation with the people who were affected and that they had a right to self-determination. Without actually spelling it out, this was obviously aimed at those regions of the British Empire, such as India, where independence movements had sprung up. It was a clear signal of American anti-imperialistic sentiment, indicating that their negotiators had been in a position of strength in the talks because Britain needed American support for its war effort. Some historians have pointed to this moment as being the one in which the balance of power in world affairs decisively tipped away from Britain and toward America.

The next four clauses concerned trade, social security, and the freedom of the seas, and gave the assurance, "that all the men in all the lands may live out their lives in freedom from fear and want." The final clause read in full:

1. 8. They believe that all of the nations of the world, for realistic as well as spiritual reasons, must come to the abandonment of the use of force. Since no future peace can be maintained if land, sea, or air armaments continue to be employed by nations which threaten, or may threaten, aggression outside of their frontiers, they believe, pending the establishment of a wider and permanent system of general security, that the disarmament of such nations is essential. They will likewise aid and encourage all other practicable measures which will lighten for peace-loving peoples the crushing burden of armaments.

These were fine words to finish off such a document, even if it could be argued that they were roundly ignored by both countries after the war came to an end. But the clause also raised the possibility of the development of an international organization to administer the diplomatic processes that would attempt to maintain peace and security in the postwar world. In this sense, the Atlantic Charter can be seen as the direct precursor of the Charter of the United Nations, the treaty signed in 1945 that set up the UN.

The joint decision by Roosevelt and Churchill to hold a conference to discuss the postwar world and then to issue the Atlantic Charter had far-reaching consequences and also established a close relationship between the two men who, along with Joseph Stalin of Russia, would lead the Allied war effort. The process of establishing a new world order that had been started by an old guard of politicians was taken up by others, a process that continues with varying degrees of success today.

EISENHOWER AND D-DAY

1944

DECISION

Social Change

Science and Innovation

Culture

Politics

Diplomacy

Military

Religion

Circumstances: Rough weather forces a postponement of the invasion of Normandy

Protagonists: General Dwight D. Eisenhower and the Allied invasion force on D-Day

Consequences: The beginning of the end for Nazi Germany in Western Europe

Our landings in the Cherbourg-Havre area have failed to gain a satisfactory foothold and I have withdrawn the troops. My decision to attack at this time and place was based on the best information available. The troops, the air, and the navy did all that bravery and devotion to duty could do. If any blame or fault attatches to the attempt, it is mine alone.

A note written by Eisenhower on the eve of D-Day in case it all went wrong

Even though he was from America, General Dwight D. Eisenhower could be forgiven if he indulged in the British national obsession with the weather during the first few days of June 1944. He was the commander-in-chief of SHAEF, the Supreme Headquarters Allied Expeditionary Force, and as such was responsible for the planning and execution of Operation Overlord, the code name given to the plan for the invasion of Normandy and the land battle that would follow it. The plan was by far the largest and most complicated amphibious invasion ever attempted, in which more than 150,000 American, Canadian, and British troops were to be landed on the Normandy beaches on the first day of the invasion alone and then followed over the next months by almost 2 million more. That first day, designated as D-Day, was the most critical part of the whole operation; its success or failure would determine not just the immediate prospects for Nazi-occupied France, but the outcome of the entire war. Eisenhower had provisionally set D-Day for June 5 and throughout much of May the weather had been ideal on those days of the month when the combination of the tides on the Normandy coast and the moonlight had been right for an invasion.

As D-Day approached, the weather turned and by the evening of June 3, when the order to go or to stand down needed to be given, storms in the Channel and low-lying cloud over much of northern France meant that launching the invasion on the morning of June 5 was all but impossible. The risks of sending an amphibious invasion force out in stormy weather were apparent enough and the overcast conditions meant that air cover could not be provided for the landings, while the airborne operation involving troops landing inland by parachute and glider to capture strategic locations could not go ahead either. Eisenhower took the decision to hold off for a day and, knowing that if he postponed again it might be weeks before everything could be reorganized, faced an even harder decision at the same time on the following day. He listened to his chief weather forecaster, who thought there might be a short break in the weather in the early morning of June 6. He then asked for the opinions of the military commanders assembled at SHAEF, some of whom thought it was worth the risk, while others advised caution. The final decision rested with Eisenhower and getting it wrong could cost the lives of thousands of the men under his command. At about 9.45 in the evening of June 4 he made up his mind and gave the order to go.

Ike, as Eisenhower was universally known, may have been in overall command of Operation Torch, the American invasion of North Africa beginning in November 1942, and then of the invasions of both Sicily and the Italian mainland in the following year, but he was by no means the only candidate for the command of SHAEF. Winston Churchill had promised the job to General Allen Brooke, the British Chief of the Imperial General Staff, while in America General George Marshall, the Chief of Staff of the US Army, was the hot favorite for the job. But Churchill came to realize that an American had to be given the position because the British Army was already operating at near its maximum capacity, so much of the men and materials for the latter stages of the war would have to come from America. Meanwhile, President Roosevelt wanted Marshall to stay in Washington as his Chief of Staff, leaving the way open for the appointment of Eisenhower.

IKE

EISENHOWER
Ike with paratroopers from the US 101st Airborne Division on June 5, 1944, as they prepared for the first assault on D-Day.

Some senior military figures were not happy about Eisenhower's appointment, despite his success in planning and overseeing three major operations involving amphibious landings. He was regarded by his critics as being a career staff officer who had no first-hand battlefield experience and had risen slowly through the ranks of the US Army in peacetime because he was a good administrator and diplomat rather than through any proven ability as a military commander. But, as it turned out, it was exactly these qualities of organization and man-management that his critics derided that made him the perfect man for the job. On numerous occasions in the build-up to the Normandy landings he proved himself capable of dealing with the huge egos of many of the senior politicians and military commanders involved, not least Churchill himself, but also including the British commander of land forces General Bernard Montgomery and the US General George Patton, who both gave the impression of being almost as keen on fighting with each other as they were on fighting the Germans.

By the time Eisenhower had been appointed as commander of SHAEF, the beaches of Normandy had already been selected as the site of the landings ahead of the Pas de Calais, the only other really viable alternative to the north. His first decision on being shown the plan, taken together with Montgomery, was to increase the scale of the initial invasion force and widen the area where it would be landing. In doing so, the initial speculative date for the invasion in early May had to be put back to June to ensure that the extra men and equipment necessary for the larger-scale attack would be ready in time. It was to be the first of numerous decisions taken by Eisenhower over the course of planning such a major undertaking, many made against the backdrop of disagreements and disputes between almost everybody else involved. Over the course of the months of planning, the need for secrecy was paramount. Erwin Rommel, the commander of the German defenses in France, was well aware of the massive build-up of American troops and equipment in Britain, which could only mean that an invasion was being planned and, as soon as he was given the command, he had ordered the Atlantic Wall, the line of defensive structures along the channel coast of northern France, to be strengthened and reinforced. If he had found out exactly when and where the attack would come, giving him the opportunity to direct his forces against the landing zones, the operation was almost certainly doomed to failure.

As well as planning for the invasion itself, a huge effort, known as Operation Fortitude, was directed at deceiving the Germans into thinking that the invasion was going to come at Pas-de-Calais. Dummy divisions were formed in East Anglia and radio traffic of the sort created by a massive build-up of forces was broadcast, while turned German agents were used to feed false information to the Nazi intelligence service. It was so effective that, even after the D-Day landings had started, some German commanders remained convinced that the real thing in Normandy was actually part of the deception plan, leading to German armed units remaining near Calais weeks after an Allied bridgehead had been established on the coast further south. It was another reason for Eisenhower to order the invasion to go ahead. A delay would not only increase the likelihood of secrecy being compromized, but would also give the Germans more chance of discovering the nature of the deception plans. It was impossible to disguise the level of activity at ports on the south coast of England, which faced Normandy rather than Calais. In any case, returning the first wave of troops, who had already embarked on ships for the invasion, back to the ports where the next

ERWIN ROMMEL, THE COMMANDER OF THE GERMAN DEFENSES IN FRANCE, WAS WELL AWARE OF THE MASSIVE BUILD-UP OF AMERICAN TROOPS AND EQUIPMENT IN BRITAIN

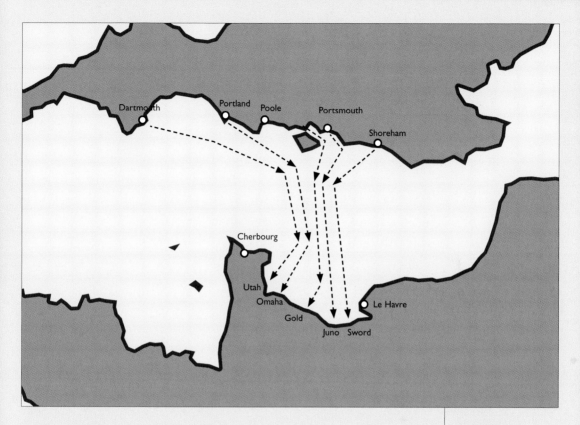

wave was being prepared would have been a logistical nightmare and doing so would have damaged the morale of all the army units involved.

Everything was in place for the invasion to proceed on time; the only obstacle stopping it was the weather, the one thing nobody could control. On that evening of June 4, as Eisenhower paused for a moment after consulting with his advisers, he must have been feeling the tremendous responsibility of command, even if he remained calm and collected. After making the decision to go, he turned to his advisers and military commanders and said, "I am quite positive we must give the order. I don't like it, but there it is." After a brief pause, everybody cheered and the mess room they had been using for the meeting immediately emptied as the rush began to get the order out. Eisenhower was left alone and, as there was nothing else he could do that would not interfere with the role of others in the plans, he found various ways to kill time for the next day and a half until the invasion began.

NORMANDY LANDINGS
On D-Day 150,000 Allied troops crossed the English Channel to take part in the assault on the Normandy beaches.

**NORMANDY
LANDINGS**
Robert F. Sargent's
photograph *Into the Jaws of
Death* showing the US Army
First Division assaulting
Omaha Beach on D-Day.

At H-Hour of D-Day, 6:30 in the morning of Tuesday June 6, 1944, the landings on the Normandy beaches began, the airborne assault having commenced a few hours earlier. The Americans went first, landing on the beaches designated as Omaha and Utah, and they were followed by the British and Canadians on Gold, Juno, and Sword. The level of surprise achieved was remarkable, given that the German forces defending the French coast had been expecting an attack. In the end, the bad weather even played into the hands of the Allies. A number of senior German commanders, believing that an attack was not possible while the rough weather persisted, had taken leave. Rommel himself had gone back to Germany for a few days to be with his wife on her birthday. But despite the chaotic and uncoordinated nature of the initial German response to the landings, they put up fierce resistance, particularly on Omaha beach, where the Americans took heavy casualties before managing to overcome the German defenses. Over the next few weeks the Allied forces established a bridgehead in Normandy where they could build up their forces for the eventual breakout, which, when it came in early August, began the long and costly process of liberating France and then crossing the River Rhine into the heartland of Germany.

Eisenhower remained in command of SHAEF until victory in Europe was achieved in May 1945, after which he served as the military governor of the US zone of occupied Germany. In later life, Eisenhower entered politics, even though he had not previously shown any great allegiance to a political party. He won the presidential election of 1952 for the Republican Party and held it for a second term before retiring to his farm in Gettysburg, Pennsylvania, where he died in 1969 at the age of 78. Posterity has not always been kind to Eisenhower in terms of his political career, but there can be no doubt about his role in the build-up to the invasion of Normandy, in which he not only took one of the biggest decisions of the Second World War, but took responsibility for it before the successful outcome of D-Day had been established. For that alone, he must surely be regarded as one of the great leaders of the twentieth century and one of the greatest military decision-makers of all time.

NORMAN BORLAUG CHANGES CAREERS

1944

DECISION

Social Change

Science and Innovation

Culture

Politics

Diplomacy

Military

Religion

Circumstances: The offer of a job in Mexico researching stem rust in wheat

Protagonists: Norman Borlaug and numerous other agricultural researchers around the world

Consequences: The Green Revolution

The green revolution has won a temporary success in man's war against hunger and deprivation; it has given man a breathing space. If fully implemented, the revolution can provide sufficient food for sustenance during the next three decades.

From the Nobel Lecture given by Norman Borlaug on December 11, 1970, after being awarded the Nobel Peace Prize

© iStockphoto

When the Nobel Committee attempted to contact Norman Borlaug in October 1970 to inform him that he had been awarded the Nobel Peace Prize for that year, he was outside at the agricultural research station in Mexico where he had worked since 1944 conducting field trials on new varieties of wheat that he and his team of researchers had bred. His wife, Margaret Borlaug, took the call from the committee and had to go and find him to relay the message. It took her some time to convince him that he really had won the prize because, at first, he thought she was joking. Even when he actually received the award, he did so on behalf of agricultural research as a whole rather than for himself, saying that, in giving him the award, the Nobel Committee was, "selecting an individual to symbolize the vital role of agriculture and food production in a world that is hungry." The point he was making was that he did not work in isolation. Nevertheless, the contribution he had made to improving food security in parts of the developing world at a time when rapidly increasing populations and stagnating agricultural production appeared to be leading to widespread famine and mass starvation certainly deserved to be individually recognized.

MEXICO It could all have been very different. After completing a Ph.D. in plant pathology and genetics at the University of Minnesota in 1942, Borlaug

© Time & Life | Getty Images

PLANT BREEDER
Norman Borlaug in 1970 on a trial plot of wheat in Mexico, holding an example of one of the varieties he developed.

got a job with the DuPont chemical company, where he worked on various materials for use by the US Army. By the time he was 30, in the summer of 1944, he was married with a young daughter and Margaret was pregnant with their second child. It was hardly the moment to give up a well-paid and steady job, and when one of his former college professors, who was setting up an agricultural research facility in Mexico, approached him about a job doing research on wheat pathogens, he did the sensible thing and turned it down. But Borlaug was from a farming background, having grown up on his family's farm in Iowa before going to the University of Minnesota, where he first studied forestry and agriculture before specializing in the control of stem rust, one of the major fungal diseases of wheat, so it is not hard to imagine him being tempted by the opportunity he had been offered. In July 1944 he changed his mind and, despite the offer of a pay raise from DuPont, made the decision to take up the position he had been offered to lead the newly established wheat research program near Texcoco, a city about 18 miles (30 km) to the north-east of Mexico City. The decision not only changed his life, but led to the work for which he was awarded the Nobel Prize, even if it intially entailed him leaving his pregnant wife and young daughter behind in America.

The agricultural research station in Mexico was originally the idea of Henry Wallace, who visited the country in 1940 when he was US Secretary of Agriculture in President Franklin D. Roosevelt's government and saw for himself the poverty and shortages of food that existed there at that time. On becoming vice president in the following year, and with the support of the Mexican President Manuel Ávila Camacho, he persuaded the Rockefeller Foundation to fund a project to set up research in Mexico aimed at improving the production of corn and wheat. Both the US Government and the Rockefeller Foundation no doubt had altruistic motives for their initiative, but there was a certain amount of self-interest behind the decision as well. Many of the fungal diseases afflicting American agricultural crops, including wheat rust, had spread north from Mexico and both the government and foundation were worried about the likelihood of civil unrest in the country turning into a communist revolution if steps were not taken to alleviate the chronic shortage of food. The US Government had no desire to see a communist regime on its southern border and the Rockefeller family had considerable holdings in the country, so were not keen on that idea either.

Borlaug was hired to set up research into the control of wheat rust in Mexican crops and to train Mexican agricultural scientists in the methods of selective breeding that had been developed in America to increase the natural immunity of wheat to its fungal disease by means of crossing different varieties of the crop. He began the long and laborious process of cross-breeding and then planting out the resulting seeds in trial plots to investigate which, if any, of the cultivars he had produced showed the best resistance to rust. After a few years of slow progress he discovered a way of speeding up the research by utilizing the different climates in central Mexico and in the Yaqui Valley of the Pacific North-west of the country to grow two crops a year, allowing him to get twice as much research done. By 1948, he had produced wheat that not only showed an enhanced resistance to rust, but produced a much heavier crop of grain than the original varieties had done. Over the next few years Borlaug's new varieties were taken up by farmers all over Mexico and by the mid 1950s the country was not only producing enough wheat for its own needs, but was exporting some as well. While this was happening, Borlaug kept breeding improved varieties, crossing the rust-resistant plants with Japanese dwarf varieties so that the new heavier cropping plants did not fall over due to the amount of grain in their ears. The success of this project can be gauged by looking at any wheat field around the world today, where almost without exception short-strawed high-yielding varieties are now grown.

THE GREEN REVOLUTION

The rapid turnaround in the fortunes of Mexican agriculture did not go unnoticed in other parts of the world that were experiencing similar problems to those that had been encountered in Mexico. The rapidly rising population of India was creating particular concern, in which the situation predicted by Thomas Malthus in the late eighteenth century of rising numbers of people outstripping the capacity of farming to feed them appeared to be coming true. In 1961 the Indian Government asked Borlaug to introduce his methods into their agricultural research stations and, even though the transformation of agriculture took longer than it did in Mexico, by 1970 the Indian wheat harvest had doubled and by 1974 the country was self-sufficient in that commodity. A similar breeding program with rice to develop short-strawed high-yielding varieties resulted in a similar outcome of increasing yields in the Indian subcontinent and other parts of Asia.

Since the Green Revolution, as the transformation of Indian farming has come to be called, numerous criticisms of the methods used to achieve it have been made, principally because high-yielding varieties of wheat and rice require the application of relatively high quantities of fertilizers and pesticides to achieve their full potential, together with the introduction of tractors and other machinery into the agricultural system. As well as having environmental consequences, some of which have been severe, the whole Green Revolution package favors large farmers over small ones because of the investment required to adopt the technology and in parts of the developing world where farming has mostly been done on a small scale, this can have a serious social impact by creating large numbers of landless poor people who are forced to move to cities in search of work. Some environmentalists have even questioned the increase in yields obtained through the use of Green Revolution technologies, saying it has come as a result of an increasing amount of land coming into cultivation rather than as a consequence of the introduction of new methods, even though the evidence does not support these conclusions.

Later in life Borlaug, who died at the age of 95 in 2009, traveled extensively around the world in an effort to increase the awareness of governments to the potential of agricultural research to find solutions to the problem of feeding ever-increasing populations. He could at times get frustrated with the level of the criticism his methods attracted, describing some environmentalists as elitists who had never experienced a shortage of food themselves or seen the devastating effects it can have, as he had himself in depression-era America, Mexico, and in numerous developing countries he had visited. And, in truth, some critics have given the impression that they would have preferred the Green Revolution never to have happened at all even if the consequences had been famine and the starvation of millions of people. More rational critics have pointed out that the Green Revolution averted a humanitarian disaster but does not provide a complete solution to alleviating hunger throughout the world, a point of view that Borlaug himself agreed with, saying that the technologies he first developed had given the world a breathing space in which to find a more permanent solution.

WHEAT FIELD
Short-stemmed high-yielding varieties of wheat based on the ones developed by Borlaug can now be seen around the world.

As the population of the world has continued to grow, agricultural capacity has managed to keep up. The agricultural system has the potential to feed all these people in the future, but it is a sobering thought that, today, there are about a billion people in the world who regularly don't have enough food to eat. Norman Borlaug and his colleagues in agricultural research made a start in addressing the pressing issue of food shortages in the developing world, and he certainly deserved the Nobel Peace Prize for his efforts, but there is clearly a great deal more work to be done.

DECISION

Social Change

Science and Innovation

Culture

Politics

Diplomacy

Military

Religion

THE MARSHALL PLAN
1947

Circumstances: The disastrous state of the economy of Western Europe in the aftermath of the Second World War

Protagonists: US Secretary of State George Marshall and the staff of the US State Department

Consequences: The beginning of recovery and reconstruction

Without further prompt and substantial aid from the United States, economic, political, and social disintegration will overwhelm Europe. Aside from the awful implications which this will have for the future peace and security of the world, the effects on our domestic economy would be disastrous: markets for our surplus production gone, unemployment, depression, a heavily unbalanced budget on the background of a momentous war debt. These things must not happen.

From a memorandum sent to US Secretary of State George Marshall on May 27, 1946, by Under Secretary of State for Economic Affairs William L. Clayton

© Getty Images

On June 5, 1947, a little more than two years after the end of the Second World War, US Secretary of State George Marshall used the occasion of his acceptance speech for an honorary doctorate awarded to him by Harvard University to introduce a change in American foreign policy in which a massive program of aid would be made available to European countries to enable the reconstruction of those infrastructures that had been destroyed in the war and to kick-start economic recovery. Marshall was well aware that this new policy may well prove unpopular with the American people and may also receive a hostile reception in Congress. This was one of the reasons why he had taken on the role of publicly introducing it rather than leaving it to President Harry Truman, because he was widely regarded in America as being the architect of the Allied victory in the war. Even so, while Marshall was making the speech, Truman was holding a press conference in Washington in which he denounced the role the Soviet Union had played in the communist takeover of Hungary, a classic case of a politician deflecting attention away from a difficult subject by making a headline-grabbing announcement on a different issue.

GEORGE MARSHALL
As US Secretary of State in 1947, Marshall was responsible for the change in American foreign policy in postwar Europe.

The European Recovery Program, or Marshall Plan as it became widely known, had been developed over the previous few months by officials in the State Department, principally Dean Acheson, William Clayton, and George Kennedy, and was a direct response to the realization that the entire European economy was in a state of almost complete collapse. All three had visited European countries in 1946 and had seen for themselves the extent of the problems faced by those countries devastated by war. They came to the conclusion that the only way Europe was going to recover was if the German economy, once the principal driver of the European economy, was reconstructed and allowed to function properly. In a series of negotiations held between Marshall and Vyacheslav Molotov, the foreign minister of the Soviet Union, it had become obvious that the Soviets would not agree to any plan that involved rebuilding Germany, and, as the British Government was effectively broke, it quickly became apparent that if anything was going to be done, America had to take the lead. It is not possible to pin down a single decision that led to the Marshall Plan, other than the one

Marshall himself made by instructing his officials to work on finding a solution to refinancing the European economy, so what we have here is really a series of decisions made over a period of months in the first half of 1946 that came together in a radical change in US Government policy concerning postwar Germany.

THE MORGENTHAU PLAN

Toward the end of the Second World War, after it had become apparent that an Allied victory was inevitable and particularly after the successful invasion of Normandy in June 1944, President Roosevelt realized the need for the Americans to adopt a policy on what to do with Germany once it had finally surrendered. The resulting plan was named after the Secretary of the Treasury at the time, Henry Morgenthau, and mostly written by Harry Dexter White, an economist in that department. Its principal aim was to restrict the development of postwar Germany to prevent the country returning to its former dominant economic position on the European continent so that it would not be in a position to start any more wars. The way this was to be achieved was to divide the country into two states and give some of its territory to neighboring countries, principally the coal-mining region of Upper Silesia to Poland and the industrial area of the Saar valley to France, while the Ruhr valley, the industrial heartland of Germany, would become a part of an internationally administered zone. In this way, Germany would be deindustrialized, becoming instead an agricultural nation that did not have the capacity to threaten anybody else.

The Morgenthau Plan was presented to the British Government at the Second Quebec Conference in September 1944 and, after initially being very reluctant to accept it, Winston Churchill had his arm twisted by President Roosevelt and eventually relented. Churchill described the plan as being the "pastoralization" of Germany, and cited the disastrous consequences of the Treaty of Versailles adopted at the end of the First World War. The draconian measures taken against Germany in the form of an enormous amount of reparations that would cripple the German economy for many years were among the driving forces behind the rise of Adolf Hitler and the Nazi Party in the 1920s and 1930s. But the British economy was reliant on American finance at the time and Roosevelt either dangled the carrot of further multibillion-dollar loans or made a veiled threat of withholding them until Churchill agreed.

After the final surrender on May 7, 1945, the Morgenthau Plan was implemented by the Allies in occupied Germany, which, among other things, involved the demolition of those factories in the Ruhr valley that had not already been bombed flat during the war. It quickly became apparent that this approach was having disastrous consequences. With no factories, there were no jobs and no wages, so the German economy effectively ceased to function, even to the point of farmers stopping bringing their produce to markets in the towns because they did not trust the currency they had previously been paid in. People were beginning to starve and they had become reliant on American aid to survive. Rising civil unrest led to US fears of a possible communist uprising, a common enough reaction in America at the time, but one later given some credence when it emerged that during the war Harry Dexter White had been regarded by Soviet intelligence as an asset in the American government. Specific evidence against White has never been presented, but it would appear that he persuaded Morgenthau of the merits of the plan to deindustrialize the German economy because he thought that communists would be able to take advantage of the ensuing chaos it would cause not only in Germany, but more widely in Western Europe.

As well as the specter of communism becoming apparent, the Americans began to realize that they would have to support the German economy for an indefinite period of time into the future if they continued with the Morgenthau Plan, so it could be argued that the decision to put a stop to it and replace it with one based on the reconstruction of Germany was as much based on pragmatism and self-interest as it was on any humanitarian desire to prevent the disastrous situation that was developing in Germany. Nevertheless, it was this decision that directly led the State Department to begin work on what would become the Marshall Plan. The scale of the problem was enormous: by the end of the war, some 5 million houses had been destroyed in Europe and there were 12 million displaced persons. Allied bombing had destroyed the center of numerous German cities, Berlin, Hamburg, Frankfurt, and Cologne included, together with much of the transport infrastructure and industrial capacity. Getting Germany back on its feet again would require a huge amount of money and, after the Marshall Plan had been

THE MARSHALL PLAN

© Gamma-Keystone | Getty Images

POSTWAR EUROPE
Many European cities lay in ruins after the end of the Second World War.

approved by the US Congress, a multibillion-dollar package was made available.

The money, in the form of both loans and grants, was offered to many other European countries as well as Germany, including the Soviet Union and those of Eastern Europe, even if this was done in the knowledge that, with the Cold War getting underway, the Soviets would almost certainly refuse. After extensive negotiations with the European countries that would be taking part in the plan, the Organisation for European Economic Co-operation (OEEC) was established to administer it and to allocate financial packages to particular countries. Over the course of the next three years, a total of $13 billion was divided among the 17 European countries taking part, of which Germany received around $2.2 billion. The transformation in the European economy began almost immediately. The period between 1948 to 1952 saw an overall increase in gross domestic product (GDP) of 35%, the fastest growth rate in European history, and while this could not be entirely put down to the Marshall Plan, there can be little doubt that it played an important role in stimulating economic activity. Agricultural production also began to rise rapidly and, with the potential food crisis averted, the threat of a communist takeover in any Western European country receded. The relaxation of trade barriers between countries required by the plan can also be seen as part of the process of European integration, even if the European Union of today has its roots in the European Coal and Steel Community, formed in 1951 by six European countries, including Germany, rather than through the Marshall Plan and the OEEC.

By the end of 1951, the Marshall Plan had ended and been replaced by a new policy. Critics have since suggested that the plan was purely a means for the Americans to further their own imperialistic and anti-communist aims and that the German economic miracle of the 1960s and 1970s came about as a consequence of the policies followed by Ludwig Erhard, the German Minister for Economics from 1949 to 1963. But if the Marshall Plan is compared to the disastrous Morgenthau Plan and to the Treaty of Versailles of 1919, it must be regarded as a triumph of American foreign policy, making the decisions taken to develop and implement it among the greatest made in US postwar history.

ROSA PARKS REFUSES TO STAND UP

1955

DECISION

Social Change

Science and Innovation

Culture

Politics

Diplomacy

Military

Religion

Circumstances: A woman takes a seat on a bus in Montgomery, Alabama

Protagonists: Rosa Parks, Martin Luther King, and other activists of the civil rights movement in America

Consequences: The end of segregation on the buses in Montgomery and the rise to international prominence of Martin Luther King

There comes a time when people get tired. We are here this evening to say to those who have mistreated us for so long that we are tired, tired of being segregated and humiliated, tired of being kicked about by the brutal feet of oppression.

From a speech given by Martin Luther King on December 5, 1955, the first day of the Montgomery Bus Boycott

In 2001 the Missouri state legislature lost a seven-year legal battle to prevent the white supremacist group the Ku Klux Klan from joining its Adopt-a-Highway clean-up program, in which any group that collected litter from the side of a stretch of road were allowed to put up a sign saying that they had sponsored it. In response, the state decided to rename the stretch of Interstate 55 in St. Louis County allocated to the KKK as the Rosa Parks Highway after the woman who, on December 1, 1955, refused to vacate her seat on a segregated bus in Montgomery, Alabama, for a white passenger and was arrested, sparking a protest in the city that became an important milestone in the struggle for civil rights in America. The KKK did not fulfill their commitment to clean up the highway, depriving the rest of us of an opportunity to have a good laugh at their expense, but the name of the road remains as one of many tributes to be found all over America to Rosa Parks, who died in 2005 at the age of 92. Her decision to commit what was, on the face of it, a relatively minor act of civil disobedience had enormous repercussions that would eventually result in that famous line from the US Declaration of Independence of 1776 that "all men are created equal" finally ringing true, even if it would probably read better if it said that, "all men and women are created equal."

NO. 2857   By all accounts Rosa Parks was a respectable, soft-spoken woman with strong religious convictions, but, as she would reveal through her actions, also one with a deep sense of injustice about the repression of black people in Alabama and an inner determination to do something about it. The Jim Crow laws legislating for the segregation of the races had been in force in the southern states of America since the 1870s and were supposedly intended to create conditions that were "separate but equal" even if in practice the actual purpose was to enforce the social and economic disadvantages faced by black people. A Montgomery city ordinance dating to 1900 specified the segregation of public transport, and by the 1950s this had been implemented by bus companies in the city in the form of reserving the front rows of seats on any bus for white people. The law did not specify any requirement for a black person to stand up if a white person did not have a seat, but this had become customary so that, when the white section of the bus was full and a white person was having to stand, the bus driver would extend the white section further back, telling any black people sitting in the row immediately behind the white section to move back or, if there was no room, to stand up. As if this was not petty enough, black people were also not allowed to walk through the white section to get to the black section if there were any white people on board, but were expected to get on the bus at the front to pay their fare to the driver, then get off and get on again through the back doors. As Rosa Parks had experienced herself, this sometimes resulted in bus drivers, who were all white men, taking a fare from a black person and then driving off before they had the chance to get back on the bus.

In the early evening of December 1, 1955, Rosa Parks got on the no. 2857 Cleveland Avenue bus in downtown Montgomery, where she worked as a seamstress in a department store, and sat down in the first row of seats allocated to black people. The bus began to fill up until there were no seats left in either the black or white sections, leaving a white man standing. As black and white people were not supposed to sit in the same row, the bus driver told the four men and women in the first row allocated to black people to stand up so the white man could sit down and, after some initial reluctance, three of the four got up. The fourth, Rosa Parks, remained seated and, on being told again to move by the bus driver, refused to get up, saying, she would later recall, after he threatened to call the police, "You may do that." More than 30 years afterward she wrote:

> People always say that I didn't give up my seat because I was tired, but that isn't true. I was not tired physically, or no more tired than I usually was at the end of a working day. I was not old, although some people have an image of me as being old then. I was forty-two. No, the only tired I was, was tired of giving in.

The police duly arrived and arrested Parks, who was taken to a police station where she was formally charged with breaking the segregation law, then transferred to the city jail.

After about two hours in the jail, Rosa Parks was bailed out by Edgar Nixon, the president of the local chapter of the NAACP (National Association for the Advancement of Colored People, which retains its name to this day out of respect to the traditions of its past). He had heard of the arrest from another passenger on the bus and went to the jail with the white lawyer Clifford Durr to ensure that the police would

ROSA PARKS
A photograph of Parks from December 1955, taken during the Montgomery Bus Boycott, with Martin Luther King in the background.

CIVIL RIGHTS

POLICE REPORT
The Montgomery Police
Department report filed on
December 1, 1955, detailing
the complaint made against
Parks by the bus driver.

deal with the bail request straight away. Dixon had been looking for a case that could be used to test the constitutional legality of the segregation laws in Montgomery and, if Parks agreed to take part in a lawsuit that could have dangerous consequences for both herself and her family, he had now been presented with the perfect opportunity. Parks was the secretary of the Montgomery NAACP and a few months previously had attended a summer school that had included classes on such subjects as the civil disobedience of Mahatma Gandhi in India, leading to some suggestion that her own actions had been premeditated. She would later say that, while the injustice of segregation had been on her mind for some time, the actual circumstances of her arrest were not planned and there is no reason not to accept her account. In the end, it actually makes little difference either way as a protest against the segregation laws was entirely justified whether it was premeditated or spontaneous.

Rosa Parks took some time to think about the proposal to challenge the segregation laws, concerned about the consequences for her husband and mother as well as for herself, then decided to do it. On Monday December 5, the day of her court appearance, a boycott of the public bus services was organized by the black community and it was observed by almost everybody. At the trial, which lasted all of five minutes, Parks was found guilty of violating the city ordinance on segregation and fined a total of $10 and $4 costs. That evening at a meeting of community leaders the decision was taken to extend the bus boycott and to form an organization, to be called the Montgomery Improvement Association, to oversee it. A vote was taken to elect a president of the new association and won by a 26-year-old Baptist minister from Atlanta, Georgia, Martin Luther King, who had recently moved to the city and had electrified meetings of the NAACP with his remarkable gift for oratory.

The bus boycott lasted for 381 days and inspired many other protests and acts of disobedience in the name of civil rights in other states in America. It lasted until the US Supreme Court ruled in the case of another woman from Montgomery, Aurelia Browder, who had experienced much the same treatment as Rosa Parks had done, finding that the segregation of buses was unconstitutional and forcing the city and the state of Alabama to integrate its transport system. It was one of a series of cases heard by the Supreme Court that challenged the remaining Jim Crow laws. It also projected King into a prominent position in the civil rights movement, where he came to national and international attention because of his adoption of the tactics of nonviolent civil disobedience and through the spellbinding power of his oratory, perhaps most famously demonstrated in the "I Have a Dream" speech delivered on August 28, 1963, as a part of the March on Washington protest. In the following year, the Civil Rights Act was signed into law by President Lyndon B. Johnson, making discrimination of any sort illegal. That was followed in 1965 by the Voting Rights Act, which outlawed all practices aimed at preventing people from any background from registering to vote. By that time, Rosa Parks had left Montgomery and was living in Detroit, where she worked for US Congressional Representative for Michigan John Conyers as a secretary and receptionist in his local office until she retired in 1988. After her death in 2005, her body lay in state for two days in the rotunda of the US Capitol building in Washington, where a bust of Martin Luther King, assassinated in 1968, also stands. The bus she was traveling on that day in Montgomery is now in the Henry Ford Museum in Detroit, where, in April 2012, it was visited by Barack Obama, the first black president of the United States of America.

THE CIVIL RIGHTS ACT WAS SIGNED INTO LAW BY PRESIDENT LYNDON B. JOHNSON, MAKING DISCRIMINATION OF ANY SORT ILLEGAL

DECISION

Social Change

Science and Innovation

Culture

Politics

Diplomacy

Military

Religion

KENNEDY AND THE CUBAN MISSILE CRISIS

1962

Circumstances: America faces the threat of nuclear warheads on its doorstep

Protagonists: President John F. Kennedy and First Secretary Nikita Khrushchev

Consequences: A nuclear war averted

This Government, as promised, has maintained the closest surveillance of the Soviet military build-up on the island of Cuba. Within the past week, unmistakable evidence has established the fact that a series of offensive missile sites is now in preparation on that imprisoned island. The purpose of these bases can be none other than to provide a nuclear strike capability against the Western Hemisphere.

From a television address to the American people given by President John F. Kennedy on October 22, 1962

The Cuban Missile Crisis lasted for only 13 days, from October 16 to October 28, 1962, but during that short time the confrontation it provoked between America and the Soviet Union came closer to nuclear war than at any other moment in the 46-year history of the Cold War, which began at the end of the Second World War and came to a close in 1991 with the collapse of the Soviet Union. At the time of the crisis, the 45-year-old President John F. Kennedy had been in the White House for only 16 months, but despite his relative youth and inexperience he made a series of decisions that brought America back from the brink of war. The most important of these was his decision not to take direct military action against Cuba, going against the advice of his senior military commanders, and instead to impose a naval blockade on the island as a means of preventing Soviet ships carrying missiles from reaching it. But perhaps his greatest contribution to averting a nuclear war and the devastating consequences that would entail was to decide on a course of action that at no time closed off the possibility of finding a diplomatic solution to the crisis. Both he and Nikita Khrushchev, the leader of the Soviet Union, were well aware that the use of military force by either side had the potential to escalate into the use of nuclear weapons and, in the end, Kennedy's strength of character and his capacity to make decisions under the most extreme pressure were two of the principal reasons why Khrushchev decided to back down.

SUMMIT MEETING
The low opinion Khrushchev formed of Kennedy at a summit in Vienna in June 1961 contributed to him underestimating the president.

BERLIN AND CUBA

One of the main points of contention between America and the Soviet Union in the late 1950s and early 1960s was over the future of Berlin, which had been split between western and eastern zones since the end of the Second World War. Khrushchev wanted Berlin to be reunited and to become part of East Germany; when, in the summer of 1961, it became clear that this solution was not going to be accepted by America or its Western allies, the Soviet Union and East Germany began the construction of what would become the Berlin Wall. After a number of diplomatic incidents in October at the crossing point between zones known as Checkpoint Charlie, in which US officials were prevented from crossing into the eastern zone, a stand-off developed between

Soviet and American tanks, defused when Kennedy decided to accept the presence of the Berlin Wall rather than risk any further escalation of the crisis.

The lack of resolve shown by Kennedy over Berlin reinforced the opinion Khrushchev had developed of him as being weak and indecisive after the Bay of Pigs fiasco earlier in the year. A force of Cuban exiles, backed and trained by the CIA, had mounted an invasion of Cuba in April 1961, landing at the Bay of Pigs, but had been comprehensively defeated by Fidel Castro's Cuban army, partly as a result of the lack of support they had received due to Kennedy's decision not to allow the American navy or airforce to provide cover. The consequence of this failure was both to increase support for Castro in Cuba and more widely in Latin America and for him to pursue closer ties with the Soviet Union, declaring that the overthrow of the American-backed dictator Batista in 1959 had been a Marxist-Leninist revolution. Castro was also concerned about the possibility of a full-scale American invasion of Cuba, leading him to accept Soviet military assistance to counter that threat, which included the deployment of defensive surface-to-air missiles. After initial reluctance to agree to such a provocative move, he also finally agreed to the Soviet plan of secretly installing intermediate-range ballistic missiles in Cuba, which would be capable of carrying nuclear warheads to locations throughout America.

Khrushchev had more than Cuban security in mind when he discussed the plan with Castro. Despite American intelligence reports that suggested that the Soviet Union had a greater capability in long-range nuclear missiles, which could strike the American mainland from sites within the Soviet Union, than America did, the truth was that they actually had many fewer than the Americans and that the guidance systems in use by the Soviets were not sophisticated enough to hit targets in America with any degree of accuracy. Cuba, on the other hand, was only 90 miles (130 km) off the coast of Florida, so shorter-range and more accurate missiles could pose a much greater threat. The US already had intermediate-range missiles stationed in Italy and, in April 1962 the Turkish Government agreed to an American request to allow the installation of similar missiles on its territory as well, from where they could target Moscow, so the Cuban missiles would act as a countermeasure to the American threat. Khrushchev also thought that, once the missiles had been installed in Cuba, Kennedy would prove himself to be a weak leader again and either accept their presence rather than risk a war with the Soviet Union or come to a negotiated settlement in which, in exchange for the removal of the missiles from Cuba, he would agree to the Soviet demand to take over all of Berlin.

For all of September 1962 and for the first two weeks of October, the Americans suspended flights of their U-2 spy planes over Cuba because of the presence of Soviet surface-to-air missiles on the island similar to the type used in April 1960 to shoot down the U-2 plane piloted by Gary Powers over Russia. But, after evidence of an increase in Soviet military activity was uncovered and rumors of the Soviets' intention to build missile platforms for surface-to-surface missiles began to circulate, on October 14 a plane was sent out to fly over Cuba despite the risks. It took pictures of a construction site in western Cuba; these were interpreted by the CIA the following day as providing irrefutable evidence of the presence of intermediate-range missiles on the island. President Kennedy was informed the next morning, October 16, and convened a meeting of government ministers and key advisers to discuss the American response. As well as Kennedy himself, the committee, which would become known as ExComm (Executive Committee of the National Security Council), included Vice President Lyndon Johnson, Secretary of State Dean Rusk, Secretary of Defense Robert McNamara, and his brother Robert Kennedy, the Attorney General, as well as specialist advisers such as General Maxwell Taylor, the chairman of the Joint Chiefs of Staff, and John McCone, the director of the CIA.

While Kennedy continued to perform the public duties in his schedule, not wanting to appear indecisive by announcing the crisis before he knew what he was going to do about it, in private the members of ExComm went through the various possible responses available to America, which ranged from a full-scale American invasion of Cuba to doing nothing at all. At meetings of ExComm on October 18 and 19 these options were discussed and the military advisers, including General Taylor, stated that their favored option was an invasion. It

THE 13 DAYS

EXCOMM MEETING
On October 29, 1962, President Kennedy chaired the ExComm meeting in the White House Cabinet Room.

became apparent that this would take months to organize, by which time it would be too late, so they next advised bombing the missile sites. Kennedy decided that it would not be possible to guarantee that all the missile sites would be put out of action by bombing and that, in doing so, it was certain to provoke an armed response from the Soviet Union that could lead to nuclear war. The idea of doing nothing was also ruled out for more political reasons: Kennedy had made a promise to the American people only the month before to act if Cuba came into possession of the means to attack the US and by doing nothing he would be both breaking that promise and would look as weak as he had over the Bay of Pigs.

LAUNCH SITE
An aerial reconnaissance photograph clearly showing a Soviet missile launch site near San Cristobal, western Cuba.

By October 22, Kennedy had reached his decision and made a television broadcast to the American people that set out the situation in straightforward language (quoted at the beginning of the chapter) and went on to explain what he intended to do about it, saying:

> To halt this offensive build-up, a strict quarantine on all offensive military equipment under shipment to Cuba is being initiated. All ships of any kind bound for Cuba, from whatever nation or port, will, if found to contain cargoes of offensive weapons, be turned back.

What he was announcing was, in effect, a blockade of Cuba, but had described it as a "quarantine" because under international law blockades were considered to be acts of war. Khrushchev replied with a broadcast of his own, describing the blockade as a "pirate action" that would lead to war. Kennedy raised the US alert level to DEFCON 2, one level below actual war and putting all US military forces on standby for immediate action. It would emerge years later that the captain of a nuclear-armed Soviet submarine that had been detected by the US navy had ordered a nuclear missile to be made ready to fire and was only stopped from doing so by the intervention of one of his junior officers. But, while the world teetered on the edge of a nuclear war, which could have been sparked by a single incident, a secret diplomatic channel had been opened between the Americans and Soviets and, on October 26, Khrushchev sent Kennedy a telegram containing an offer that had the potential to lead to a peaceful solution to the crisis.

Khrushchev said he would remove the missiles from Cuba in exchange for a public commitment from Kennedy not to invade and an end to the blockade of Cuba.

The next day, another communication was received from Khrushchev that was not so conciliatory as the first and contained a demand for the removal of American missiles from Italy and Turkey. Kennedy decided to publicly reply to the first message, accepting the proposals to lift the blockade and making a commitment not to invade Cuba. He then informed Khrushchev through the diplomatic back-channel that he would also remove the missiles from Italy and Turkey in secret within the next six months, which was not actually a huge concession because, unknown to the Soviets, these missiles were on the way to becoming obsolete anyway due to the development of submarine-based Polaris missiles. Khrushchev agreed, bringing the crisis to an abrupt and unexpectedly successful end on October 28, after which the Soviet technicians in Cuba immediately began dismantling the missile sites. By November 20, they had dispatched the missiles that had been in Cuba back to the Soviet Union. The secret nature of the agreement to remove the US missiles from Italy and Turkey gave the impression that Khrushchev had settled for a solution to the crisis that favored America, diminishing his own reputation for hard bargaining, while, at the same time, enhancing that of Kennedy. In the meantime, Berlin stayed divided until the fall of the Berlin Wall in November 1989 and the reunification of Germany in the following year, and Cuba remained a thorn in America's side, as it does today under the presidency of Fidel Castro's younger brother Raúl.

DECISION

Social Change

Science and Innovation

Culture

Politics

Diplomacy

Military

Religion

GEORGE MARTIN SIGNS THE BEATLES

1962

Circumstances: A record producer listens to a band that has been turned down by every other record company

Protagonists: John, Paul, George, and Ringo, along with Brian Epstein and George Martin

Consequences: The emergence of the most popular and biggest-selling band in the history of popular music

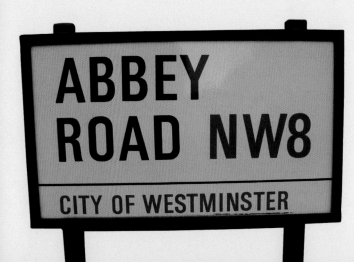

There was an unusual quality of sound, a certain roughness that I had not encountered before. There was also the fact that more than one person was singing, which in itself was unusual. There was something tangible that made me want to hear more, meet and see what they could do.

George Martin, *All You Need is Ears*

On New Year's Day, 1962, The Beatles attended their first proper audition for a record company, recording a demo tape of 15 songs over the course of an hour in the Decca Records recording studio in West Hampstead, London. The demo consisted of only three songs written by John Lennon and Paul McCartney, the rest being cover versions of songs the band regularly played live, which, at least according to their manager Brian Epstein, would better show off the range of their musical skills. By that time, the band were playing regularly in Liverpool, most famously at the Cavern Club, and had been to Hamburg on two occasions, each time playing three-month residencies in clubs in the city where they could end up playing all day and half the night as well. The experience had brought them together as a band musically, even if John, Paul, and the lead guitarist George Harrison did not always see eye to eye with their drummer, Pete Best. After the audition, the band went back to Liverpool and waited for the outcome. It took a month for Decca to make up their minds and, when they finally did, they made what is now considered to be the worst decision in the history of popular music by turning The Beatles down. A record producer from Decca phoned Brian Epstein to give him the bad news. He is reported to have said by way of an explanation, "Guitar groups are on the way out, Mr. Epstein," and had then gone on to suggest that, as Epstein was already running a very successful record shop in Liverpool, perhaps it would be better if he stuck to the business he knew best.

CAVERN CLUB
The Beatles with Pete Best on drums playing the Cavern Club on December 8, 1961, shortly before their failed audition with Decca Records.

To be fair to Decca, they may have been the first record company to turn The Beatles down, but they were by no means the last. Over the course of the next few months, Epstein approached all the major British record companies and was turned down by, among others, Pye, Columbia, and HMV. Three of the four record producers employed by EMI listened to the demo tape, which, it would later emerge, Epstein had paid the Decca record producer to make, and each of them said no. The fourth one was on holiday at the time, so did not get a chance to listen for himself. In April the band went back to Hamburg for their third residency in a club, finding out once they were there that Stuart Sutcliffe, the original bass player in the band who had left in

GEORGE MARTIN

the previous year to study art in Hamburg, had died suddenly at the age of 21 after suffering a brain haemorrhage. In May, while they were still in the city, Epstein made what he considered at the time to be one final effort to get them signed to a record company. He took the demo tape to London and, through a friend who worked in HMV's flagship record store on Oxford Street, managed to get it passed on to George Martin, the fourth EMI record producer who had yet to hear it and who primarily worked for the record company's Parlophone label.

Martin heard something in the recording that he liked, although he would later struggle to say exactly what that something was. But, whatever it had been, it was enough for him to want to meet the band in person and to hear them play live. On June 6, after they had finished their contract in Hamburg, The Beatles auditioned for Martin at EMI's Abbey Road studios in St. John's Wood, London, hardly two miles from where they had failed to impress Decca five months earlier. As before, they played a few of their own songs, but mostly the covers they played in their normal live set. Once they had finished, Martin said it had been very nice and that he would let them know. If they were expecting to be signed on the spot, then they left the recording studios disappointed. Back in Liverpool, they played more gigs at the Cavern and at various other venues around the city without hearing anything from Martin, until he finally telephoned Brian Epstein and offered them a recording contract. It was the standard one-year deal EMI offered to new artists, with an option to extend beyond the single year if the record company was happy with the outcome of the recording sessions, and it paid a royalty to the band of one penny for every single sold.

BEATLEMANIA

In September 1962, The Beatles made their first record with George Martin at Abbey Road studios. By that time, Pete Best had been sacked from the band, just at the moment when it was about to become enormously successful, and replaced by Ringo Starr, who had been playing with the Liverpool-based band Rory Storm and the Hurricanes. Martin had not been happy with Best's drumming, but the decision to fire him rested with John, Paul, and George, even if they actually got Brian Epstein to break the news. After the first recording, Martin was not overly impressed with Ringo either and booked a session drummer to rerecord the band's first single, "Love Me Do," with Ringo only playing the maracas. It was released the following month and, by

Christmas, had sold 17,000 copies, making each member of the band all of £17 in royalties, and had reached No. 17 in the charts.

The band recorded again on November 26 and this time Martin was much happier with Ringo and with the overall outcome of the session, saying to the band over the intercom from the control room as they finished playing, "Gentleman, you've just recorded your first number one record." He was not wrong. After its release in January, "Please Please Me" went to No. 1 and stayed there for 30 weeks. The album of the same name, featuring eight Lennon and McCartney compositions and six covers, also went to No. 1 in the album chart and the next single, "From Me to You," came out in April and went to No. 1 as well. Then the fourth single, "She Loves You," sold a million copies after it came out in August, holding the record as the highest-selling UK single in Britain until it was finally beaten in 1977 by Paul McCartney's song "Mull of Kintyre." Live performances and appearances on TV followed and, what with the moptop haircuts, the suits, and the band's irreverent sense of humor, Beatlemania was born. In the first three years of their association with EMI, The Beatles sold 9 million singles in Britain alone and toward the end of their recording career in 1969, the band accounted for 20% of the record company's entire sales. By one estimate, worldwide sales figures in all formats have now surpassed the 1 billion mark, making The Beatles by far and away the most successful recording artists of all time. So, if Decca's decision to turn down The Beatles was the worst one taken in popular music history, then surely it is equally true to say that George Martin's decision to sign the band for EMI was the best one, not least for the phenomenal sales figures they have achieved over the years, but also because of the huge amount of enjoyment people from around the world have gained from their songs.

THE FIFTH BEATLE
John, Paul, George, and Ringo posing with George Martin, who heard something in their sound that no other record producer did.

DECISION

Social Change

Science and Innovation

Culture

Politics

Diplomacy

Military

Religion

ANWAR SADAT FLIES TO JERUSALEM

1977

Circumstances: The Egyptian president takes the initiative to bring about peace negotiations with Israel

Protagonists: Anwar Sadat, Menachem Begin, and Jimmy Carter

Consequences: the first peace treaty between an Arab country and Israel

I have come to you so that together we should build a durable peace based on justice to avoid the shedding of one single drop of blood by both sides. It is for this reason that I have proclaimed my readiness to go to the farthest corner of the earth.

From the speech given by President Anwar Sadat to the Israeli Knesset on November 20, 1977

On November 19, 1977, the Egyptian President Anwar Sadat flew from Cairo to Jerusalem to meet with Israeli Prime Minister Menachem Begin and to give a speech in the Knesset, the chamber of the Israeli parliament. In most other parts of the world, the arrival of the head of state of a neighboring country would be considered a normal part of the maintenance of friendly relations between the two, but this was certainly not the case on this occasion. Egypt and Israel had technically been at war since 1948 and, as well as engaging in numerous minor military encounters since that time, had also been involved in major confrontations in June 1967 during the Six Day War and again in the Yom Kippur War of October 1973. It was a brave decision by Sadat to go to Israel, not only because he would be visiting a sworn enemy, but also because he knew that by becoming the first Arab leader to visit Israel since its creation he would be viewed by many in Egypt and the Arab world as a traitor to his people. This was particularly the case in Jordan, Syria, and Lebanon, the Arab states immediately bordering Israel, and within the Palestinian community in the occupied territories of the West Bank and Gaza Strip, as a consequence of both the long-held animosity toward Israel over the seizure of Palestinian land in the late 1940s and because of the loss of territory to it in 1967, when Israel annexed the occupied territories, together with the Golan Heights from Syria and the Sinai peninsula from Egypt. But the visit would also demonstrate to the Israelis and the rest of the world that Sadat was serious about negotiating a peace settlement with Israel and would lead directly to the Camp David Accords of 1978 and the signing of the Egypt–Israel Peace Treaty in the following year.

SADAT AND BEGIN

The two leaders of Egypt and Israel did not, at first sight, appear the most obvious candidates to engage in peace negotiations. Both were fiercely nationalistic and had come into politics from the military of their respective countries. Sadat was one of the Egyptian army officers who instigated the Egyptian Revolution of 1952 against the British that led to the presidency of Gamal Abdel Nasser. He served in a number of different posts in Nasser's government and, after Nasser's death in 1970, went on to succeed him as president. During the Yom Kippur War, which also saw simultaneous attacks on Israel by Syria and Jordan, Sadat attempted to regain the Sinai and, even though the Egyptian forces only actually managed to reclaim a small amount of the territory lost in 1967, it was the first time an Arab country had achieved any success at all against Israel and it made him a hero in the Arab world. One of his primary objectives as president of Egypt, as well as regaining the whole of the Sinai, was to make Egypt a fully independent country, which meant severing the ties Nasser had formed with the Soviet Union. Sadat's strategy to achieve this involved realigning Egypt with America, which he thought would also boost his territorial aspirations if America could be persuaded to put pressure on Israel to return the Sinai.

Menachem Begin came to what was, at the time, British Mandatory Palestine in 1942 from Poland and had fought against British and Arab forces in the wars that led to the foundation of the State of Israel. He entered politics at the establishment of the first Israeli parliament in 1948 and remained in opposition for the entire period of time up until the Likud Party, of which he was leader, won the 1977 Knesset elections. He had been prime minister of Israel for only six months at the time of Sadat's visit, which had come about after Sadat had made a speech in the Egyptian parliament saying he would go to the ends of the earth to achieve peace, even if that meant going to Jerusalem. Begin was as keen to maintain an alliance with the Americans as Sadat was, and the chances of doing so could only be enhanced by taking the opportunity of establishing peace with Egypt, which would also serve to secure Israel's southern border. He responded to Sadat's speech by sending him a formal invitation to come to Israel, passed through an American intermediary, thereby paving the way for the historic visit.

THE PEACE PROCESS

Sadat and Begin hardly established friendly relations during the trip or in the subsequent peace negotiations, but they may have been able to arrive at a mutual understanding because of their common experiences in the military and political fields. The fact that both men had come into politics through a sense of nationalism rather than because of any deep-seated ideological convictions probably also helped, because neither had any other agenda than attempting to achieve the best outcome for their countries. But despite the mutual advantages of a peace settlement, it took an extensive diplomatic effort by the Americans to get the two sides together in talks under the mediation of President Jimmy Carter, which began in September 1978 at Camp David, the presidential country retreat in Maryland. Even then the diplomatic missions from both countries refused to occupy the same room as the other; Carter was forced to hold separate meetings with Sadat and Begin and then convey the details of his negotiation with each to the other. It is hard to imagine many US presidents being prepared to act in this way, but after 13 days of intensive negotiations carried out in this bizarre manner, an agreement was reached. It was a remarkable achievement by Carter given the circumstances and resulted in the Camp David Accords, signed by Sadat and Begin in the presence of Carter on September 17 at the White House.

SADAT AND BEGIN
The Egyptian and Israeli leaders at a joint session of the US Congress on September 18, 1978, as the Camp David Accords are announced.

The first of the two accords, "A Framework for Peace in the Middle East," called for both sides to work toward finding a solution to the Palestinian question, a problem that remains the most intractable in the Middle East to this day, while the second, "A Framework for the Conclusion of a Peace Treaty between Egypt and Israel" achieved exactly what was set out in its title. On March 26, 1979, Sadat and Begin signed the Egypt–Israel Peace Treaty, again at the White House, and witnessed by Jimmy Carter, which formally ended all hostilities between the two countries. In exchange for a complete Israeli withdrawal from the Sinai, including all Israeli settlers, Egypt undertook to maintain the region as a demilitarized zone and to recognize the legitimacy of Israel as a nation, the first Arab nation to do so. It was a watershed moment in the history of the Middle East, even if it did not lead to the beginning of negotiations between Israel and any other Arab nations.

On October 6, 1981, Anwar Sadat was assassinated by Islamic extremists in the Egyptian army while he was attending a parade to mark the anniversary of the Yom Kippur War. At the subsequent trial, the leader of the assassins cited the Camp David Accords as his motivation for the killing of the president, demonstrating yet again the huge difficulties involved in finding any sort of solution to the Arab and Israeli conflict. But the peace between Egypt and Israel has now been in place for over 30 years, though it remains to be seen how all of the changes brought about by the ongoing Arab Spring, as the movement for open government and democracy across the Arab world has been called, will affect the long-term picture in the Middle East.

DECISION

Social Change

Science and Innovation

Culture

Politics

Diplomacy

Military

Religion

DENG XIAOPING AND ECONOMIC REFORM IN CHINA

1979

Circumstances: The uncertainty over how China would be governed after the death of Mao Tse-tung

Protagonists: Deng Xiaoping, the Communist Party of China and the Chinese people

Consequences: The Chinese economic miracle

It doesn't matter if a cat is black or white as long as it catches mice.

Response by Deng Xiaoping to being asked if the nature of his reforms were communist or capitalist

© Neftali | Shutterstock

Over the past 30 years, China has undergone an unprecedented economic transformation that has seen an average annual economic growth rate of 10% over the entire period. By 2011 its gross domestic product (GDP) had overtaken that of both Germany and Japan to make it the second largest in the world, trailing only America, which, at least if some economic forecasts are to be believed, it will surpass at some point over the next 20 years. No economist, or anybody else for that matter, was making such predictions in the mid 1970s, when the Chinese economy had stagnated and the political situation in the country after the death of Mao Tse-tung in 1976 was in turmoil. Mao had been chairman of the Chinese Communist Party since the successful revolution that in 1949 led to the foundation of the People's Republic of China and, after taking power, he implemented a centrally planned economic system based on that of the Soviet Union. Coming after more than ten years of war, which included the Japanese invasion of China and occupation of large parts of the country, the Second World War and the civil war that culminated in the revolution, Mao's economic policies proved to be disastrous. The collectivization of agriculture in the so-called Great Leap Forward of the late 1950s was a catastrophic failure, resulting in widespread famine and the deaths of tens of millions of people, while the Cultural Revolution of the 1960s, in which Mao attempted to impose his own particular version of communism across all sections of Chinese society, effectively paralyzed the economy.

The secretive nature of the Chinese Communist Party makes it difficult to know exactly how the movement for the reform of the economy began, but it is widely accepted that the man responsible for it was Deng Xiaoping. He had been a prominent member of the party since its very early days in the 1920s and had taken part in the Long March (the retreat of the Red Army from the Chinese nationalist forces, the Kuomintang, led by Chiang Kai-shek), which would allow the Red Army to regroup and, after the wars of the 1930s and 40s, eventually defeat the Kuomintang. By the 1960s, Deng had been sidelined by Mao, purged from the government for expressing his opposition to the hardline communism of the Cultural Revolution. In his later years, Mao suffered from a number of debilitating illnesses; by the early 1970s China was effectively being ruled by a faction led by his wife Jiang Qing and known as the Gang of Four, who had come to prominence

DENG

DENG XIAOPING

Deng was treated as if he
was the Chinese head of
state by President Jimmy
Carter on a visit to America
in January 1979.

during the Cultural Revolution. Afer Mao's death in September 1976, a power struggle erupted between the Gang of Four and other factions within the Communist Party for overall control of China and, although we don't know the exact circumstances, the outcome was the arrest of Jiang Qing and the other three members of her group at a party meeting in October 1976 on charges of treason. This opened the way for the rehabilitation of Deng, who returned to the government and, by the time of the Congress of the Central Committee of the Communist Party of China, held in December 1978, he had maneuvered himself into a position from which he effectively became the party leader.

At no stage did Deng actually hold any of the highest political offices in China, but while other people were styled as the chairman of the Central Committee or the president of China, it was widely accepted both within China and internationally that up until his death in February 1997, Deng was the one who was really in charge. On an official visit to America in early 1979, he was treated as the Chinese head of state by President Jimmy Carter, and when British Prime Minister Margaret Thatcher went to China in December 1984 to finalize the negotiations over the return of Hong Kong after the end of the lease agreement between the two countries, which ran out in 1997, she held meetings with Deng, even if the final agreement was signed by Chinese Prime Minister Zhao Ziyang rather than Deng himself. But the most prominent role he was to play in China after becoming what is sometimes called its "paramount leader" was the introduction of widespread economic reform, beginning in early 1979, almost as soon as he had taken control of the country.

THE REFORMS

Because of the opaque nature of Chinese politics, it is impossible to say for certain exactly when Deng made the decision to liberalize the Chinese economy, opening it up to the rest of the world and allowing the emergence of free enterprise. The date given here of 1979 only indicates when Deng began to implement his reforms, and there can be little doubt that he had been arguing in favor of the measures he took for at least the past 20 years by that time. Deng described his program of reform as falling into four areas, known as the Four Modernizations:

he fundamentally reorganized the agricultural system to allow family farmers to take over the management of the land and to sell their surplus produce on the free market; the educational system was restructured to place a particular emphasis on science and technology; industry was reorientated toward producing goods for export; and the military was modernized, leading to smaller and more professionally organized armed forces separate from the political structures of the country.

Deng continued to describe himself as a Marxist-Leninist throughout his life, even if the reforms he initiated moved China away from the centrally planned economies characteristic of communism toward the capitalist system of market-orientated free enterprise. The system he introduced has been described as a "socialist market economy," even if the only element of it that could really be described as socialist is the structure of the government itself. In fact, the one area of the Chinese state that has been largely untouched by reform has been politics, which remains as secretive and as undemocratic as it has ever been. After Deng came to power in the late 1970s, a relaxation in both the state control of the media and the repression of opposition to the Communist Party resulted in what appeared to be the beginnings of the adoption of a more democratic system of government, but in the aftermath of the Tiananmen Square protests of 1989 a more hardline approach has been reintroduced. Deng formally retired in 1992, even if he was widely perceived to still be pulling the strings behind the scenes in the Chinese government, and died at the age of 92 in 1997, by which time the Chinese economy was firmly set on the path it continues to follow today. As the Chinese people become increasingly affluent, it remains to be seen if the government can continue to put off the sort of political reform that might have been expected to accompany the economic reforms. By opening up the economy, Deng laid the foundation for the huge economic expansion of China and the full impact of his reforms may not yet have become fully apparent. If this is the case, then Deng's greatest legacy to the Chinese people may be still to come.

CobbleCC | Creative Commons

ECONOMIC BOOM
The rising skyline of Beijing is one indicator of the transformation of the Chinese economy brought about by Deng's reforms.

DECISION

Social Change

Science and Innovation

Culture

Politics

Diplomacy

Military

Religion

NELSON MANDELA REFUSES TO GIVE IN

1985

Circumstances: The long fight against apartheid in South Africa

Protagonists: Nelson Mandela and President P. W. Botha

Consequences: The creation of a new South Africa

During my lifetime I have dedicated myself to this struggle of the African people. I have fought against white domination, and I have fought against black domination. I have cherished the ideal of a democratic and free society in which all persons live together in harmony and with equal opportunities. It is an ideal which I hope to live for and to achieve. But if needs be, it is an ideal for which I am prepared to die.

From the opening statement for the defense made by Nelson Mandela at his trial in Pretoria on April 20, 1964

© Pierre-Jean Durieu | Shutterstock

ROBBEN ISLAND

On January 31, 1985, the president of South Africa, P. W. Botha, announced in parliament that he was prepared to release Nelson Mandela from prison if he "unconditionally rejected violence as a political weapon." It was not the first time Botha had made such an offer, except on previous occasions a further condition had been attached that Mandela go into voluntary exile in the Transkei, one of the territories known as Bantustans set up by Botha's government as "homelands" for the black inhabitants of the country. On February 10, Mandela released a statement, read out by his daughter Zindzi at a mass meeting in Jabulani Stadium, Soweto, in which he said, "I am surprised at the conditions that the government wants to impose on me. I am not a violent man." He then spoke directly of Botha, saying:

> Let him renounce violence. Let him say that he will dismantle apartheid. Let him unban the people's organization, the African National Congress. Let him free all who have been imprisoned, banished, or exiled for their opposition to apartheid. Let him guarantee free political activity so that people may decide who will govern them.

He went on to say, "Only free men can negotiate. Prisoners cannot enter into contracts," and stated his position in words that nobody could misinterpret: "I cannot and will not give any undertaking at a time when I and you, the people, are not free."

By the time Mandela made this statement he had served 22 years of the life sentence he had received in 1964 for sabotage, the first 18 of which had involved hard labor in the lime quarry of the notorious prison on Robben Island. In such circumstances it would have been understandable, to say the least, if he had decided that he had done his bit for the cause of ending apartheid in South Africa and agreed to the terms of Botha's offer, particularly considering that he had long since embraced the Gandhian philosophy of civil disobedience and nonviolent protest. In not only rejecting the offer but also refusing to enter into any dealings with Botha he both retained the moral high ground and refocused the attention of the rest of the world on the situation in South Africa. It could be argued that as Mandela had been committed to the antiapartheid cause since the 1950s, he did not actually have to make a decision on this occasion as he had long ago made up his mind to commit himself to ending apartheid or dying in the attempt. Nevertheless, whatever his convictions had been in the past,

"I AM SURPRISED AT THE CONDITIONS THAT THE GOVERNMENT WANTS TO IMPOSE ON ME. I AM NOT A VIOLENT MAN."

when faced with the choice of immediate release after 22 years in prison or continuing with a struggle in which there were few indications at the time of the likelihood of a successful outcome, it must have required an extraordinary level of fortitude and inner strength to make the decision to carry on.

MANDELA   Rolihlahla Mandela was born in 1918 in the Transkei region of the Eastern Cape Province. His father, who died from tuberculosis when Mandela was nine, was the chief of his village and came from a junior branch of the Thembu royal family of the region. He was the first member of his family to go to school, where, as a young child, he was given the English name of Nelson. The first sign of political activism came in 1938 when he was attending the University of Fort Hare in the Eastern Cape, where he met Oliver Tambo, the future president of the African National Congress. After his first year he was forced to leave the university because of his activism; he then moved to Johannesburg, initially as a means of avoiding a marriage his family had arranged for him. He found a job as a clerk in a law firm and completed the degree he had started at Fort Hare by correspondence course before going on to study law at the University of Witwatersrand.

By this time he had become friends with Walter Sisulu, a member of the ANC, who would become something of a mentor to Mandela's political development; they would later spend many years together imprisoned on Robben Island. In 1944 Mandela, Sisulu, and Tambo were instrumental in setting up the Youth League of the ANC, created to take a more active role in resisting repression than was then being pursued by the leadership of the ANC. By the end of that decade all three had become prominent in the ANC and had stepped up their activism as a consequence of the 1948 general election in which only white people, who made up about 20% of the population at that time, could vote. It was won by the Afrikaner-dominated National Party, which immediately began to introduce a raft of legislation to implement its policy of apartheid, an Afrikaans word that means "apart," in which people were classified as belonging to one of four racial groups: "white," "native" (black African), "Indian," and "colored," which included people of mixed race and anybody else

© Gallo Images | Getty

ANC ACTIVISTS
Nelson Mandela (on the right) with Oliver Tambo in 1960 during the period when both were on trial for treason.

who did not fit into any of the other categories. The apartheid laws were enacted to keep these groups apart and, as all racist legislation tends to do, the official line was that each group would be "separate but equal." In practice, of course, the laws were intended to maintain the privileged position of white people, who were assigned the use of the best hospitals and schools, while those who belonged to what was considered the lowest class, the black Africans who made up over 70% of the population, faced constant discrimination in almost every aspect of their lives.

One of the consequences of the introduction of the apartheid laws was constant police violence and harassment against members of the ANC, including Mandela. In 1955 the ANC produced a Freedom Charter setting out its core principles of opposition to apartheid and committing the organization to campaigning for a fully democratic and nonracial South Africa. This was declared to be treasonous by the government, and Mandela, together with 150 other members of the ANC, was arrested. The subsequent trial for the capital crime of treason lasted for five years and ultimately ended with all the defendants being acquitted. Mandela cemented his reputation in the ANC at this time and, in 1961, became the leader of Umkhonto we Sizwe (the Spear of the Nation), the armed wing of the ANC formed in response to the Sharpsville massacre of the previous year in which white South African policemen opened fire on a crowd of black antiapartheid protestors, killing 69 people. Up until this point, Mandela had followed the course of nonviolent protest espoused by Mahatma Gandhi, who had developed his methods of protest after personally experiencing racism while living in South Africa, but Mandela came to the conclusion that, as all means of nonviolent protest had been outlawed, the only course of action left open to him was to begin a campaign of sabotage against government-owned property and infrastructure.

On August 5, 1962, Mandela was arrested after 18 months of the campaign of sabotage. He was initially charged with inciting workers to strike and with leaving the country illegally, for which he received a five-year sentence, and then, after the arrest of 19 more ANC members, including Walter Sisulu, he was charged along with nine others with committing over 200 acts of sabotage. The Rivonia Trial, as it became known, after the suburb of Johannesburg where the arrests had been

PRISON

ROBBEN ISLAND
The cell where Nelson Mandela was imprisoned for 18 of the 27 years he spent in jail, now preserved as a museum.

© Miguel Pereira

made, was widely condemned around the world as a sham. Eight of the ten accused, including Mandela and Sisulu, were found guilty, sentenced to life imprisonment, and sent to Robben Island. Conditions in the prison were harsh, particularly for black inmates, and Mandela and Sisulu were held there until 1982, when both were transferred to Pollsmoor Maximum Security Prison in Cape Town. The government would later say that this was done so that contact between Mandela and P. W. Botha could be established, but a more likely explanation is that he was moved to stop the influence he was having on younger ANC activists who had also been imprisoned on Robben Island in what had become known as the Mandela University.

By this time Mandela had become famous around the world as the leader of the antiapartheid movement and was the focus of numerous campaigns aimed at putting pressure on the South African government. It was under these circumstance that President Botha made the offer to release him under condition that he reject violence, which was almost a tacit admission that the South African government had no better idea how to deal with Mandela than the British had done with Gandhi more than 50 years beforehand. In 1988, Mandela, now 70 years old, was moved to the low-security Victor Verster Prison in the Western Cape, an indication that the government was actively considering releasing him. Botha suffered a mild stroke in the following year and, against his wishes, was maneuvered out of office by reform-minded colleagues in the National Party, paving the way for the more progressive F. W. de Clerk to become president.

Almost as soon as he entered office in September 1989, de Clerk announced that the ban on the ANC, in force since the 1950s, was to be lifted and he began the process of dismantling the apartheid system. On February 2, 1990, he announced that Mandela was to be released and, nine days later and in front of the world's media, he walked out of Victor Verster Prison, a free man for the first time in 27 years. After being released, Mandela was elected as president of the ANC and entered into multiparty negotiations with the South African government aimed at establishing the first fully democratic elections in the country's history. The process was marred by violent confrontations between ANC supporters and those of the Inkatha Freedom Party, leading to fears of a descent into factional fighting between different antiapartheid groups as well as the chance of the eruption of a more widespread conflict based on racial differences. The murder of the ANC leader Chris Hani on April 10, 1993, by a white man who had received help from a member of the right-wing Conservative Party, caused all sides participating in the negotiations to renew their efforts to reach a settlement before chaos ensued, and Mandela made a television address to the nation appealing for calm, looking very much like the president-in-waiting.

At the general election held on April 27, 1994, the ANC won a landslide victory and Nelson Mandela became the first black president of South Africa. The date symbolically marked the end of the apartheid era and has become a national holiday in South Africa, known as Freedom Day, while Nelson Mandela's birthday, July 18, has been declared Mandela Day by the United Nations, one of numerous tributes paid to the great man that have also included the Nobel Peace Prize, awarded in 1993 jointly to Mandela and F. W. de Clerk. In 1999, Mandela retired from politics at the age of 80, having served one term as president and in the knowledge that his life's work had been successfully completed, even if the process of reconciliation that he began still has a long way to go.

GORBACHEV INSTITUTES PERESTROIKA

1986

Circumstances: The disastrous economic situation of the Soviet Union in the 1980s

Protagonists: Mikhail Gorbachev and the people of Eastern Europe and the Soviet Union

Consequences: The collapse of the Soviet Union, the end of the Cold War, and the beginnings of democracy in Eastern Europe

He had no grand plan and no predetermined policies; but if Gorbachev had not been Party General Secretary, the decisions of summer 1986 would have been different. The USSR's long-lasting order would have endured for many more years, and almost certainly the eventual collapse of the order would have been much bloodier than it was to be in 1991. The irony was that Gorbachev, in trying to prevent the descent of the system into general crisis, proved instrumental in bringing forward that crisis and destroying the USSR.

Robert Service, *A History of Twentieth-Century Russia*

At the 27th Congress of the Communist Party of the Soviet Union, held in Moscow in February 1986, Mikhail Gorbachev, who had become general secretary of the party in March of the previous year, made a speech in which he set out his intention to revive the Soviet economy. In doing so he used two words, *perestroika* and *glasnost*, which were picked up by the Western media and came to represent a sea change in both the method of government employed within the Soviet Union and how it was perceived by other countries. Perestroika means "restructuring" and referred to the changes Gorbachev was in the process of instituting in the political and economic structures of the Soviet Union, while glasnost is usually translated into English as "openness" and, in the sense in which it was being used, referred to a policy of transparency in the workings of government and a willingness to discuss the failures of the past publicly by allowing more freedom of the press and of the individual to express opinions contrary to the party line.

Two other words he used in the same speech that did not find such wide acceptance outside the Soviet Union but were equally important in describing his plan were *demokratizatsiya* (democratization) and *uskoreniye*, which means "acceleration" and was used by Gorbachev to highlight the urgency of the need for change and to express his desire to take the necessary measures as quickly as possible. What the speech did not contain was any detail about what these changes actually would entail or how he intended to go about implementing them and it is generally accepted now that he most probably did not know himself at the time. But the decisions made by Gorbachev had consequences far beyond what he had envisaged, and the eventual outcome was almost exactly the opposite to what had been intended, not only transforming the Soviet Union, but leading to its dissolution, as well as playing a part in the reunification of Germany, the revolutions throughout Eastern Europe and the end of the Cold War.

The situation Gorbachev inherited on becoming general secretary was both politically and economically dire. The policy of Leonid Brezhnev, the Soviet leader from 1966 to 1982, had been to build up the military capability of the USSR in order to compete with the Americans, but in doing so he had starved the domestic economy of investment and it had stagnated. Over the course of his premiership, the government heirarchy had become stuffed with aging party officials, leading to high

THE SOVIET ECONOMY

levels of corruption and a resistance to change in any form, while the Soviet Union and the Warsaw Pact countries of Eastern Europe had been kept together by the threat of military force, much as it had been during the Stalinist era of the past. Productivity rates in industry and agriculture had been falling for decades, while the state had attempted to conceal the disastrous nature of the economic decline from the people of the Soviet Union by means of the repression of free speech. At the same time as the economy was falling apart, Gorbachev also had to deal with the continuing war in Afghanistan, which the Soviet Union had started in 1978 in support of the failing communist regime there and that showed no sign of coming to an end, and, from April 1986, he also had to contend with the Chernobyl nuclear disaster, the worst accident to occur in a nuclear power station in history.

GORBACHEV

Gorbachev had risen through the ranks of the Communist Party to gain a position on the Politburo, its central committee and governing body, in 1979 and had come to prominence under the leadership of Yuri Andropov after he became general secretary on the death of Brezhnev. Andropov died at the age of 70 after only 15 months in charge and was succeeded by an even older man, Konstantin Chernenko, who was also in ill health and died in February 1984. It had become obvious that the next general secretary needed to be a younger and healthier man and, as Gorbachev was the youngest member of the Politiburo at 54 and was not tarnished by association with his predecessors, he became the obvious choice to become the next general secretary. He immediately attempted to begin the process of change that was essential for the future of the Soviet Union, but quickly came to realize that the only way he could bring about reform in the face of resistance from the old guard in the party was to make the disastrous state of the economy and the mistakes of the past known to the people of the country, who had previously only been kept informed by party propaganda.

The policy of glasnost was supposed to be the method by which Gorbachev could make his case for reform more widely known, but once he had allowed the Soviet media the freedom to criticize the past performance of the party in maintaining the economy, they began to go much further than he had anticipated. Gorbachev's idea of democratization had been limited to introducing elections to appoint party members to positions within the Communist Party and he had no intention of extending this to include free elections in a multiparty democratic system, but once he had allowed people to freely express their opinions, they not only began to demand full democracy, but the republics making up the Soviet Union, with the exception of Russia, saw it as an opportunity to demand independence. Much the same occurred in the Eastern European countries of the Warsaw Pact and when it became apparent that Gorbachev was not going to use military force to prevent them from breaking away, as previous Soviet regimes had done, the slow movement toward democracy suddenly gained momentum. In 1989 a wave of revolutions swept through Eastern Europe and by 1991 the communist governments had been abolished in Hungary, Poland, Bulgaria, Czechoslovakia, and East Germany.

POLITICAL RIVALS
Mikhail Gorbachev and Boris Yeltsin shake hands after the failure of an attempted coup d'état against Gorbachev in August 1991.

© Time & Life | Getty Images

At the same time as Eastern European countries were abolishing communism, the Soviet republics were agitating for independence and once the first one, Lithuania, had declared itself independent without Russian interference, most of the others immediately followed suit. In August 1991, hardliners in the communist regime attempted to stage a coup d'état against Gorbachev so that they could reimpose an authoritarian central government. Gorbachev was held under house arrest for two days, until a popular uprising in Moscow led by his political opponent Boris Yeltsin overcame the coup and Gorbachev was released. In December the remaining members of the Soviet Union, now only made up of Russia, Ukraine, and Belarus, agreed on a formal dissolution. Gorbachev resigned his position and, after the first democratic election ever to be held in Russia, Yeltsin was voted in as its new president.

As events overtook him, Gorbachev hardly had the chance to begin the process of perestroika before the entire edifice of the communist state came crashing down, so in this sense his decision to transform the Soviet Union could be considered a disastrous failure. But given that the Soviet Union could only have been maintained in the long run by the use of military force, then what Gorbachev achieved, unintended as it may have been, was a relatively peaceful transition to a more democratic form of government.

DECISION

Social Change

Science and Innovation

Culture

Politics

Diplomacy

Military

Religion

AUNG SAN SUU KYI RETURNS TO BURMA

1988

Circumstances: A Burmese expatriate returns home to look after her sick mother

Protagonists: Aung San Suu Kyi, her family, and the pro-democracy campaigners of Burma

Consequences: A slim chance that Burma is heading toward democracy

To conclude I would like to reiterate our emphatic demands and protests, namely that we have no desire at all for a referendum, that the one-party system should be dismantled, that a multiparty system of government should be established, and we call for free and fair elections to be arranged as quickly as possible. These are our demands.

The conclusion to the first public speech given by Aung San Suu Kyi on August 26, 1988, at Shwedagon Pagoda in Rangoon

Before returning to Burma in April 1988, Aung San Suu Kyi described herself as being an Oxford housewife. She was married to Michael Avis, an academic specializing in Tibetan literature and culture, and had two teenage sons, so in some respects it was an accurate description. But she was also the daughter of Aung San, the man revered in Burma as "the father of the country" who in 1947 had been instrumental in negotiating Burmese independence from Britain and had been set to become its first prime minister when he and other members of his government-in-waiting had been assassinated by their political rivals. Suu Kyi was only two years old at the time of her father's assassination and at the age of 15 had left Burma when her mother was appointed as the Burmese ambassador to India. After studying in India and then taking a degree in Philosophy, Politics, and Economics at St. Hugh's College, Oxford, she worked at the headquarters of the United Nations in New York for three years and then, after getting married to Avis, studied in India and at the School of African and Oriental Studies in London. It was hardly the normal background of an Oxford housewife and, as Michael Avis would later write, after she had received a telephone call from Burma early in April 1988 to inform her that her 76-year-old mother had suffered a stroke, he instantly knew that their lives of comfortable domesticity would never be the same again.

SUU KYI
Aung San Suu Kyi campaigning in a by-election for the Burmese parliament in March 2012, which she went on to win.

© Htoo Tay Zar | Creative Commons

THE RETURN

The decision to go to Burma had initially been taken so Suu Kyi could look after her mother, who was in hospital in Rangoon (now known as Yangon). When she was well enough, she was moved back to the family home, a colonial-era house situated on Inya Lake on the outskirts of the city. Suu Kyi was 42 years old and had not lived in Burma for any length of time since leaving the country at 15, only returning occasionally for short visits to see her family. Her visit on this occasion coincided with a tumultuous period in the post-independence history of Burma, which had been under military rule since a coup d'état in 1962 ousted the democratically elected civilian government. The coup had been led by General Ne Min and he and his military government attempted to impose a Soviet-style system on the country with disastrous results. Through a combination of ineptitude and corruption, the country had become one of the most impoverished in the world, despite being rich in natural resources, and in the summer of 1988 dissatisfaction with the military government boiled over into mass protests. Ne Min unexpectedly resigned on July 23, warning during the announcement that if the protests continued the army would open fire and would not be shooting into the air. On the auspicious date of August 8, 1988, leading to the protests becoming known as the 8888 Uprising, a general strike was called, together with marches and demonstrations across the country. The government responded in the way Ne Min had said it would, with a show of force in which soldiers fired into unarmed crowds, killing many hundreds of people.

Up until this point, Suu Kyi had not become actively involved in the protests. She remained at home with her mother, but had been visited there over the course of the previous few months by a number of activists in the pro-democracy movement. Even though she had not lived in Burma for almost 30 years, she was a well-known figure in the country because of the reputation of her father and, after the terrible loss of life inflicted on unarmed civilians by the Burmese army, which had been founded by her father, she felt compelled to become involved in the protests. After giving a speech to a small number of people in the hospital where her mother was being treated, her first ever public oratory, on August 26 she addressed a huge crowd, estimated at being at least half a million strong, gathered at the Shwedagon Pagoda in central Rangoon. It was the place where her father had given speeches himself in the fight for independence from the British more than 40 years previously and after his assassination he had been buried near the pagoda. In choosing this spot, Suu Kyi was associating herself with his memory and, as well as calling for free and fair multiparty elections in the country, she also described the uprising as the "second struggle for national independence."

SUU KYI WAS A WELL-KNOWN FIGURE IN THE COUNTRY BECAUSE OF THE REPUTATION OF HER FATHER

On September 18, and with the protests in the streets continuing, General Saw Maung assumed control of the government in what was effectively another coup and began an even harsher crackdown on the protest movement. In the expectation of all opposition political parties being banned by the new military government, Suu Kyi and a number of other prominent pro-democracy campaigners formed their own party, the National League for Democracy, of which she became general secretary. Maung announced that his government would only be in place until elections could be organized, which would take place in May 1990. In July of 1989, Suu Kyi and other members of the National League for Democracy were placed under house arrest, where they would remain throughout the run-up to the election. Despite these restrictions, Suu Kyi's party gained more than 50% of the vote in the election, which translated into 392 of the 492 seats available in the Burmese parliament. At first Maung said that he would only remain in power while a new constitution was being written, but two months later the military government annulled the result of the election.

Suu Kyi was already renowned in Burma even before the pro-democracy protests began, but she became internationally known for the role she played in them and in 1991 was awarded the Nobel Peace Price. Over the next 20 years, she would spend a total of 15 years confined to her house on Inya Lake with only short visits being allowed from her family. In 1997 Michael Avis was diagnosed with terminal cancer and was refused permission to enter the country to visit his wife for one last time. The military government offered to allow Suu Kyi to travel to Britain, but she was aware that if she left Burma she would not be allowed to come back again, so stayed under house arrest. Finally, she was released in November 2010 as part of what appears to be a thaw in the authoritarian military government, which has since permitted her to travel abroad, where she has been showered with accolades and treated as if she were a visiting head of state.

Soe Zeya Tun | Reuters | Corbis

LAKE HOUSE
The family home on Inya Lake where Aung San Suu Kyi spent a total of 15 years under house arrest.

Elections have been held in Burma, even if the government has reserved the majority of the seats in both its chambers of parliament for military candidates and, in May 2012, Suu Kyi won a by-election, taking up her seat in the lower house in July of that year. It is currently too early to tell if the relaxation of military rule that has occurred over the past few years is a genuine attempt to lead Burma toward democracy or is a cynical move by the government to try to ingratiate itself with the international community in order to exploit Burma's natural resources for their own profit. Given the propensity of military rulers, wherever they are from, to cling to power until forced to give it up, the second of these two scenarios would appear to be the more likely, suggesting that Suu Kyi's campaign for reform in Burma is not over yet.

DECISION

Social Change

Science and Innovation

Culture

Politics

Diplomacy

Military

Religion

TIM BERNERS-LEE INVENTS THE WORLD WIDE WEB

1990

Circumstances: A software engineer attempts to find the solution to the problem of how to share information between scientists in a large research institution

Protagonists: Tim Berners-Lee and his fellow workers at CERN

Consequences: The development of the most widely used application on the internet

This is for everybody.

Tweet sent by Tim Berners-Lee while participating in the opening ceremony of the London 2012 Olympic Games

© drserg | Shutterstock

In the late 1980s, Tim Berners-Lee was working as a software engineer at CERN, the European Organization for Nuclear Research in Geneva, which altogether had over 10,000 scientists either working for it directly or affiliated to it in one way or another from universities and research institutions around the world. Even though the internet made life easier for all these people to stay in touch, they could only do so by email and through file sharing, making it time-consuming and not particularly efficient as a means of keeping everybody informed about what everybody else was doing. Berners-Lee had briefly worked for CERN previously, for six months in 1980, when he had developed a prototype of an information-sharing system that he called ENQUIRE. It used hypertext, highlighted words in a piece of text that can be used to link to other texts, as a way of managing large amounts of data, and while this research did not actually lead anywhere and appears to have been lost after he left CERN at the end of the initial six-month contract, the need for a convenient way of managing information remained when he returned some years later.

TIM BERNERS-LEE
The inventor of the World Wide Web making a point at a meeting in the UK Home Office in March 2010.

Between his two stints at CERN, Berners-Lee had been working for a British software firm on developing uses of the internet and, in 1989, decided to try combining the old research he had done on hypertext with the internet as a means of producing a system for sharing information between CERN scientists, wherever they happened to be in the world. In a typically self-deprecating manner, he would later write of how he achieved this: "I just had to take the hypertext idea and connect it to the Transmission Control Protocol and domain name system ideas [on the internet] and—ta-da!—the World Wide Web." Needless to say, it was actually a little more complicated than that, but over the following year, and in collaboration with Robert Cailliau, a computer scientist from Belgium also working at CERN, he designed the first web browser. Then, while the two of them were chatting in the cafeteria about possible names for what they had developed, he suggested it be called the World Wide Web, having realized by then that it had a much wider application than simply as a means for CERN scientists to stay in touch with each other.

WORLD WIDE WEB

By the end of 1990, Berners-Lee and Cailliau had developed a web server and connected a Hypertext Transfer Protocol (HTTP) to it over the internet. By August of the following year, they had put up the first website with the address, Info.cern.ch, which contained the first webpage, http://info.cern.ch/hypertext/WWW/TheProject.html, giving details about the project at CERN and instructions on how to use the World Wide Web. Over the next few years, more servers began to appear in scientific institutions around the world that were not necessarily involved with CERN, including at the National Center for Supercomputing Applications in Illinois, where the Mosaic web browser was developed. As well as allowing images to be placed within text pages for the first time, it was simple to install, easy to use, and worked on PCs and Macs, opening up the web to a much wider number of users among the general public as well as scientists, and setting the standard that has been followed by almost all subsequent web browsers such as Internet Explorer, Mozilla Firefox, and Google Chrome.

ANOTHER DECISION As if making one great decision was not enough, Berners-Lee, together with the management at CERN, then went on to make another one. In 1993, all the software written by Berners-Lee concerning the World Wide Web was placed in the public domain, enabling anybody who wanted to use it for any purpose they had in mind to do so without paying royalties to either Berners-Lee or CERN. In a statement, CERN said:

> CERN relinquishes all intellectual property rights to this code, both source and binary form, and permission is granted for anybody to use, duplicate, modify, or redistribute it.

The statement also explained that CERN was making the code freely available to, "further compatability, common practices, and standards in networking and computer supported collaboration." Berners-Lee later wrote of this decision:

> CERN's decision to make the Web foundations and protocols available on a royalty-free basis, and without additional impediments, was crucial to the Web's existence. Without this commitment, the enormous individual and corporate investment in Web technology simply would never have happened, and we wouldn't have the Web today.

He was again being very modest about his own role in the decision and failed to mention that if commercial companies had been forced to pay royalties for using his code, he could potentially have become a very rich man indeed. But it was this act of selfless generosity, together with the development of the Mosaic browser, which really allowed the Web to flourish. In October 1994, Berners-Lee left CERN to found the World Wide Web Consortium (W3C) at the Massachusetts Institute of Technology to set industry standards for the further development of the Web and to ensure that access to it stays free to everybody.

Berners-Lee remains the director of W3C and in 2009 also set up the World Wide Web Foundation, which describes itself as being, "a nonprofit organization devoted to achieving a world in which all people can use the Web to communicate, collaborate, and innovate freely, building bridges across the divides that threaten our shared future." One of the recent projects of the foundation is the development of the Web Index, which sets out to measure the growth and usage of the Web in numerous countries around the world and ranks them according to how open and inclusive they are in allowing free access to information.

© SSPL | Getty Images

NeXT COMPUTER
Berners-Lee used a computer terminal like this one made by NeXT when developing the World Wide Web.

The contribution Berners-Lee has made to the development and spread of the internet through his invention of the World Wide Web has been extensively recognized over the years. In 2004 he was knighted for "services to the global development of the Internet" and he also took part in the opening ceremony of the London Olympics 2012. In a moment of calm among the madness of the ceremony, Berners-Lee appeared seated at a NeXT computer terminal like the one he used to invent the World Wide Web. As he was working for a European organization at the time, located in Switzerland and France, had a Belgian collaborator, and was using computer equipment made in America by the company set up by Steve Jobs after he left Apple in 1985, it is debatable just how much the World Wide Web can be considered a British contribution to international culture. But, minor quibbles aside, the decisions that led to the development of the World Wide Web and then to making it freely available to everybody must surely be among the greatest made in the history of information technology, on a level with the inventions of writing and the printing press. The potential of the internet is still being explored, but there can be little doubt that the work done by Tim Berners-Lee will continue to play a part in its future development, which, if Berners-Lee has anything to do with it, whatever the next development may be, it will also be made freely available to us all.

DECISION

Social Change

Science and Innovation

Culture

Politics

Diplomacy

Military

Religion

APPLE REEMPLOYS STEVE JOBS

1996

Circumstances: After being forced out of the company he founded, Steve Jobs is offered an opportunity to return

Protagonists: Steve Jobs and other past and present employees of Apple

Consequences: The struggling computer company was transformed into the market leader in consumer electronics

Jobs, exuding confidence, style, and sheer magnetism, was the antithesis of the fumbling Amelio [the CEO of Apple at the time] as he strode onstage. The return of Elvis would not have provoked a bigger sensation.

From a report on Macworld 1997, Steve Jobs' first public appearance after returning to Apple, by Jim Carlton of the *Wall Street Journal*

© Yutaka Tsutano

Steve Jobs, who died in October 2011 after suffering from pancreatic cancer for a number of years, set up Apple in his garage at the age of 21 along with his old school friend Steve Wozniak and Ronald Wayne, who was 20 years older than Jobs and described his role in the fledgling company as being one of "adult supervision." Wayne sold his 10% share in the company for $800 shortly after it was incorporated, which, with the benefit of hindsight, was probably not the best business deal he had ever done. In 2012, its market capitalization (the value of one share multiplied by the number of shares issued) was $625 billion, making it the most valuable publicly traded company in the world and worth more than two and a half times as much as Microsoft. The phenomenal success of the company can mostly be attributed to the diversification of its business, from concentrating solely on computers and software to include innovative consumer electronics like the iPod, iPhone, and iPad, and to its marketing strategy, which has made these products the must-have accessories for much of the past 15 years even though, or perhaps because, they have often been more expensive than their competitors. Much of the credit for this success goes to Jobs, who right from the start was not heavily involved in the technical side of product development, but had an extraordinary ability to spot the commercial potential of new technology and recognized the importance of design and marketing in placing new products into the marketplace.

STEVE JOBS
Jobs was described as inspirational and mercurial by some and abrasive and impossible to work with by others.

The fortunes of Apple have not always been so bright, particularly in the mid 1980s when, despite having what was widely regarded as a superior product, the company began to fall behind Microsoft in the lucrative and expanding market in personal computers. In 1983, Jobs had hired John Sculley as chairman and chief executive of Apple, persuading him to move from Pepsi. Jobs remained in his role as operations director for the Macintosh division of the company, with a management style that could be inspirational at one moment and abusive at another. The relationship between Jobs and Sculley broke down over the pricing policy of a new Macintosh model and was not helped by Jobs frequently describing Sculley behind his back as a "bozo" who was wrecking the company. Tensions came to a head at a board meeting in May 1985 at

STEVE LEAVES

which Jobs attempted to regain control of the company, but was out-voted and removed from his managerial position. He resigned a few weeks later and took five other disillusioned employees with him to start NeXT, which specialized in producing personal computer workstations for universities and research institutions and supplied the computer used by Tim Berners-Lee at CERN to invent the World Wide Web.

AND COMES BACK AGAIN

In the early 1990s, the performance of Apple dipped badly as a result of the launch of a number of unsuccessful products. By 1994, Martin Spindler had replaced John Sculley as CEO of the company and had identified the outdated nature of the Macintosh platform and its operating system as being the main cause of the company's problems. He attempted to rectify this situation by effectively buying in new technology rather than developing it themselves, but his efforts yielded few results. In February 1996, Spindler was replaced by Gil Amelio, who did not get along very well with Jobs, but nevertheless was aware that the best solution to the problems at Apple, which had begun to lose significant amounts of money, was to use the operating system that had been developed by NeXT.

By the time Amelio made Jobs an offer to buy NeXT, Jobs was in his 40s and married with children. The animation company Pixar, which he had bought in 1985, had also just had a major success with the movie *Toy Story*. He remained as driven and inspirational as he had ever been, but perhaps the changing circumstances of his life had made him less abrasive and, as the founder of Apple, he appears to have wanted the opportunity to revitalize the struggling company. A deal was struck between Amelio and Jobs in which Apple paid $427 million in shares for NeXT and Jobs was given a seat on the board of directors. It would prove to be a brilliant decision for Apple as a company, but not so great for Amelio personally because Jobs soon replaced him as CEO. The iMac range of desktop computers was released in 1998 and sold well, marking the beginning of a change in fortunes that continued with other "i" products launched by Jobs himself in a series of highly publicized events at which he was always seen wearing his trademark pair of Levi's and black turtleneck sweater. The enthusiasm he brought to these demonstrations was certainly a key reason for the turnaround of the company, but what really did the trick was making things that a huge number of people wanted to buy. It remains to be seen whether the company can continue its remarkable run of success without the man who started it all in the first place.

THE GOOD FRIDAY AGREEMENT

1998

DECISION

Social Change

Science and Innovation

Culture

Politics

Diplomacy

Military

Religion

Circumstances: The long and difficult peace process in Northern Ireland

Protagonists: David Trimble, John Hume, Ian Paisley, Martin McGuinness, Gerry Adams, together with many political leaders from Britain, the Republic of Ireland, and America, and the long-suffering people of Northern Ireland

Consequences: The chance of peace

1. (1) It is hereby declared that Northern Ireland in its entirety remains part of the United Kingdom and shall not cease to be so without the consent of a majority of the people of Northern Ireland voting in a poll held for the purposes of this section in accordance with Schedule 1.

(2) But if the wish expressed by a majority in such a poll is that Northern Ireland should cease to be part of the United Kingdom and form part of a united Ireland, the Secretary of State shall lay before Parliament such proposals to give effect to that wish as may be agreed between Her Majesty's Government in the United Kingdom and the Government of Ireland.

The first clause of the Good Friday Agreement

The signing of the agreement in Belfast on Good Friday, April 10, 1998, by representatives of the British and Irish Governments together with those from most of the main political parties of Northern Ireland was a major milestone in the long and often tortuous peace process in that country. It was not actually a peace treaty because there was never any declaration of war in the first place, but it provided a framework through which it was hoped that the armed conflict, the Troubles as it was commonly called, would finally come to an end. One of the provisions set out in the final document was for a referendum to be held in Northern Ireland to either accept or reject the terms set out in the agreement and a separate referendum for the Republic of Ireland to vote on the required amendments to the Irish constitution. Both were held on May 22 of that year and both results were emphatic endorsements of the agreement: in Northern Ireland 71% of those taking part voted in favor of accepting the agreement, while in the Republic an emphatic 94% voted to change the constitution, giving up the Republic's claim on the territory of Northern Ireland and extending the right to Irish citizenship to include the whole of Ireland. The implementation of the Good Friday Agreement, then, was not only the result of decisions taken by politicians in Britain, the Republic of Ireland, and Northern Ireland, but was also a collective decision taken throughout Ireland, North and South, to, in the words of John Lennon, "give peace a chance."

THE TROUBLES The conflict is often said to have begun in 1969, when serious rioting occurred in a number of cities in Northern Ireland resulting in the deployment of the British Army, and came to an end with the signing of the Good Friday Agreement. But the roots of the Troubles can be traced back all the way to the sixteenth and seventeenth centuries, when Protestant immigrants from England and Scotland were given land formally belonging to Irish Catholics in what were known as the Irish plantations. And, while the Troubles may be formally over, the peace process is an ongoing one, occasionally interrupted by acts of sectarian violence, even if most of the paramilitary organizations on both sides have declared an end to the conflict and, to use the terminology employed, put their weapons "beyond use." The British Army operation in the province was drastically scaled down after the Good Friday Agreement was signed and, in August 2007, also formally came to an end.

The direct cause of the Troubles was the everyday discrimination faced by the Catholic minority of Northern Ireland after the partition of Ireland in 1922, when the 26 counties of the mainly Catholic South became the Irish Free State and subsequently, in 1937, the Republic of Ireland, while the six counties of the North, where Protestants made up about two-thirds of the population, remained part of Britain. The purpose of this partition was to avoid a civil war threatened by armed volunteer forces loyal to the British Crown, who thought that, in a united Ireland, the Protestants of the North would face discrimination from the Catholic-dominated government in Dublin. Despite being well aware of the problem, the government of Northern Ireland allowed discriminatory practices to occur in the province and took measures to ensure that the Protestant majority would continue to dominate the political process. There were no actual laws in place to enforce the discrimination, but the inbuilt bias in the political system together with the police force, the Royal Ulster Constabulary, being made up entirely of Protestants led to a deep sense of resentment in the Catholic community. The fact that government jobs and public housing were also allocated along sectarian lines, with Catholics always being last in line, only served to increase the frustration further.

© Fribbler | Creative Commons

BELFAST 1970
A loyalist banner on a street off the Shankill Road, scene of numerous acts of violence during the 30 years of the Troubles.

The bewildering array of political parties and paramilitary groups in Northern Ireland throughout the period of the Troubles makes an already complex situation even more confusing. In a nutshell, the Protestant majority are described as unionists and loyalists because of their desire to remain part of the union of Britain and their loyalty to the British Crown. The two main unionist political parties involved in the peace process were the Ulster Unionist Party, led by David Trimble, and the Democratic Unionist Party, led by Ian Paisley, both of whom, prior to the peace process, had been fiercely against any dealings with anybody from the opposite side. The republicans, almost exclusively made up of Catholics who wanted a united Ireland, leading to them also being known as nationalists, were represented by the moderate Social Democratic and Labour Party, under the leadership of the highly respected John Hume, and Sinn Féin. This was the political wing of the

THE OPPOSING SIDES

Provisional Irish Republican Army, originally a splinter group of the the IRA, which had fought against the British in the struggle for Irish independence, which, after its formation in December 1969, became by far the most effective of the numerous paramilitary organizations in the province. The two key figures in Sinn Féin were Martin McGuinness and Gerry Adams, both of whom, it has been alleged, had at one time held senior positions in the IRA.

THE PROCESS The peace process gradually emerged out of secret meetings held between representatives of the British Government and Sinn Féin, beginning in the late 1980s, together with the development of a perception on both sides that there could be no military solution to the Troubles. Over the years, these talks developed into a wider set of negotiations that included the Irish Government as well and in which John Hume and David Trimble played significant roles, recognized in 1998 by the joint award of the Nobel Peace Prize. President Bill Clinton was also involved in getting the process going, inviting Gerry Adams for what was at the time considered a controversial visit to America in January 1994 and personally visiting the province on a number of occasions. The month before Adams's visit to America, the British prime minister, John Major, and Irish Taoiseach, Albert Reynolds, issued the joint Downing Street Declaration, which contained much of what would later form the Good Friday Agreement, in which both recognized the right of the people of Northern Ireland to self-determination and the British Government stated that it had "no selfish strategic or economic interest in Northern Ireland."

In April 1994, the IRA announced a three-day ceasefire, which it described as a "temporary cessation of hostilities," and this was followed five months later by a "cessation of military operations," taken by most people, but by no means all, to mean a permanent ceasefire. It was followed by a ceasefire announcement from the main loyalist paramilitary organizations, including the Ulster Volunteer Force and Ulster Defence Association, and a long and acrimonious argument developed between the politicians from both sides concerning the issue of the decommissioning of the arms held by the various paramilitaries in which one party or another would find a reason to boycott the negotiations, and Ian Paisley regularly lived up to his nickname of Dr. No for refusing to have anything to do with just about everybody else.

The logjam was in part broken by Clinton, first in appointing Senator George Mitchell as the US Special Envoy to Northern Ireland, a position he used to develop a set of principles to get the peace process moving and to negotiate the decommissioning of weapons, and second by visiting the province in November 1995 and speaking at a mass rally in Belfast in which he described terrorists of both sides as being "yesterday's men."

George Mitchell went on to chair the formal peace negotiations and his great patience and good sense were two of the main reasons for the eventual success of the talks. He had, for instance, to deal with the apparently insurmountable obstacle of some loyalist politicians, including Paisley, refusing to join negotiations before the IRA had decommissioned its arms, while the IRA refused to give up its weapons until the talks had begun. Somehow Mitchell managed to find a way through this minefield and even continued with the talks after the IRA returned to its campaign of violence in 1996, setting off huge bombs in the City of London and the center of Manchester. The ceasefire was reestablished in July 1997 and the peace process was pushed along by newly elected Prime Minister Tony Blair.

After two years of interrupted negotiations, the Good Friday Agreement was finally signed and, as well as setting out the position of the British and Irish Governments, it contained clauses concerning weapons decommissioning and the setting up of a devolved assembly in Northern Ireland. At the first session of the assembly government, Ian Paisley was sworn in as first minister with Martin McGuinness as his deputy, while Tony Blair watched the proceedings from the gallery of the parliament, apparently sitting a few seats away from the senior leadership of the IRA. In what must be the most remarkable turnaround in the history of Northern Irish politics, the 81-year-old Paisley not only embraced the peace process, but appeared to get on very well personally with his former archenemy McGuinness. As Paisley remarked at the first meeting of the assembly, it was very much the start of peace in Northern Ireland, not the complete solution, but if he can put the past behind him and look toward a brighter future for all the people of Northern Ireland, then surely there must be hope that the hard-won peace can last.

PEACE MAKERS
British Prime Minister Tony Blair, former Senator George Mitchell, and Irish Taoiseach Bertie Ahern at a press conference in July 1999.

© AFP | Getty Images

FURTHER READING

The First Stone Tools

Scarre, Chris, Ed. The Human Past: World Prehistory and the Development of Human Societies. London: Thames and Hudson, 2009.

Stringer, Chris, and Peter Andrews. The Complete World of Human Evolution. London: Thames and Hudson, 2005.

Stringer, Chris. The Origin of Our Species. London: Allen Lane, 2011.

The Migration Out of Africa

Oppenheimer, Stephen. Out of Eden: The Peopling of the World. London: Constable, 2003.

Roberts, Alice. The Incredible Human Journey. London: Bloomsbury, 2009.

An interactive map showing human migrations, www.bradshawfoundation.com/journey

The First Farmers

Barker, Graeme. The Agricultural Revolution in Prehistory: Why did Foragers become Farmers? Oxford: OUP, 2006.

Cauvin, Jacques. The Birth of the Gods and the Origins of Agriculture. Cambridge: CUP, 2000.

Dietrich, Oliver et al. The role of cult and feasting in the emergence of Neolithic communities. New evidence from Göbekli Tepe, south-eastern Turkey. Antiquity 86 (2012), p. 674–695.

The Sumerians Begin to Write

Glassner, Jean-Jaques. The Invention of Cuneiform: Writing in Sumer. Baltimore: John Hopkins University Press, 2003.

Van De Mieroop, Marc. A History of the Ancient Near East: ca. 3000–323 BC (2nd edition.). Oxford: Blackwell, 2007.

The Egyptian and Hittite Peace Treaty

Bryce, Trevor. The Kingdom of the Hittites. Oxford: OUP, 2005.

Shaw, Ian. The Oxford History of Ancient Egypt. Oxford: OUP, 2000.

The Athenians Choose Democracy

Dunn, John. Democracy: The Unfinished Journey 508 BC to AD 1993. Oxford: OUP, 1992.

Keane, John. The Life and Death of Democracy. London: Simon and Schuster, 2009.

Miles, Richard. Ancient Worlds: The Search for the Origins of Western Civilisation. London: Allen Lane, 2010.

Siddhartha Gotama Goes in Search of Enlightenment

Armstrong, Karen. Buddha. London: Weidenfeld and Nicholson, 2000.

Keown, Damien. Buddhism: A Very Short Introduction. Oxford: OUP, 1996.

Ashoka the Great Renounces War

Allen, Charles. Ashoka: The Search for India's Lost Emperor. London: Little Brown, 2012.

Keay, John. India: A History from the Earliest Civilisations to the Boom of the Twenty-First Century. London: HarperCollins, 2000.

Julius Caesar Crosses the Rubicon

Caesar, Julius. The Civil War. London: Penguin, 1967.

Goldsworthy, Adrian. Caesar: The Life of a Colossus. London: Weidenfeld and Nicholson, 2006.

Holland, Tom. Rubicon: The Triumph and Tragedy of the Roman Republic. London: Little Brown, 2003.

Paul on the Road to Damascus

Freeman, Charles. A New History of Early Christianity. New Haven: Yale University Press, 2009.

Grant, Michael. Saint Paul. London: Weidenfeld and Nicholson, 1976.

Wilson, A. N. Paul: The Mind of the Apostle. London: Sinclair Stevenson, 1997.

An episode of the BBC Radio 4 program In Our Time on St. Paul, www.bbc.co.uk/programmes/b00kjk8z

Constantine Converts to Christianity

Cameron, Averil. *The Later Roman Empire: AD 284–430*. London: Fontana Press, 1993.

Odahl, Charles Matson. *Constantine and the Christian Empire*. London: Routledge, 2004.

Stephenson, Paul. *Constantine: Unconquered Emperor, Christian Victor*. London: Quercus, 2009.

The Magna Carta

Danziger, Danny and John Gillingham. *1215: The Year of the Magna Carta*. London: Hodder and Stoughton, 2003.

Holt, J. C. *Magna Carta*. 2nd edition. Cambridge: CUP, 1992.

Vincent, Nicholas. *Magna Carta: A Very Short Introduction*. Oxford: OUP, 2012.

Webpage about the British Library's copies of Magna Carta, www.bl.uk/treasures/magnacarta/index.html

The Medici Open a Bank

Jardine, Lisa. *Worldly Goods*. London: MacMillan, 1996.

Parks, Tim. *Medici Money: Banking, Metaphysics, and Art in Fifteenth-Century Florence*. London: Profile Books, 2005.

Strathern, Paul. *The Medici: Godfathers of the Renaissance*. London: Jonathan Cape, 2003.

Gutenberg Prints a Bible

Eisenstein, Elizabeth L. *The Printing Revolution in Early Modern Europe*. Cambridge: CUP, 2005.

Kapr, Albert. *Johann Gutenberg: The Man and his Invention*. Aldershot: Scholar Press, 1996.

Man, John. *The Gutenberg Revolution: The Story of a Genius and an Invention that Changed the World*. London: Review, 2002.

Ferdinand and Isabella Commission Christopher Columbus

Columbus, Christopher. *The Four Voyages of Christopher Columbus*. Harmondsworth: Penguin, 1969.

Sale, Kirkpatrick. *The Conquest of Paradise: Christopher Columbus and the Columbian Legacy*. London: Hodder and Stoughton, 1991.

Thomas, Hugh. *Rivers of Gold: The Rise of the Spanish Empire*. London: Weidenfeld and Nicholson, 2003.

The Siege of Vienna

Finkel, Caroline, *Osman's Dream: The Story of the Ottoman Empire 1300–1923*. London: John Murray, 2005.

Reston, James. *Defenders of the Faith: Christianity and Islam Battle for the Soul of Europe, 1520–1536*. New York: The Penguin Press, 2009.

Copernicus Publishes *On the Revolutions of Celestial Spheres*

Repcheck, Jack. *Copernicus' Secret: How the Scientific Revolution Began*. London: JR Books, 2009.

Sobel, Dava. *A More Perfect Heaven: How Copernicus Revolutionised the Cosmos*. London: Bloomsbury, 2011.

Michel de Montaigne Retires from Public Life

Bakewell, Sarah. *How to Live: A Life of Montaigne in One Question and Twenty Attempts at an Answer*. London: Chatto and Windus, 2010.

Langer, Ullrich, Ed. *The Cambridge Companion to Montaigne*. Cambridge: CUP, 2005.

Montaigne, Michel de. *The Complete Essays*. London: Penguin, 2003.

Descartes Finds His Reason

Grayling, A. C. *Descartes: The Life of Réne Descartes and its Place in His Times*. London: The Free Press, 2005.

Southwell, Gareth. *A Beginner's Guide to Descartes's Meditations*. Oxford: Wiley-Blackwell, 2007.

Newton Goes Back to School

Aughton, Peter. *Newton's Apple: Isaac Newton and the English Scientific Renaissance*. London: Weidenfeld and Nicholson, 2003.

Gleik, James. *Isaac Newton*. London: Fourth Estate, 2003.

The Newton Project webpage, an attempt to publish all of his writings, www.newtonproject.sussex.ac.uk

National Trust webpage on Newton's birthplace, www.nationaltrust.org.uk/woolsthorpe-manor

Peter the Great Reforms Russia

Crackcraft, James. *The Revolution of Peter the Great*. Cambridge, Massachusetts: Harvard University Press, 2003.

Massie, Robert K. *Peter the Great: His Life and World*. London: Victor Gollancz, 1981.

The Declaration of Independence

Armitage, David. *The Declaration of Independence: A Global History*. Cambridge, Massachusetts: Harvard University Press, 2007.

Ellis, Joseph J. *American Creation: Triumphs and Tragedies at the Founding of the Republic*. New York: Alfred A. Knopf, 2007.

The Library of Congress webpage on the declaration, www.loc.gov/rr/program/bib/ourdocs/DeclarInd.html

The Storming of the Bastille

Doyle, William. *The French Revolution: A Very Short Introduction*. Oxford: OUP, 2001.

Hibbert, Christopher. *The French Revolution*. London: Allen Lane, 1980.

Schama, Simon. *Citizens: A Chronicle of the French Revolution*. London: Viking, 1989.

The Louisiana Purchase

Kennedy, Roger G. *Mr. Jefferson's Lost Cause: Land, Farmers, Slavery, and the Louisiana Purchase*. Oxford: OUP, 2004.

Kukla, Jon. *A Wilderness So Immense: The Louisiana Purchase and the Destiny of America*. New York: Alfred A. Knopf, 2003.

The collection of papers relating to the Louisiana Purchase held by the Library of Congress in Washington, www.loc.gov/rr/program/bib/ourdocs/Louisiana.html

The Congress of Vienna

Hobsbawm, Eric. *The Age of Revolution: Europe 1789–1848*. London: Weidenfeld and Nicholson, 1962.

Thompson, David. *Europe Since Napoleon*. Harmondsworth: Pelican Books, 1966.

Zamoyski, Adam. *Rites of Passage: The Fall of Napoleon and the Congress of Vienna*. London: HarperPress, 2007.

A series of interactive maps showing the changes to European borders decided at the Congress of Vienna, www.the-map-as-history.com/maps/1_history-europe-XIX-congress-vienna.php

Karl Drais and the Laufmaschine

Herlihy, David V. *Bicycle: The History*. New Haven: Yale University Press, 2004.

A *New Scientist* article on Drais, www.newscientist.com/article/mg18524841.900-brimstone-and-bicycles

The Monroe Doctrine

Cunningham, Noble E. *The Presidency of James Monroe*. Lawrence: University of Kansas, 1996.

Howe, Daniel Walker. *What Hath God Wrought: The Transformation of America, 1815–1848*. Oxford: OUP, 2007.

Darwin Joins the Voyage of HMS *Beagle*

Brown, Janet. *Charles Darwin: Voyaging: Volume 1 of a Biography*. London: Jonathan Cape, 1995.

Darwin, Charles. *Autobiographies*. London: Penguin Books, 2002.

Darwin, Charles. *Voyage of the Beagle*. London: Penguin Books, 1989.

Lincoln and Emancipation

Goodwin, Doris Kearns. *Team of Rivals: The Political Genius of Abraham Lincoln*. New York: Simon and Schuster, 2005.

McPherson, James M. *Battle Cry of Freedom: The Civil War Era*. Oxford: OUP, 1988.

Striner, Richard. *Father Abraham: Lincoln's Relentless Struggle to End Slavery*. Oxford: OUP, 2006.

The Wright Brothers Build an Airplane

Tobin, James. *First to Fly: The Unlikely Triumph of Wilbur and Orville Wright*. London: John Murray, 2003.

Link to the Smithsonian National Air and Space Museum exhibition on the Wright Brothers, airandspace.si.edu/wrightbrothers

D. W. Griffith Makes a Movie in Hollywood

Schickel, Richard. *D. W. Griffith*. London: Pavilion Books, 1984.

Gandhi and Civil Disobedience

Fischer, Louis. *The Life Of Mahatma Gandhi*. London: Cape, 1951.

Gandhi, M. K. *An Autobiography: or My Experiments with the Truth*. London: Penguin Books, 1982.

Robert Johnson at the Crossroads

Gioia, Ted. *Delta Blues: The Life and Times of the Mississippi Masters who Revolutionised American Music*. New York: W.W. Norton and Company, 2008.

Wald, Elijah. *Escaping the Delta: Robert Johnson and the Invention of the Blues*. London: Amistad, 2004.

Roosevelt's New Deal

Kennedy, David M. *Freedom from Fear: The American People in Depression and War, 1929–1945*. New York: OUP, 1999.

Leuchtenburg, William E. *Franklin D. Roosevelt and the New Deal*. New York: Harper and Row, 1963.

The British Cabinet Resolves to Fight On

Beevor, Anthony. *The Second World War*. London: Weidenfeld and Nicholson, 2012.

Gilbert, Martin. *Churchill: A Life*. London: William Heinemann Ltd, 1999.

Hastings, Max. *Finest Years: Churchill as Warlord 1940–45*. London: Harper Press, 2009.

The Atlantic Charter

Brinkley, Douglas, and David R Facey-Crowther. *The Atlantic Charter*. London: Palgrave Macmillan, 1994.

Kimball, Warren F. *Forged in War: Churchill, Roosevelt and the Second World War*. London: HarperCollins, 1997.

Eisenhower and D-Day

Ambrose, Stephen E. *Eisenhower: Soldier and President*. New York: Simon and Schuster, 1990.

Eisenhower, Dwight D. *Crusade in Europe*. New York: Doubleday, 1948.

Hastings, Max. *Overlord: D-Day and the Battle for Normandy 1944*. London: Michael Joseph Ltd., 1984.

Norman Borlaug Changes Careers

Conway, Gordon. *One Billion Hungry: Can We Feed the World?* Ithaca: Cornell University Press, 2012.

Lipton, Michael, and Richard Longhurst. *New Seeds and Poor People*. London: Routledge, 1989.

Thurow, Roger, and Scott Kilman. *Enough: Why the World's Poorest Starve in an Age of Plenty*. New York: PublicAffairs, 2009.

The Marshall Plan

Hogan, Michael J. *The Marshall Plan: America, Britain, and the Reconstruction of Western Europe, 1947–1952*. Cambridge: CUP, 1987.

Lowe, Keith. *Savage Continent: Europe in the Aftermath of World War II*. London: Viking, 2012.

Pogue, Forrest C. *George C. Marshall: Statesman, 1945-1959*. New York: Viking, 1987.

Rosa Parks Refuses to Stand Up

Brinkley, Douglas. *Mine Eyes Have Seen the Glory: The Life of Rosa Parks*. London: Weidenfeld and Nicholson, 2000.

Tuck, Stephen. *We Ain't What We Ought To Be: The Black Freedom Struggle from Emancipation to Obama*. Cambridge, Mass: The Belknap Press, 2010.

Kennedy and the Cuban Missile Crisis

Dallek, Robert. *John F. Kennedy: An Unfinished Life, 1917–1963*. London: Allen Lane, 2003.

Fursenko, Aleksandr, and Timothy Naftali. *One Hell of a Gamble: Khrushchev, Castro, Kennedy and the Cuban Missile Crisis 1958–1964*. London: John Murray, 1997.

Kennedy, Robert F. *13 Days: The Cuban Missile Crisis, October 1962*. London: MacMillan, 1969.

George Martin Signs The Beatles

Davies, Hunter. *The Beatles: The Authorised Biography*. London: Heinemann, 1968.

Lewisohn, Mark. *The Complete Beatles Chronicle: The Definitive Day-By-Day Guide to The Beatles' Entire Career*. Chicago: Chicago Review Press, 2010.

Martland, Peter. *Since Records Began: EMI, the First 100 Years*. London: Batsford, 1997.

Anwar Sadat Flies to Jerusalem

Morris, Benny. *Righteous Victims: A History of the Zionist-Arab Conflict, 1881–1999*. London: John Murray, 2000.

Shlaim, Avi. *The Iron Wall: Israel and the Arab World*. London: Allen Lane, 2000.

Deng Xiaoping and Economic Reform in China

Brandt, Loren, Ed., and Thomas G. Rawski. *China's Great Economic Transformation*. Cambridge: CUP, 2008.

Dillon, Michael. *China: A Modern History*. London: I.B. Tauris, 2010.

Vogel, Ezra F. *Deng Xiaoping and the Transformation of China*. Cambridge, Massachusetts: Belknap Press of Harvard University Press, 2011.

Nelson Mandela Refuses to Give In

Johnson, R. W. *South Africa's Brave New World: The Beloved Country Since the End of Apartheid*. London: Allen Lane, 2009.

Mandela, Nelson. *Long Walk to Freedom: The Autobiography of Nelson Mandela*. London: Little Brown, 1994.

Ross, Robert, Ed., Anne Kelk Mager and Bill Nasson. *The Cambridge History of South Africa Vol. 2: 1885–1994*. Cambridge: CUP, 2011.

Gorbachev Institutes Perestroika

Gorbachev, Mikhail. *Memoirs*. London: Doubleday, 1996.

Service, Robert. *A History of Twentieth-Century Russia*. London: Allen Lane, 1997.

Aung San Suu Kyi Returns to Burma

Aung San Suu Kyi. *Freedom from Fear and Other Writings*. London: Viking, 1991.

Popham, Peter. *The Lady and the Peacock: The Life of Aung San Suu Kyi*. London: Rider, 2011.

Rogers, Benedict. *Burma: A Nation at the Crossroads*. London: Rider Books, 2012.

Tim Berners-Lee Invents the World Wide Web

Berners-Lee, Tim. *Weaving the Web: The Past, Present and Future of the World Wide Web by its Inventor*. London: Orion Business, 1999.

Tim Berners-Lee's websites, www.webfoundation.org, www.w3.org, thewebindex.org

Apple Reemploys Steve Jobs

Isaacson, Walter. *Steve Jobs*. London: Little Brown, 2011.

The Apple website, www.apple.com

The Good Friday Agreement

McKittrick, David, and David McVea. *Making Sense of the Troubles*. Belfast: The Blackstaff Press, 2000.

Powell, Jonathan. *Great Hatred, Little Room: Making Peace in Northern Ireland*. London: The Bodley Head, 2008.

Link to a PDF of the Good Friday Agreement, www.dfa.ie/uploads/documents/Anglo-Irish/agreement.pdf